James Mumford

The Catholic Scripturist

Or the Plea of the Roman Catholics

James Mumford

The Catholic Scripturist
Or the Plea of the Roman Catholics

ISBN/EAN: 9783337202545

Printed in Europe, USA, Canada, Australia, Japan

Cover: Foto ©Lupo / pixelio.de

More available books at **www.hansebooks.com**

THE

CATHOLIC SCRIPTURIST;

OR,

The Plea of the Roman Catholics,

SHOWING

THE SCRIPTURES TO HOLD THE ROMAN CATHOLIC FAITH IN ABOVE
FORTY OF THE CHIEF CONTROVERSIES NOW UNDER DEBATE.

"Now I beseech you, brethren, mark them which cause divisions and offences contrary to the doctrine which ye have learned; and avoid them."
ROM. xvi. 17.

By JAMES MUMFORD, PRIEST,
OF THE SOCIETY OF JESUS.

A New Edition.

LONDON:
BURNS & LAMBERT, 17 & 18 PORTMAN STREET,
AND 63 PATERNOSTER ROW.

1863.

BIOGRAPHICAL NOTICE OF THE AUTHOR.

THE REV. JAMES MUMFORD was born in Norfolk in the year 1606; at the age of twenty he joined the Society of Jesus, and made his religious profession on the 29th of September 1641. The provincial returns state that he was of a delicate constitution of body; that he had passed the highest collegiate offices of the order; that he served the English Mission twenty-six years; that some years before his death, which happened in England on the 9th of March 1666, he was apprehended at Norwich, and led round the city in his priestly vestments, amidst the scoffs of the rabble, and then sent off to Yarmouth, but in consequence of a dispute between the two towns respecting their chartered rights, he was remanded to Norwich, where, after some months' imprisonment, he was enlarged on bail. Father MUMFORD was distinguished for his charitable compassion for the suffering souls in Purgatory. He wrote several works, the most celebrated of which are *The Question of Questions* and *The Catholic Scripturist*. *The Question of Questions* was first published under the assumed name of "Optatus Ductor," 4to, Ghent, 1658, and was reprinted at London 1686-7. *The Catholic Scripturist* was originally printed at Ghent in 1662; a second edition appeared in London in 1686; and a third was printed at Holyrood House, Edinburgh, in 1687, by James Watson, printer to King James II.; a fourth edition was published at London in 1767.

A TABLE OF THE POINTS

CONTAINED IN THIS TREATISE.

	PAGE
THE PREFACE	1

POINT
- I. That Scripture alone cannot be a rule sufficient to direct us in all necessary controversies 7
- II. Tradition, besides Scripture, must direct us in many necessary controversies 15
- III. Of the never failing of the Church, which, being perpetual, can preserve perpetual traditions. Also of succession of true pastors and professors . . . 21
- IV. Of the universality and vast extent of this perpetual Church, which also must be the converter of Gentiles. This no Church differing from the Roman ever was . 30
- V. Of the infallibility of the Church, and consequently of her fitness to be judge of controversies . . . 38
- VI. That the Roman Church is this infallible Church, and our judge in all points of controversy 53
- VII. That the chief pastor of this Church is the successor of St. Peter 54
- VIII. That this our chief pastor or pope is not Antichrist . 60
- IX. Of the sacraments of the Church, and of the ceremonies which the Church useth in administering these sacraments, as also in other occasions 64
- X. Of baptism, which is the first sacrament 68
- XI. Of confirmation 69
- XII. Of the holy Eucharist 71
- XIII. Of communion under one kind 83
- XIV. Of the Mass, or of the holy Eucharist, as it is a sacrifice 85
- XV. Of saying Masses, and other public prayers, in the Latin tongue 92
- XVI. Of the sacrament of penance, or confession . . . 100
- XVII. Of the sacrament of extreme unction 103
- XVIII. Of the sacrament of holy order 105
- XIX. Of the sacrament of matrimony 106
- XX. Of the single life of priests 108
- XXI. Of the single life of such as have vowed perpetual chastity 114
- XXII. Of the works of counsel and supererogation . . . 118
- XXIII. Of voluntary austerity of life 121

A TABLE OF THE POINTS, ETC.

POINT		PAGE
XXIV.	Of satisfactory good works	125
XXV.	Of purgatory, and prayer for the dead . . .	131
XXVI.	Of indulgences	143
XXVII.	That faith alone doth not justify	148
XXVIII.	Whether our justification be any thing inherent in us	151
XXIX.	Whether our justification may not be lost . . .	154
XXX.	To justification it is necessary to keep the commandments. This is possible	157
XXXI.	How still we have free will to do good or evil . .	160
XXXII.	How this free will is still helped with sufficient grace	163
XXXIII.	This sufficient grace is denied to none, Christ dying even for reprobates	166
XXXIV.	How our good works done in grace, and by the help of Christ's grace, are meritorious, and merit life everlasting	169
XXXV.	It is laudable to do good works for reward . . .	175
XXXVI.	We laudably worship angels and saints . . .	177
XXXVII.	The angels and saints can hear our prayers . .	185
XXXVIII.	That saints can and will help us, and therefore it is laudable to pray to them	191
XXXIX.	That among the saints it is most laudable to pray to our Lady: and of the beads said to her honour .	199
XL.	It is laudable to worship the images of saints . .	207
XLI.	It is laudable to worship the relics of saints . .	219
XLII.	Some places are more holy than others: we therefore laudably make pilgrimages and processions to such holy places	224
XLIII.	That we laudably keep feasts in the honour of saints .	231
XLIV.	That we laudably observe fasts, saints' eves, and other days	235
XLV.	That we laudably in our fasts abstain from certain meats	239

TO THE PROTESTANT READER.

I HUMBLY beg of thee to peruse this Table of the Points here treated, and to turn first to that very Point in which thou thinkest we are less able to give thee satisfaction. And according as thou findest what I shall say, even in that Point, to be more or less satisfactory, so judge of the rest.

THE PREFACE.

1. "Now I beseech you, brethren, mark those which cause divisions and offences, contrary to the doctrine which ye have learned, and avoid them," Rom. xvi. 17. These words were the words of God and of truth, as well in the year 1517 as at this present year. Had any good Christian spoken these words in that aforesaid year 1517, all who had heard them could have made no other sense of them, but that they were forewarned by them both to *mark* and to *avoid* all authors *of divisions and offences contrary to the doctrine which they had learned.* Yet, as then, there was not any good Christian (unless you will account them for such, whom you yourselves acknowledge to have maintained gross heresies) who did not believe and profess the Roman faith. This was the *faith and doctrine* which they had learned. Wherefore, when in that year Luther first appeared, causing *divisions and offences contrary to the doctrine which they had learned*, all were bound, by the advice of the Apostle, to *mark* and *avoid* the said Luther, and all his adherents and followers.

2. But the world, then no less addicted to old vices than to new doctrines, did shut their ears to this advice of the Apostle, and did open their arms to em-

brace that which was (in so very many points) *contrary to the doctrine which they had learned*. And the misery is, that all those new teachers, which ensued in whole swarms, though they all taught *contrary to what they had learned*, yea, and the one contrary to the other, yet all pretended to teach nothing but Scripture rightly understood, which they all affirmed not to have been rightly understood for the foregoing thousand years, in such points as then they began to question. Yet with the same breath they said, that in all those several points in which they contradicted the former doctrine (and by doing so caused so great *divisions and offences*) they did affirm only that to which they were enforced by evident, manifest, and most clear texts of Scripture. Which was to say that, for the precedent thousand years, nobody had rightly understood, or at least every body had by word and practice contradicted, evident, manifest, and most clear texts of Scripture.

3. The good Christians of those ages, and we who adhere unto them, being in the quiet and peaceable possession of what we had learned, were bound (according to the advice of the Apostle) to avoid those new teachers; and it was sufficient for us to show they taught *contrary to what we had learned*, which they themselves confessed to be true, and was too evident to require proof. But because we stood constantly to maintain *what we had learned*, upon this ground, as the Apostle did bid us, our adversaries, desirous to bring us from believing to disputing, would be still importunely pressing us to prove, point by point, every point which we held, by evident, manifest, and most clear Scripture. We well

understood that it was their parts (who affirmed all former ages, for some thousand years at least, to have thus grossly erred against clear Scripture) to make good so great and so scandalous an accusation by producing texts (in the points under question) of so manifest, undeniable evidence against us, that their texts, compared to ours alleged in defence of the same points, should make the truth so clear on their side that all might be forced to confess they had reason to revolt (as they did) from all their ecclesiastical and civil magistrates, and to frame also a new body by themselves wholly and entirely, both in doctrine and discipline, quite different, yea, and contrary to all congregations, as then, upon the face of the earth.

4. The exorbitancy of this their proceeding will be unjustifiable when I shall here produce so many and so loud-speaking texts for above forty of those points which they misliked in our religion; yea, it was our holding those points for which, they said, they were enforced to this so unfortunate *a division*. But how weakly they were enforced, upon this account, to *cause such divisions and offences*, will easily be seen by any impartial eye, which shall attentively peruse on the one side all the texts which I shall here allege for forty-five of those points (for which chiefly they have caused this division), and on the other the few and inconsiderable, and a thousand-times-answered, texts which they bring to the contrary.

5. This, then, is the plea of us Roman Catholics, that we, ever since our ancestors in England were Christians, have held *the doctrine which we have learned,*

still avoiding those who taught the contrary. For that we have done this in no fewer than fifty points, in which we are most accused of novelty, hath been demonstrated in a late book, entitled *England's Old Religion, out of Bede's own words.* And though Bede had not been (as he was) the most grave and learned author which ever England had, but had been only a Jack-Straw, living and writing before the year 731 (that is, about nine hundred years ago), yet to see, in *his words then written,* those fifty points all held and all practised in our England, when England's religion was at the purest, cannot but abundantly convince that we Roman Catholics did then hold and practise what we hold and practise now. What is this but to *hold the doctrine we have learned, avoiding those who teach the contrary?*

6. Yet this is not our whole plea; for we know it will be objected that what we then learnt was contrary to Scripture; and they must mean clear and manifest Scripture, or else why do they go against the doctrine and practice which they found agreeing so exactly with the doctrine and practice of old England, as unanswerably demonstrated in that book? But we furthermore plead, that in those very points to which contradiction, yea, and manifest contradiction to Scripture, is objected against us, we have Scripture speaking so fully for us, that no one of those many religions now tolerated in England can, with any colour of probability, challenge greater evidence of Scripture for their opposite tenets than we here produce for our undoubtedly ancient doctrine; and therefore this our doctrine, even in this respect, ought in all reason to be at least as much tolerated

as any of those religions lately sprung up in England. The proof of what I say must rely upon what shall appear to be made good by me, in each point of those forty-five here ensuing.

7. It only remains that I advertise the reader how impossible it is that I, or any one else, should cite all texts just in those very words in which he will find them in his English Bible; for you have so many several translations of the English Bible, that whilst I oblige myself to follow one, I shall make sure not to follow the other. I conceived the best expedient to avoid this difficulty would be to follow always either the very words or the full sense of that English Bible which is most universally received. And in this point I have been so very scrupulous, that I continually admonish my reader, if at any one time I chance to put down any single text differing in sense from the English Bible which I have made choice of, as the best edition of their most received Bible, which is that which was set forth at Cambridge, 1635, printed by Thomas and John Buck, printers to that University, which Bible king James did cause to be set forth *out of his deep judgment, apprehending how convenient it was that, out of the original sacred tongues, there should be a more exact translation*, as is said in the preface of this translation, dedicated to his majesty.

A NOTE TO THE CATHOLIC READER.

LET the Catholic reader observe, that when we cite the two books of *Samuel*, the texts cited will be found in our two first books of *Kings;* and when we cite here their two books of *Kings*, the text will be found in our Bibles in the two last books of *Kings*. For our third is their first, our fourth their second. So also, with them, the books of *Paralip.* be called *Chronicles;* the second of *Esdras* they call *Nehemiah*. In numbering also the *Psalms*, they do, from the 10th *Psalm*, differ from us, counting still one more than we, until they come to *Psalm* 147, which from the eleventh verse includes our *Psalm* 147. And thence we go forward with the same account.

THE
CATHOLIC SCRIPTURIST,

ETC.

POINT I.

THAT SCRIPTURE ALONE CANNOT BE A RULE SUFFICIENT TO DIRECT US IN ALL NECESSARY CONTROVERSIES.

1. No Roman Catholic doth deny the Scripture to be a sufficient rule to direct us in all controversies, if we take the Scripture rightly interpreted. And therefore all those many texts which Protestants bring, to prove the Scripture to be our sole rule of faith, are very clearly answered by saying, that all those texts speak of the Scripture not taken as the letter sounds,—"for the letter kills," 2 Cor. iii. 6,—but they speak of the Scripture as rightly interpreted. And Protestants cannot but grant the Scripture rightly interpreted to be a sufficient rule of faith. But what are we the nearer? For now comes the great question of questions, Who be those that give the right interpretation to Scripture?

2. The very ground of all religions, but the Roman, is the Scripture as interpreted by their own selves, after they have carefully conferred one place with another. For I ask, and ask them again and again, by whom Scripture ought to be interpreted?

They will say, By Scripture conferred with Scripture. Here I must yet ask them again, By whom the conference of one Scripture with another can be made so exactly that from hence we may come undoubtedly to know the true interpretation? This question I will be still asking them until they can answer it. For I am sure that if I press this question home, they must be at last enforced to say, that the ground of their whole religion is the Scripture interpreted by themselves, when it hath been carefully conferred by themselves: so that the very ground of their whole faith is deceitful and fallible, if they themselves be fallible, either in interpreting or in conferring Scripture carefully or skilfully. If they say, their interpretation thus made is undoubted and infallible, then they cannot blame us for saying that the interpretation of the Church, made with as great care and skill, used by her in the exact conference of one Scripture with another, is infallible.

3. Stay here, dear reader; and as thou lovest thy salvation, before thou goest any further, ponder attentively how fallible and subject to a world of errors the ground of all such religions must needs be, which wholly and entirely are found at last to rely upon a mere human interpretation, after that a mere human and most fallible diligence and skill hath been employed in conferring one text with another. Then, ponder on the other side how incomparably surer and more justifiable in the sight of God and man the ground of that faith is which relieth indeed on the Scripture; but not on the Scripture as interpreted by private and fallible interpreters after their most fallible exactness of conferring Scripture with Scripture; but which relieth upon Scripture as interpreted by the Church, after that she, with no less exactness, hath conferred one Scripture with another in a general council, having incomparably greater human abilities than those of any private man's be, and having the special assistance of the Holy Ghost leading his

THE RULE OF FAITH. 9

Church into all truth. Of this infallibility we shall speak fully, Point V.

4. Now the Scripture, as rightly interpreted by the Church, will send us, for the clearing of many doubts, unto the Church authorised by Christ to instruct and teach us, as in that fifth point shall be evidenced out of Scripture. The difference then between our adversaries and us is, that we affirm the Scripture as it is rightly interpreted by the Church after she hath exactly conferred, in a general council, Scripture with Scripture, to be the rule of faith by which she decideth all necessary controversies. But our adversaries, misliking the dependence on the Church, will have the Scripture, by itself alone, to be a rule sufficient to direct each one who shall carefully confer it to judge all necessary controversies. This we deny; and though they say it in words, yet in very deed they also come to deny what they say; for, let a man mark it well, and he shall see that all these sectaries, when they come to the main controversy, do not take Scripture alone, as conferred with Scripture only, but they all take Scripture with their own interpretation made upon their own conference. And if you tell them they have failed by not taking due notice of several other texts in Scripture which should have been pondered in their conference, and would have produced a different interpretation, they will say their own spirit tells them the contrary: so that, finally, they who laugh at the Church for trusting to be securely guided by the Holy Ghost, come to ground their whole faith upon the assurance of being truly guided by their own spirit or judgment. But let us come to what we propound, and let us prove by Scripture that Scripture, taken as they take it, cannot be a sufficient rule to direct us in all necessary controversies. This I prove:

5. First, Because, to end all controversies, we must at least rule ourselves by all the books of Scripture,

and we must be assured we do so. This is clear, because by no text of Scripture can it be proved that any determined book, or number of books, is sufficient to end all controversies. But to do this, the whole number of books written by any Scripture writer is wholly requisite, seeing that no text speaks of any one, or any determinate number; but all speak of all. Now mark to what pass this opinion brings you. For, if we be to judge all necessary controversies by all the books which ever were written by any Scripture writer, we must necessarily have these books amongst us. But we have not in the whole world extant amongst us divers books of sacred prophetical Scriptures. For no fewer than twenty books of the prophetical penmen of the Holy Ghost have quite perished, as the learned Contzen proveth in his preface upon the four Gospels; and I will prove this as far as is sufficient by these following texts: Josh. x. 13, "Is not this written in the book of Jasher?" Again, 1 Kings iv. 32, "Solomon spoke three thousand proverbs, and his songs were one thousand and five." Again, 1 Chron. xxix. 29, "The acts of David first and last are written in the book of Samuel the seer, and the book of Nathan the prophet, and the book of Gad the seer." Where be these two prophets' books? Again, 2 Chron. ix. 29, mention is made of the "books of Nathan the prophet, and the prophecy of Aijah, and the visions of Iddo the seer." And chap. xii. 15, in the book of "Schemiah the prophet, and Iddo the seer, concerning genealogies;" which seems to be a different book from his *book of visions* before specified. And chap. xiii. 22, mention is made of the "story of the prophet Iddo." And chap. xx. 34, mention is made of the "book of Jehu son of Hanani." And chap. xxxiii. 19, we find mention of the works of the "sayings of the seers." We know then by Scripture that what is said by those books is said by prophets; and we also know by Scripture that "God spoke in time past unto the fathers by the prophets," 2 Peter i. 21. Moreover, we know by Scripture, that "Prophecy came not in old time by the will of man; but the holy men of God spake as they were moved by the Holy Ghost," 2 Peter i. 21. Standing therefore to what is known by Scripture, these books which have perished did deliver what was spoken by the Holy Ghost, and contained the true word of God. Whence is proved that we have not now entirely the whole word of God written. And this is further proved by the ensuing text of St. Paul, 1 Cor. v. 9, "I wrote to you in one Epistle." Note that he saith this in his first Epistle *to them;* where is this Epistle which St. Paul wrote *to them,* before he wrote the first to them? *I wrote to you.* We then say, give us all sacred prophetical writings which ever were written, or give us at least some one single clear text, which tells us that we are to end all necessary controversies by such books alone as be now extant in the true canon of Scripture, or else be ashamed to speak without a text in this very question, in which you affirm that all our necessary controversies must be ended by only clear Scripture. The controversy about this very question is one of the greatest of all controversies, and yet you would have us credit you, without being able to bring clear Scripture for what you say; especially Scripture conferred with these now-cited texts, of which, I dare say, you never thought. And though you should bring me a clear text to prove what is desired, yet where would you find a clear text to show me that all those twelve books, yea, or any one of them, which you have rejected amongst the *Apocrypha,* do not belong to the true canon of the whole Scripture? Remember, I call for a text as you bid me, and not for a reason against which we have our reasons; the text says, you must end all necessary controversies. Let then some text be brought able to end this, even in your own judgment.

6. Secondly, If Scripture only be the rule to end

all necessary controversies, then some ages had no such rule at all, but were destitute of all assured rule to end their necessary controversies, and that for two thousand and four hundred years together. For Moses, who was the first Scripture writer, was not born but after the world had stood two thousand and four hundred years, as may be made apparent by Scripture, in calculating the ages of such as successively lived one after the other, according to his own history of *Genesis*: so long, therefore, the world was without any Scripture. Scripture, then, is not the only rule of true faith, seeing that Sarah, Rebecca, and others of those times had true faith, though their faith was only squared by the rule of the tradition of their Church, as we shall see in the next point, No. 2.

7. Thirdly, The rule by which all men should be ruled in all necessary points should be in a language understood by all. But it is clear that most of the Jews, in the captivity of Babylon, had lost the knowledge of the Hebrew tongue, wherein the old Scripture was written. Neither was the Bible translated into the Syriac language till some years after our Saviour's death. Syriac differs as much from Hebrew as Italian from Latin; and the very letters differ as much as Greek and Latin. The Jews, then, for about fourteen generations understood the Hebrew no more than your people now understand the Bible in Latin. But of all this I shall speak more fully in Point XV. No. 1.

8. Fourthly, That cannot be a sufficient rule to decide all necessary controversies, which speaks not one word of many necessary controversies; but the Scripture speaks not a word of many necessary controversies; *ergo*, and first, it is necessary to know which books of Scripture be canonical, and which not; also, whether the canonical books we now have be alone sufficient to guide us in all necessary controversies. Then whether they can do this if they

be not incorrupt. And how we shall assuredly know whether they be incorrupted or not? Or which is the copy that is incorrupt? Again, which is the true translation of this copy? Again, which is the true sense of this translation, and that assuredly with a clear text for this assurance? Of these and many more particular controversies not a word in Scripture. Again, standing to Scripture alone, the heresy of Helvidius, denying our blessed Lady ever to have remained a virgin, seemeth rather to have had some colorable defence than any clear judgment given against it by Scripture only. For Matt. i. 25, "He knew her not till she brought forth her first-born Son." In which text these words, *till she brought forth*, and those others, *her first-born Son*, give some colour to say she had other sons afterwards. For which doctrine Helvidius was held an heretic by St. Augustine (*Hær.* 84), and by St. Hieron, *contra Helvidium*. You may see four-and-twenty necessary points set down all at large by Optatus Ductor, in his *Question of Questions*, no one of which is clearly decided in Scripture.

9. Fifthly, That cannot be a sufficient rule to decide all necessary controversies, which in such controversies speaks not clearly, but is very hard to be understood, as the Scripture is. Whence we see all controversies arise about the true meaning of such and such texts. So 2 Pet. iii. 16, "In the which (Epistles of St. Paul) are certain things hard to be understood, which the unlearned and unstable wrest, as they do the other Scriptures, unto their own damnation." Whence it is evident that *damnable errors* may be incurred by misinterpreting *places hard to be understood*, and so this *hardness* is found in *points necessary to salvation;* for in such only *damnable errors* can be incurred.

10. Sixthly, Christ did not command any one of the Evangelists to write his Gospel. They all did write of themselves, upon particular occasions, ex-

pressed by Eusebius. St. Luke tells you, in his preface, why he did write uncommanded. Christ then intended to leave us some other rule than this, which he never commanded to be written at all, much less to be written so as to be to us the only rule of faith.

11. Seventhly, By reading the ceremonial law, given by God to Moses, so clearly, so distinctly, and so close together, in the compass of no great book, I evidently infer, that if the self-same most prudent law-maker had intended, in the books of canonical Scripture, to have delivered unto us the sole rule of faith, and which alone we are to follow, he would not only have clearly told us so, but he would with no less, but rather with more, clarity and distinction, and in a far less compass, have set down unto us this rule, entirely and completely together in some one part of the canonical Scripture, distinctly expressing all those points, the belief of which he exacts of us under pain of damnation. For this did much more import to be done thus plainly and distinctly, than the setting down of the Jewish ceremonies: for is it likely that the same God who prescribed unnecessary ceremonies to be so clearly and distinctly set down in a few leaves, to direct the Jewish Church, which is but the handmaid, would not, for the Church of Christ, which is the mistress, give as clear a direction in points wholly necessary to salvation; but would send every one of her children to read over the whole Bible, and to pick out here one place, and there another; as Protestants say God sends us to seek even the most necessary points of our belief (which He requires of us under pain of damnation), now in this place of so vast a volume as the Bible is, now in another place hard by, now in another a great way off; and so to go seeking from the beginning of *Genesis* to the end of the *Apocalypse*: and this, though the number of points necessary to salvation be but small, as Protestants all agree? I cannot, therefore, think it was God's intention to leave us to the Bible only, as to the sole rule of faith.

POINT II.

TRADITION, BESIDES SCRIPTURE, MUST DIRECT US IN MANY NECESSARY CONTROVERSIES.

1. FIRST, The word of God may be notified either by tradition, without writing; or by Scripture, or writing. It is undoubted that the word of God, written or unwritten, is the rule of faith; wherefore, seeing it hath been proved (in the former Point) that the written word of God is not our only rule of faith, it evidently followeth that God's unwritten word, notified by tradition, must be taken as part of this rule.

2. Secondly, Moses was the first Scripture writer; and he, according to his own story, did not write till the world had continued above two thousand and four hundred years: so long, then, all the faithful in the world were truly faithful without any Scripture. All this long time, then, the unwritten word of God (that is, tradition) was the only rule of faith; for even then many had that faith which is defined by St. Paul, Heb. ii. 1; which I prove, because in that very place he numbers Abel, Enoch, Noah, Abraham, and Sarah, all having the faith he there described; and yet Sarah cannot be shown to have had her faith grounded on any other word of God but that which was delivered by the tradition of the Church in her times. And generally, then, the faith of all true believers was grounded upon tradition only. By this tradition they knew that God "blessed the seventh day, and sanctified it," Gen. ii. 3: and so all held themselves obliged to keep the sabbath. By this tradition they knew the distinction of beasts "clean and unclean," Gen. vii. 2. By this tradition they knew themselves obliged "not to eat the flesh with the blood," Gen. ix. 4; so likewise, that the tithes were to be paid to the "priest," Gen. xiv. 20. By only tradition they knew the fall of Adam; their future salvation by the

Messias to come; their remedy from sin by penance and repentance; their reward of good, and punishment of evil. Again, from Abraham until the written law (that is, for some four hundred years), they knew by tradition only that "this is the covenant which ye shall keep between me and you, all mankind shall be circumcised, an infant of eight days," Gen. xvii. 10. Now give me one text, if you can, which bids us not take tradition for a rule of faith after the writing of Scripture.

3. Thirdly, Even after the writing of Scripture, the Gentiles had not the Scripture, yet by tradition only many of them (as appears by the book of *Job*) retained true faith. And even among the Jews, after they had the Scripture, several necessary points were left to be known by tradition only; as the remedy for original sin before the eighth day, and for women children both before and after; as also by only tradition they knew that all the virtue that sacrifices had to take away sin was from the blood of their Redeemer to come. The observing of all these traditions was not any unlawful addition to the written word of God; whence you may understand the clear meaning of those words so often objected against us, Deut. iv. 2, "You shall not add to the word I command you, neither shall you diminish aught from it." For here is only forbidden to add contrary to the law. So that other place, Chron. xii. 32, "Whatsoever I command you, observe, thou shalt not add thereunto, nor diminish from it." For this place is meant only of not offering any other sacrifices besides those which were in the law prescribed: but it was ever lawful for lawful superiors to add more precepts agreeable to the law. So, chap. ii. 30, 31, after the children of Israel, according to law, had kept the solemnity of Azymes seven days, ver. 23, "the whole assembly took good counsel to keep other seven days." And ver. 27, "Their prayer came to the holy habitation of heaven." This addition, then, did not displease God.

Again, Esth. ix. 27, "The Jews ordained, and took upon them and their seed, and upon all that would be joined with them, so as it should not fail that they keep these two days, and that these days should be kept throughout every generation, every family:" behold here another addition. And behold also another again of the "dedication of the altar, made for eight days from year to year," 1 Macc. iv. 56, 59. And that you may know that this book is Scripture, or at least that a feast is to be kept not appointed in Scripture, our Saviour himself did keep this feast, John x. 22, as I shall show, Point XXXVIII. Again, the change of the Sabbath into the Sunday is only clearly known by tradition: yea, the manner of keeping it is contrary to all Scripture we have; for Scripture saith, Lev. xxiii. 32, "From even unto even shall you celebrate your Sabbath." Yet we do not begin the Sunday the even before, neither dare we work after the even upon Sunday. Who taught us this? Tradition only.

4. Fourthly, Tradition is (and therefore is truly to be held) the word of God, making us fully assured of what is not written. For example, for some years after the death of our Saviour, his glorification after death was not written so as to express that Jesus was that Christ whom God had glorified; and yet, before this was written, St. Peter said truly, Acts ii. 36, "Therefore, let all the house of Israel know assuredly (mark the word *assuredly*), that God hath made the same Jesus, whom you have crucified, both Lord and Christ." We may then have an infallible faith of what is not written; yea, we are forbidden to believe otherwise than was delivered by tradition; 2 Thess. ii. 14, "Therefore, brethren, stand and hold the traditions you have been taught, whether by word or by our epistle." For what he taught by his tongue only was as truly the word of God as what he did also write with his pen. Yea, this which I call tradition is the epistle of Christ, 2 Cor. iii. 3, "You are the

epistle of Christ: not written with ink, but with the Spirit of the living God." This epistle *written with the Spirit of the living God* is no less true, nor of less credit than what is written with ink in papers. Wherefore most of the Apostles did give their converts no other form of belief but what (by their preaching) they had written in their hearts, *not with ink, but with the Spirit of the living God*. For the proper subject to receive and retain the word of God is not paper, but the hearts of the faithful. Whence, St. Irenæus, lib. iii. cap. 4, "What if the Apostles had also left no Scripture! Ought not we to follow the order of tradition which they delivered to them to whom they committed the churches? To which ordinance many nations of those barbarous people who had believed in Christ do consent without letter or ink, having salvation (that is, soul-saving doctrine) written in their hearts." For a world of the first believers did never so much as see all Scripture. It was the year 99 before St. John wrote his Gospel, and when the canon of Scripture was fully ended; there is no mention made even of the least care taken by the Apostles to divulge the Scripture in barbarous languages; no, nor to divulge it in Latin itself, as you must needs say who deny primitive antiquity to all Latin editions. All this clearly proves that tradition was relied upon as upon the word of God itself. Whence St. Paul did not only counsel but also command the Thessalonians to withdraw themselves from all who walked not after the tradition they had received of their pastors, 2 Thess. iii. 6, "Now," said he, "we command you, brethren, in the name of our Lord, that ye withdraw yourselves from every brother that walketh disorderly, and not after the tradition which he received of us."

5. It was for the keeping this tradition and form of faith why he praised the Romans, chap. vi. 17, "You have obeyed from your heart the form of doctrine which was delivered you." This form could not

be a form contained in the whole canon of Scripture, for the whole canon was not finished when St. Paul did write this. It was, therefore, *the form of uniform tradition* delivered in each church, which taught by word of mouth all things necessary: for this he praised the Corinthians, 1 Cor. xi. 2, "Now I praise you, brethren, that you keep the traditions" (so you put it in the margin, but in the text you read *ordinances*) "as I delivered them to you." This *form*, these *traditions*, these *ordinances*, are inculcated again and again: 1 Tim. vi. 20, "O Timothy, keep that which is committed to thy trust;" and, ver. 3, "If any one teach otherwise, he is proud, knowing nothing." Again, 2 Tim. i. 13, "Hold fast the form of good words which thou hast heard of me: that good thing which was committed to thee, keep by the Holy Ghost." Again, chap. iii. 14, "But thou continue in those things which thou hast learned and been assured of, knowing of whom thou hast learned them;"—learned, I say, by word of mouth, for by writing he had received but little. So, also, when as yet by writing he had taught the Romans nothing, he, in his first and only Epistle to them, wrote thus, Rom. xvi. 17, "Now I beseech you, brethren, mark them which cause divisions and offences contrary to the doctrine which you have learned." Likewise, when as yet he had written nothing to the Galatians (for where is any such writing?), he begins thus, Gal. i. 6, "I marvel that so soon you are removed from him who called you into the grace of Christ unto another Gospel." I say *removed*, that is, changed *from the form of faith* which I delivered, which was a true though not a written Gospel, *into another Gospel* taught by these new *otherwise teachers;* yet, saith he, with all earnestness, "Although we, or an angel from heaven, preach any other Gospel unto you than that ye have received, let them be accursed," ver. 8. St. Paul as yet had preached nothing to them in writing, but they had received all by *oral tradition;* and yet notwithstanding once again more vehemently, ver. 9, "As we have said before, so I say now again, If any man preach any other Gospel unto you than that you have received, be he accursed." Note the word *received* intimateth that they had all by tradition. For what, as then, had they received from him in writing? And he saith no more than other Apostles (who did write nothing, but delivered all by oral tradition) might truly have said of the Gospel so delivered by them. Neither did St. Paul speak of what they should receive many years after, but of what they had *as then received;* for that was true as any thing they should receive by writing. And, therefore, for their forsaking of what they had received thus, he most deservedly saith unto them, "O, foolish Galatians, who hath bewitched you?" chap. iii. 1. For, indeed, they seemed bewitched out of their senses, who, to follow the private judgment of some *otherwise teachers*, reject what they had *received* by the full and still continued report of all Christianity, from the first teachers of the faith.

6. They object tradition to be the word of men ; but all these arguments show this apostolical tradition (for which only we now contend) to be the word of God—*a form of sound words.* And, 1 Thess. ii. 13, "Ye received the word of God which ye heard of us; ye received it not as the word of men, but (as it is in truth) the word of God." Behold, what was heard by them only by word of mouth was *in truth the word of God.* Therefore a fit rule of faith, even before it was written.

7. They ask, how we know a true apostolical tradition from a false one, which is the tradition of men? I answer, that a true apostolical tradition cometh down handed by a full unanimous report of all Catholic nations in all ages, attested by their universal practice and uniform doctrine ; what is thus delivered is the doctrine of the Church diffused, and therefore infallible; upon this ground (for other in-

fallible grounds you have none) you receive only such and such Scripture for canonical, and such and such copies of the Scripture for authentical. We can therefore, to the full, as well distinguish true traditions from false ones, or apostolical traditions from traditions of ordinary men, as you can distinguish the authentic copy of their writings from such as are forged or corrupted; for you must first distinguish the truth of the tradition which recommends such books unto you from all false traditions.

POINT III.

OF THE NEVER FAILING OF THE CHURCH, WHICH, BEING PERPETUAL, CAN PRESERVE PERPETUAL TRADITIONS. ALSO OF SUCCESSION OF TRUE PASTORS AND PROFESSORS.

1. IF the Church of Christ could fail, or cease to be, it is evident tradition might fail, and not be preserved in its purity. The true Church is both infallible, as long as she lasts (of which see Point V.), and is also sure to last to the end of the world. Yea, she is assured all this time to have a lawful succession of true pastors, and under them true professors of the faith in a vast number: find any such Church besides the Roman, if you can, and I give you leave to call that the true Church. And lest perhaps the great number of powerful texts, which we are to cite, should work small effect with minds prepossessed with one or two objections to the contrary, we will first clear them, and then pass to the manifold clear texts which demonstrate the true Church at no time to be a lurking invisibility.

2. The prime objection is from the words of Elias, 1 Kings xviii. 22, "I, even I, only remain a prophet of our Lord." And in the next chap. v. 10, "I, even I,

only am left," which again he repeats ver. 14. I answer, that at least he is told presently by God, ver. 18, "That there were left in Israel seven thousand men whose knees had not been bowed before Baal." And in the former chapter it is manifest he knew of a hundred prophets. For, ver. 13, Abdias told him, "I hid of the prophets of our Lord a hundred men, by fifty and fifty, in caves." Wherefore he well knew that there were many faithful, amongst whom so many prophets were known to him; yea, hence it is clear that he was not the only prophet left. Wherefore those words, "I, only I, remain a prophet of our Lord," are to be understood thus: "I, only I, remain a prophet," standing openly to oppose their fury amongst the apostate tribes of Israel. For Elias knew full well, that not all the children of Israel, but only ten tribes, were fallen from God, 1 Kings xii. He knew also that the still faithful tribe of Juda (including Benjamin) afforded "Rehoboam a hundred and fourscore thousand chosen men" to fight against the other revolted ten tribes, ver. 21; which is again repeated 2 Chron. xi. with a notable declaration how much the true Church, even then, flourished in Judah and Benjamin, Rehoboam himself building "fifteen cities enclosed with walls." And, ver. 13, "The priests and Levites that were in all Israel resorted to him out of all their coasts." And, ver. 16, "Of all the tribes of Israel, whosoever had given their hearts to seek their Lord God of Israel, came into Jerusalem to sacrifice, and they strengthened the kingdom of Judah." All this Elias knew very well, and also that which follows, to wit, that Asa reigned over all Judah in all piety and peace, 2 Chron. xiv. And "he built other fenced cities in Judah." And, ver. 8, "Asa had of Judah an army of three hundred thousand, and of Benjamin two hundred and eighty thousand." And he defeated "ten hundred thousand Ethiopians." And, 2 Chron. xvii., Josaphat, who lived in the days of Elias, was yet greater than Asa his father both in piety and power. For, ver. 10, "The dread of our Lord came about all the kingdoms of the lands that were about Judah, neither durst they make battle against Josaphat." And he built many strong cities, and stupendous was the number of his forces, ver. 14: of Judah under Abnath three hundred thousand; and two hundred and eighty thousand under Johanan; and two hundred thousand under Amasias; and two hundred thousand under Eliada; and two hundred and eighty thousand under Josabad. All these make eleven hundred thousand and sixty thousand soldiers. And yet the Scripture saith, "All these were at the hand of the king, besides others whom he had put in walled cities in Judah." Behold the Jewish Church, even at her lowest ebb. Christ's Church is the mistress, and of higher dignity. Wherefore at all times after her beginning, you must find me at least as many visible professors of her doctrine as the Jewish Church had in her meanest condition. "For the New Testament is established in far better promises," Heb. viii. 6. As also appears by the texts which here shall be cited. All which texts convince such a perpetual, conspicuous, and visibly flourishing state at all times, that no Church differing from the Roman can be showed to have had any thing like it.

3. The other only considerable objection is, that perhaps these promises, made by God to his Church, concerning his always protecting her, were made upon this condition, that he would do this if she should persevere to keep his commandments; for so all his promises to David and Solomon are made. I answer, that it is evident that some promises which seem made to them and their posterity are not to be literally understood of their posterity according to the flesh, but as they by grace be sons of Christ, who was the son of David. And divers of these promises are made so absolutely, that absolutely they admit of no such condition. Take for proof hereof that convincing text, Psalm lxxxix. 4, "I have made a cove-

nant with my chosen, I have sworn to David my servant, Thy seed will I establish for ever, and I will build up thy throne to all generations." All which is only verified in Christ, who, in his Church, "hath given him the seat of David his father, and he shall reign in the house of Jacob for ever, and of his kingdom there shall be no end." As the angel said, Luke i. 32. After this promise of everlasting perpetuity to his Church, lest any one should think his promises might be made void by any sins of hers, or to be made only upon condition of their walking in his commandments, he added in the same Psalm, ver. 29, "And I will put him the first-begotten high above the kings of the earth; I will keep my mercy unto him for ever, and my testament faithful unto him. I will put his seed for ever and ever, and his throne as the days of heaven. But if his children shall forsake my law [this cannot be possibly in your doctrine spoken of the elect] and will not walk in my judgments; if they will profane my justices, and not keep my commandments, I will visit their iniquities with a rod, and their sins with stripes: but my loving kindness I will not take away from him, nor suffer my faithfulness to fail. My covenant will I not break, nor the thing which is gone out of my lips. Once I have sworn in my holiness, if I lie to David, his seed shall continue for ever, and his throne as the sun in my sight, and as the moon perfect for ever." This text speaks home to prove what I intend, to wit, that these promises be made upon Christ, "the son of David, the son of Abraham," Matt. i. 1; and as St. Paul teacheth, that only those who believe in Christ be the true children of Israel and Abraham, so they only be the true children of David; and concerning them is verified the promise, which, as is here said, for no sins of theirs shall ever be frustrated. "Not as though the word of God had taken no effect, but they that are the children of the promise are counted for the seed," Rom. ix. 6.

4. And in this sense the sacred text speaks, 2 Sam. vii. 16, "And thine house and thy kingdom shall be established for ever before thee, thy throne shall be established for ever. According to all these words did Nathan speak to David." So Psalm lxxii. 5, "They shall fear thee as long as the sun and moon endure, throughout all generations. He shall have dominion also from sea to sea, and from the river to the ends of the earth." In whom can these texts of Scripture be verified but in Christ, ever reigning in his Church diffused, even in a flourishing condition, over the face of the earth. According to what is said, Luke i. 32, "The Lord God shall give him the throne of his father David; and he shall reign over the house of Jacob for ever [by having still the kingdom of his Church, consisting of those true Israelites of whom St. Paul spoke], and of his kingdom [or Church] there shall be no end."

5. Isaias every where is very full to this purpose; chap. xlix. 14, "And Sion said, Our Lord hath forsaken me, and our Lord hath forgotten me. Why, can a woman forget her infant, that she will not have pity on the son of her womb? And if she should forget, yet I will not forget thee. Behold, I have written thee in my hands." And again, chap. liv. 9, "As in the days of Noah is this thing to me, to whom I swore I would bring in no more the waters of Noah upon the earth, so have I sworn not to be angry with thee, nor to rebuke thee. For the mountains shall (sooner) be moved, and hills tremble: but my mercy shall not depart from thee, and the covenant of my peace shall not be moved, said our Lord, thy miserator. Poor little one, shaken with tempest, without all comfort, behold I will lay thy stones in order, and will found thee in sapphires, and I will put the jasperstone for thy munitions." And again, chap. lx. 15, "I will make thee the pride of worlds, a joy unto generation and generation." Ver. 18, "Iniquity shall be no more heard in thy land, waste and de-

struction in thy borders, and salvation shall occupy thy walls, and praise thy gates. Thou shalt have no more the sun by day, neither shall the brightness of the moon enlighten thee (these are too mean lights for thee); but the Lord shall be to thee an everlasting light, and thy Lord God for thy glory. Thy sun shall go down no more, and thy moon shall not be diminished, because the Lord shall be unto thee an everlasting light, and the days of thy mourning shall be ended." Again, chap. lxi. 6, "You shall eat the strength of Gentiles, and in their glory you shall be proud, everlasting joy shall be to them. I will give their work in truth, and make a perpetual covenant with them, and they shall know their seed in the Gentiles. All that shall see them shall know that these are the seed which the Lord hath blessed." Again, chap. lxii. 3, "Thou shalt be a crown of glory in the hand of our Lord, and the diadem of a kingdom in the hand of thy God. Thou shalt no more be called forsaken, and thy land shall be called no more desolate; but thou shalt be called my will in her, and thy land inhabited, because it hath well pleased our Lord in thee, and thy land shall be inhabited. Thy God shall rejoice upon thee; upon thy walls, Jerusalem, I have placed watchmen all the day, and all the night; for ever they shall not hold their peace." See here the continual visibility of the Church in her watchmen and pastors, of which consequently there must be a perpetual succession. And, ver. 8, "Our Lord hath sworn by his right hand, and by the arm of his strength, If I shall give thy wheat any more to be meat to thy enemies, and if the strange children shall drink thy wine." And he concludeth, ver. 12, "Thou shalt be called a city sought for and not forsaken." That the true Church also shall have a perpetual succession of priests and Levites is clearly expressed in the last chapter of Isaias; in which, after the prophet had named Africa, Lydia, Italy, Greece, and the islands afar off, he addeth, lxvi. 21,

"And I will take of them to be priests and Levites, saith our Lord: for as the new heavens, and the new earth, which I make to stand before me, so shall stand the seed of your name." Note, that these Levites be now not by birth, but by election, ordained to be such out of several countries, Italy, Greece, and other islands, which names your Bible avoids to translate.

6. St. Jeremy is no less copious, chap. xxx. 11, "Though I make a full end of all nations, yet I will not make a full end of thee; but I will correct thee in measure." The Church, indeed, may be chastised for a while, but never be brought to consummation. For, chap. xxxi. 35, "Thus saith our Lord, that giveth the sun for the light of the day, the order of the moon and the stars for the light of the night, &c. If these laws shall fail before me (saith our Lord), then also the seed of Israel shall fail from being a nation before me for ever. If the heavens above shall be able to be measured, and the foundations of the earth to be searched out, I also will cast away all the seed of Israel." Again, chap. xxxii. 38, "And they shall be my people, and I will be their God; and I will give them one heart and one way, that they may fear me all their days, and it may be well with them, and with their children after them; and I will not cease to do them good. And I will make an everlasting covenant with them; and I will give my fear in their heart, that they may not revolt from me." Again, chap. xxxiii. 14, "Behold, the days will come, saith our Lord, and I will raise up the good word that I have spoken to the house of Israel; in that time I will make the spring of justice to bud forth unto David, and he shall do judgment and justice on the earth. This saith our Lord, There shall not fail of David a man to sit upon the throne of the house of Israel [Christ must successively have his vicar or vicegerent in all ages], and of the priests and Levites there shall not fail before my face a man to offer holocausts and to burn sacrifices, and to kill

victims all days." Behold a succession of lawful priests still offering sacrifices, expressed by the priests and sacrifices as were then only known. Again it followeth, "And the word was made to Jeremy, saying, If my covenant with the day can be made void, also my covenant may be made void with David my servant, that there may not be of him a son (a vicar or vicegerent) to reign in his throne, and the Levites and priests my ministers; yea (ver. 22) even as the stars in heaven cannot be numbered and the sand of the sea be measured, so will I multiply the seed of David my servant, and the Levites my ministers." Whence it is evident that the number of lawful priests by lawful mission and ordination shall not only never fail, but also never fail *to be a great number.* There followeth again, in the same chapter, the former covenant repeated once more.

7. Ezekiel also speaks very home, ch. xxxiv. 22, "I will save my flock, and it shall be no more a spoil, and I will raise up over them one pastor, who shall lead them; my servant David he shall feed them, and he shall be their pastor; and I the Lord will be their God, and my servant David the prince of them." And, ver. 28, "And they shall be no more a spoil to the Gentiles." Again, chap. xxxvii. 23, "Neither shall they be polluted any more in their idols; and I will cleanse them, and they shall be my people, and I their God, and my servant David king over them, *and there shall be one pastor over them all.* They shall walk in my judgments, and they shall keep my commandments, and they shall do them, and they shall dwell on the land which I gave to my servant Jacob, themselves and their children, and their children's children, even for ever, and David my servant a prince for ever. And I will make a peace to them, an everlasting covenant shall be to them; and I will found them, and will multiply them, and will give my sanctification in the midst of them for ever," &c. And the very last verse of the last chapter: "The name of the city from that day: Our Lord there."

8. Clearly also Daniel, chap. ii. 44, " In the days of those kingdoms the God of heaven shall raise us a kingdom that shall not be dissipated for ever [but still continue in the quality of a kingdom] ; and this kingdom shall not be delivered to another people; and it shall consume all the [idolatrous] kingdoms, and it shall stand for ever in quality of a kingdom."

There is little need to pass to the New Testament, the Old sufficing, if any thing will suffice. Of Christ's gospel St. Paul says, 2 Cor. iv. 3, "If our gospel be hid, it is hid to them that are lost." Either you must confess yourselves lost men, or you must say that at no time Christ's gospel lay hid, so as you could not tell who professed it. I insist not in the known places, as that the Church (Matt. xvi. 18) "is built upon a rock, and that the gates of hell shall not prevail against it." Again, it is evident that she must still be visible in all ages, that we *may still* at any time *tell the Church,* and *hear her,* Matt. xviii. 17 ; and be still *fed by her* doctrine and sacraments. For these be the two essential marks of a true Church, as Protestants say. Hence, Ephes. iv. 11, "He gave some apostles, some prophets, and other some evangelists, and other some pastors and doctors, &c., until we meet all in the unity of faith," which will not be till the world's end. "These be the light of the world, still set upon the candlesticks, never hid under a bushel," Matt. v. 14. *A city upon a hill,* still to be seen. And though the *mustard seed* was the least at the beginning, yet in the growing it proves a tree, and all fowls repair to it, Matt. xiii. 32. Yea, this must be a Church perpetually continuing in such reverence to our blessed Lady, that her words must be fulfilled, Luke i. 48, "all generations shall call me blessed." And, ver. 33, "Her son shall reign in the house of Jacob for ever, and of his kingdom there shall be no end." And so himself saith to his apostles, Matt. xxviii. 20, "Behold I am with you all days, even to the consummation of the world." His apostles were not to be in the world even to the end of the world. The promise therefore is, to be with them in the person of such as should succeed them in teaching and preaching, &c. Again, in the like sense, he saith, John xiv. 16, " And he will give another Paraclete, that he may abide with you for ever."

All these texts demonstrate what we have undertaken to prove. And hence it doth unavoidably follow that the Church must in all ages have a continual succession of true preachers of the word of God and true administration of sacraments; for these two things (even according to the Thirty-nine Articles of the Church of England) are the two essential signs or notes of a true Church, which must ever accompany her in all ages. And if a Church be (as St. Cyprian saith) *a flock adhering to their shepherd*, then as in all ages there is a flock of Christ, so there must be a shepherd to whom this flock may and must adhere. And therefore a lawful succession of true pastors must needs in all ages be found in the Church, at least without any considerable interruption; and this is expressed in several texts here cited. Now ponder that this is to be found in no Church but the Roman. See more in the next Point.

POINT IV.

OF THE UNIVERSALITY AND VAST EXTENT OF THIS PERPETUAL CHURCH, WHICH ALSO MUST BE THE CONVERTER OF GENTILES. THIS, NO CHURCH DIFFERING FROM THE ROMAN, EVER WAS.

1. IF the Church were to remain perpetually in any very small extent or bigness, perhaps we might hear little news of her in some ages. But the true perpetual Church (foretold to be in all ages in the texts

now cited) is likewise in Scripture no less clearly foretold to be in all ages so universally spread and so visibly numerous, that the very recital of these texts is enough to put quite out of countenance any other Church but the Roman, especially being that this true Church is so manifestly said to gain this, her vast extent, by the multitude of Gentiles which she is to convert to her,—a thing which evidently must be verified in the true Church; and yet it is evident that this only is verified in the Roman Church; that is, no Church (but such as was joined to her in communion) ever converted any one parish of Gentiles.

2. The texts which evidence this vast extent of the true Church are Gen. xiii. 16, "I will make thy seed as the dust of the earth," and chap. xv. 5, "Look up to heaven, and number the stars if thou canst. And he said to him, So shall thy seed be." Again, chap. xxii. 16, "By my own self I have sworn, saith the Lord, I will bless thee, and I will multiply thy seed as the stars of heaven, and as the sand that is by the sea. And in thy seed shall be blessed all nations of the earth." Now St. Paul tells us, Rom. ix. 8, "Not they that are the children of the flesh [of Abraham], they are the children of God; but they that are the children of promise are esteemed for the seed." And if still you contend that these texts are only for the Jewish Church, you must also remember that Christ's Church is the mistress, she the handmaid; and that, as St. Paul says, "the New Testament is established in far better promises," Heb. viii. 6; and must flourish far more than ever the Jewish synagogue did. Hence, Apoc. vii. 5, St. John, after "twelve thousand of every tribe of Israel were signed, saw a great multitude which no man could number, of all nations, tribes, peoples, and tongues." But let us go on.

3. David, Psalm ii. 8, "Ask of me, and I will give thee the Gentiles for thy inheritance, and thy possession to the end of the earth." Psalm xxii. 27,

"All the ends of the earth shall remember and be converted to our Lord. All the kindreds of the nations shall adore in his sight." Again, Psalm lxxii. 7, "In his [Christ's] days shall the righteous flourish so long as the moon endureth. And he shall rule from sea to sea, and from the river even to the ends of the round world. Yea, all the kings of the earth shall adore him; and all nations shall serve him." Psalm xcviii. 3, "All the ends of the earth have seen the salvation of our God." Of what Church is this true besides the Roman?

4. In this point of the multitude of Gentiles to be converted, none more eloquent and copious than the prophet Isaias, chap. ii. 2, "And in the latter days [the New Testament is called the last hour, John ii. 18] the mountain of the house of our Lord shall be prepared in the top of mountains, and all nations shall flow unto it: and he shall judge the Gentiles," &c. Again, chap. xlix. 1, "Listen, O you islands, and attend, you people from afar." And then, ver. 6, "It is a small thing that thou shouldst be my servant to raise up the tribes of Jacob, and to convert the dregs of Israel. [It is too poor a thing for Christ to be author of so small a Church as the Jewish Church was.] Behold I have given thee to be the light of the Gentiles, that thou mayest be salvation even to the farthest parts of the earth. Kings shall see, and princes arise, and adore for our Lord's sake. Behold, these shall come from far, and behold, they from the north and the sea; and these from the south country. Lift up thy eyes round about, and see all these are gathered together,—they are come to thee." And, ver. 19, "Thy deserts, and thy solitary places [in which nobody before served God], and the land of thy ruin shall now be strait, by reason of the inhabitants. And yet shall the children of the barrenness say in thine ears, The place is strait for me; make me space to dwell." Then, ver. 22, "Behold, I will lift up my hands to the Gentiles, and to

the people I will exalt my signs. And they shall carry thy sons in their arms, and thy daughters upon their shoulders. And kings shall be thy nursing fathers, and queens thy nurses. With a countenance cast down to the ground they shall adore thee, and they shall lick up the dust of thy feet." [Kings prostrating themselves at the feet of Christ's vicar, and kissing them.] Again, chap. liv. 2, "Enlarge the place of thy tents, and stretch out the skins of thy tabernacle: for thou shalt penetrate to the right hand and the left. And thy seed shall inherit the Gentiles, and shall inhabit the desolate cities." Here note, that these things were spoken to the Jewish Church, telling her how much the future glory of Christ's Church should exceed her; and so to her the prophet said in the first verse: "Praise, O barren woman which barest not: sing praise, and make joyful noise, because many are the children of the desolate [Gentiles] more than of her that hath a husband." To wit, the synagogue to which he had been so long espoused. So that it is flatly against Scripture to make the Church of Christ at any time so barren as the synagogue was in the days of Elias. Although, even then, she had in the field far above eleven hundred thousand men, besides many thousands of soldiers in her walled cities, as we showed Point III. No. 2. Much more is it against Scripture to make her so little as not to be visible or known. And therefore again, chap. lx. 1, "Arise, be illuminated, Jerusalem, because thy light is come, and the glory of our Lord is risen upon thee. Gentiles shall walk in thy light, and kings in the brightness of thy rising. Lift up thine eyes and see round about: all these are gathered together, they are come to thee. Thy sons shall come from afar, and thy daughters shall rise from thy side. Then shalt thou see, and abound, and thy heart shall be enlarged, when the multitude of the sea shall be converted to thee. The strength of the Gentiles shall come to thee, the inundation of camels shall cover thee." Ver. 10, "The children of strangers shall build thy walls, and their kings shall minister to thee, and thy gates shall be open continually, [never shalt thou be invisible, for] day and night they shall not be shut, that the strength of the Gentiles may be brought to thee: for the nations and the kingdoms that shall not serve thee shall perish." What nations can serve (yea, and be bound, under pain of perishing, to serve) an invisible Church? Again, ver. 15, "I will make thee an eternal excellency, a joy unto generation and generation; and thou shalt suck the milk of Gentiles, and thou shalt be nourished with the teats of kings." Again, chap. lxii. 2, "And the Gentiles shall see thy righteousness, and all the kings thy glory."

5. Jeremy also every where fully; chap. xxx. 19, "I will multiply them, and they shall not be few: and I will glorify them, and they shall not be small." Christ's Church still shall ever contain a vast number of people. Again, chap. xxxi. 34, "And a man shall no more teach his neighbour, and a man his brother, saying, Know our Lord; for all shall know me, from the least of them to the greatest, saith our Lord. Thus saith our Lord, that gives the sun for the light of the day, the order of the moon and stars for the light of the night. If these laws shall fail before me, saith our Lord, then also the seed of Israel shall fail that it be not a nation for ever before me." This text cometh convincingly home to prove that this universality shall be perpetual, and no more fail in any age than the light of the sun and moon. As long as they last, this Church shall be a flourishing *nation for ever*. For again, ver. 37, "Thus saith our Lord, If the heavens shall be able to be measured, and the foundations of the earth beneath to be searched out, I also will cast away all the seed of Israel." And then, in a metaphor of a city built upon hills far distant from one another, he says, this so vastly extended city

"shall not be plucked up, and it shall no more be destroyed for ever;" which is a gallant expression of the perpetual universality of the Church, for ever retaining a vast great extent in any ages whatsoever. The same follows, chap. xxxiii. 20, "Thus saith our Lord, If my covenant with the day can be void, and my covenant with the night, that there be no day nor night in their time, also my covenant may be made void with David my servant, that there be not a son of him to reign in his throne, and Levites and priests my ministers. Even as the stars of heaven cannot be numbered, and the sand of the sea be measured, so will I multiply the seed of David my servant, and the Levites my ministers." Now, if the number of priests, pastors, and teachers shall be so great at all times, how great at all times, and how exceeding visible, must be the number of the people who are visibly to be ruled, fed, and taught? And yet again, ver. 25, "If I have not set my covenant between night and day, and laws to heaven and earth, surely I will also cast off the seed of Jacob, and of David my servant, that I take not of his seed princes of the seed of Abraham, Isaac, and Jacob." These Levites and priests shall not be so by birth, but they shall be taken out of Italians, Africans, Grecians, the islands, as Isaias saith in his last chapter, ver. 21, though your Bible did not interpret the Hebrew names of the countries. These texts, then, manifestly tell the perpetual succession of priests and pastors in Christ's Church, so that we are no less assured of having lawful princes in the Church lawfully, still governing the same, than we are assured of having night and day, and the heavens moving above us, and the earth standing under us. A point much to be noted; yet we may confidently say, No Church, no Church but the Roman, can do this.

6. Ezekiel, chap. xvii. 22, "Thus saith our Lord, And I will take the marrow of the high cedar, and will set it, and will plant it upon a mountain, a moun-

tain high and eminent. On the high mountains of Israel will I plant it, and it shall shoot forth into a bud, and shall yield fruit, and it shall be into a great cedar, and all birds and every fowl shall dwell under the shadow of the boughs thereof, and shall there make their nests." Behold Christ's Church, which in her beginning was but a small grain of mustard-seed, now grown up to the greatness of such a cedar as this is. And not grown, and grown, until at last she was grown quite invincible. Memorable is that text, chap. xxxvi. 25, "And I will pour out upon you clear water, and you shall be cleansed from all your contaminations, and from all your idols will I cleanse you, and give you a new heart, and will put a new spirit in the midst of you, and will [by my grace] make that you shall walk in my precepts, and keep my judgments and do them." [Before we go farther, I pray take special notice, that the Church by the grace of Christ is freed from fear of being abandoned, because she did not at any time grow to forsake God's judgments, for He will still give her grace to keep them.] "In that day that I shall cleanse you from all your iniquities, and shall make the cities to be inhabited, and shall repair the ruinous places, and the desert land shall be tilled; and they shall say, This land untilled is become a garden of pleasure." And, ver. 37, "I will increase them with men like a flock, as the flock of Jerusalem in her solemn feasts [in which feasts many thousand men, gathered out of every household of that nation, did use to go up to Jerusalem]; so shall the desert cities be full of flocks of men." How can universality, and a most visible numerosity, be more fully expressed; when even the desert places shall be filled, as Jerusalem was thronged and crowded in the solemnities thereof? Daniel, chap. ii. 35, makes the Church of a little stone grown into a mountain, filling the whole earth; how ridiculously, then, do you tell me, you can scarce see it for this thousand years before Luther?

7. Mich. chap. iv. 1, "And it shall be in the latter end of the days [1 Joh. ii. 18, the time of the New Testament is called the last hour], there shall be the mount of the house of our Lord prepared in the top of mountains, and high above all the hills [what more visible?], and people shall flow unto it, and many nations shall hasten, and shall say, Come, let us go up to the mountain of our Lord, and to the house of the God of Jacob," &c. And, ver. 7, "I will make her that labours into a mighty nation, and our Lord will reign over them from this time, now and for ever." So that "from this time, now and for ever," the Church was promised still for all ages to be a *mighty* or *strong nation*. Never a small invisible unknown company.

8. Zach. chap. xiv. 8, "And it shall be in that day, living waters shall issue forth from Jerusalem; half of them to the east sea, and half of them to the last sea; in summer and winter shall they be, and our Lord God shall be king over all the earth: and in that day shall be one Lord, and his name shall be one." And by and by he tells us at large, even to the end of the chapter, how all nations shall be accursed that come not up to adore in his Church. A manifest sign of her perpetual purity in doctrine. For how would God lay such curses and plagues upon men for refusing to follow the Church erring?

9. Malach, chap. i. 11, tells us, the Church shall be extended as far as the sunbeams among the Gentiles. "From the rising of the sun, even to the going down thereof, great is my name among the Gentiles; and in every place there is sacrificing, and there is offered a clean oblation, because my name is great among the Gentiles, saith the Lord of Hosts." Behold the true Church, all the world over, offering a pure and grateful sacrifice.

10. The places of the New Testament are more known, as that the Church, by reason of her continual universality, is a *city upon a hill*, still to be seen

from all places. *A candle upon a candlestick*, as well seen to the whole world, as a candle to the whole room in which it burns. The Apostles are sent to *preach to all nations*. The little *mustard-seed* grows to be the biggest of all plants, like the cedar in Ezekiel, chap. xvii. 22. St. Peter's net is even broken with the taking of fish, &c. But because the New Testament writes no farther than the Acts of the Apostles, and contained but a small part of them, the subsequent conversion of the multitude of nations, of the strength of Gentiles, and of all the kings of the earth (as the above-cited texts declare) is to be taken out of history, in which manifestly the truth of all that was foretold doth appear. But all this, wholly and entirely, was performed by the Roman Church only, that is, by such as have been known to have joined in communion with her. If you say the Roman is not the true Church, here foretold by the prophets, then I pray ponder well how impossible it is for you upon earth to find any other Church to which those manifold prophecies, with any show of probability, can be applied.

POINT V.

OF THE INFALLIBILITY OF THE CHURCH, AND CONSEQUENTLY OF HER FITNESS TO BE JUDGE OF CONTROVERSIES.

1. NOTE, that in two manners or ways, things of belief and practice may be delivered by a community: The first is, when such things, once received by the said community, are perpetually retained by the same in all places by the public practice; and also, upon all occasions, taught by word of mouth, and expressed in written books. Thus our common-law in England (though never written by any law-maker) is notwithstanding by daily practice most faithfully

kept, and hath been so for so many hundred years by
the whole nation diffused. And in this manner the
Church diffused keepeth in perpetual practice, and
delivereth to her children as infallible truth, what
was first delivered unto her, by commission from God,
either in writing or by word of mouth. The other
way of making and delivering laws, is to call together
the representative body of the community. So here
in England our statute-laws are made, not by the
king alone, nor by the parliament alone, but by the
order both of the king and parliament. And what is
thus enacted is the decree of the nation representative. Now as the representative of our nation is the
king and parliament, so the Church representative is
the chief pastor thereof, together with a lawful general council. And the definitions and decrees set forth
by their authority are called the definitions and the
decrees of the Church representative. All such definitions we Roman Catholics hold infallible. Whether the definition of a council alone, defining without
their chief pastor, or the definitions of the chief pastor alone, defining without a council, be infallible or
no, there be several opinions amongst us; in which
we do and may vary without any prejudice to our
faith, which is not built upon what is yet under opinion, but upon that which is delivered as infallible;
and we all unanimously hold that to be so, which the
universal Church representative, consisting jointly of
the chief pastor of the said Church voting in and
with a general council; not that this representative,
made wholly of men, is not, of its own nature, subject to error. For this we never affirm. And so our
adversaries say nothing at all to the purpose, whilst
they labour to prove this. Let them disprove, if they
can (and that out of Scripture alone), that which we
say, namely, That this Church representative is infallible merely and purely by the special assistance of
the Divine Providence, always affording to his Church
a sufficient measure of *the spirit of truth to lead*

her into all truth. And that he is ever so surely resolved to do this, that no sins of his Church shall ever hinder him from doing it, as is most expressly delivered by God himself, Psalm lxxxix., in the words cited by me at large, Point III. No. 3. Which place the reader shall find most convincing to prove, that notwithstanding all the sins that shall ever happen in his Church, the sun and moon shall sooner fail than God will fail to provide a successor in Christ's throne, to govern his Church in the profession of truth, so as *his faithfulness shall not fail,* or *none of his words be frustrated;* which you shall see delivered again and again in the ensuing places of Scripture. All which (to the number of thirty) I gather so fully, because the Protestants exclaim against nothing more than the Church's claim to infallibility, which Dr. Ferne calls *the very bane of Christendom,* though it be the very groundwork of Christianity. For all the interpretation of Scripture is fallible, if the interpretation of the Church be fallible, even then when she hath carefully conferred Scripture with Scripture.

2. And to avoid confusion, I will divide these thirty texts into these three several sorts. The first sort shall contain either such as command us absolutely to follow and obey the Church in such a manner as would wholly misbeseem God to command us, if she could thrust errors upon us for divine verities; or such texts as teach us to rely more upon the Church than could prudently be done, if she could teach error. The second sort shall contain a multitude of such glorious expressions made every where of the Church, as would be most empty and truthless if the Church should ever prove a mistress of errors, and press them on her children for divine verities. The third and last sort shall be such texts as plainly affirm truth to be still taught in the Church, and to be entailed upon her, promising she shall not revolt from it, but stand still a true pillar and ground of truth.

3. *Of the first sort of texts,* we have these, by which

either God commands us universally to follow his Church, or speaks that of his Church which could not be delivered as it is, if this Church could err. For example, how could God glory in the multitude of such as follow his Church, if, by so doing, they should be led into error? And yet (Isaias ii.) God seems to glory in the multitude of those who confidently resort to the Church, as to a mistress of assured truth, to be instructed by her, saying, ver. 3, "Let us go up to the mountain of our Lord, and he will teach us his ways, and we shall walk in his paths, and he shall judge among the nations." Behold Christ erecting a court of tribunal in his Church, *to judge among nations, and decide all their controversies;* which must needs suppose obedience to be yielded to this judgment. Yea, the same prophet adds, liv. 17, "That no weapon that is formed against thee shall prosper: and every tongue resisting thee in judgment thou shalt condemn." And the prophet, there, from the beginning manifestly speaks of Christ's Church. Thirdly, Isaias lx. 12, "The nation and kingdom that will not serve thee shall perish." Under pain of perishing, the Church must be obeyed. Whence, fourthly, Ezech. xliv. 23, "They [that is, the priests] shall teach the people what is between a holy thing and a thing polluted, and the difference between clean and unclean they shall show them. And when there shall be controversy, they shall stand in judgment, and shall judge according to my judgments." This being their office, the people's office must needs be, not to judge them, but obey them.

4. Whence, fifthly, Christ (Matt. xviii. 17) commands all to obey the Church, under pain of being held here on earth as *publicans* and *heathens*, and of having this sentence ratified in heaven. "Tell the Church, saith he; and if he will not hear the Church, let him be unto thee as a heathen and a publican. Amen, I say unto you, whatsoever you shall bind on earth shall be bound in heaven; and whatsoever you

shall loose upon earth shall be loosed also in heaven."
Here you see obedience to be yielded under pain of
being held *as a publican or a heathen*, and this sentence
to be ratified in heaven. Now, if the Church could err
in teaching,—for example, that Christ is truly present
in the sacrament, and hence oblige all to adore him
therein as much as they adore him in heaven, and
could oblige them to this under pain of being held as
publicans and heathens, and held so as well in heaven
as upon earth,—surely this cannot be an error. For
then in heaven this sentence would never be ratified.
And tell me not that this text speaks of private differences between brother and brother; though I deny
not but this is also true in such differences as belong
to the court or tribunal of the Church. Yet hence it
evidently follows, that this text doth much more concern those differences in point of religion between
brother and brother. Both because these do more properly belong to the court of the Church and to her tribunal, as also because when scandal and offence is given
to our brother in point of heresy, tending to the seduc-
tion of his soul, our brother, seeing this soul-murder-
ing sin broached to his own ruin and to the eternal
ruin of his brother, hath far greater reason in this
case than in any other to *tell the Church his mother*, to
whom, in this difference above all other *differences*, it
properly belongeth to look to the safety of her children. For this is an offence and scandal to the
whole brotherhood of all Christianity. Therefore, in
these points of highest concernment, we are most
bound to *hear the Church*, under pain of being accounted *publicans* and *heathens*, and of having this
heavy sentence *ratified in heaven*.

5. Sixthly, Matt. xxiii. 1, "Then Jesus spoke to
the multitude and to his disciples, saying, Upon the
chair of Moses have sitten the Scribes and Pharisees [by which sitting, with lawful succession, they,
as wicked as they were, are known to be lawfully
authorised prelates]; all therefore whatsoever they

shall say unto you, observe and do." Behold here a precept of obeying in *all whatsoever*. And therefore behold a precept, which could not be given, if that which is delivered by public authority of the Church were not secured from error in *all whatsoever*.

6. Seventhly, The first and best Christians did practically acknowledge their belief of the infallibility of the Church. For, to have a decision of the most important controversies, Acts xv. 2, " They appointed Paul and Barnabas to go up, and certain others of the rest, to the apostles and priests, unto Jerusalem, upon this question." And the Church assembled the first council, in which, though this council were assisted by the Holy Ghost, yet "there was made a great disputation," ver. 7. And then the definition of the Church came forth in these words : " It seemeth good to the Holy Ghost and us," ver. 28. Other lawful councils, knowing the Holy Ghost also promised to them, do use to set forth their definitions with the same words, and this most agreeable to Scripture. For, John xv. 26, " When the Paraclete cometh, whom I shall send from my Father, the spirit of truth, he shall give testimony of me, and you shall give testimony." Mark this conjunction of *he* and *you;* he the *spirit of truth,* and *you* governors of my Church; so that you in giving testimony may freely say, " It seemeth good to the Holy Ghost and us."

7. Eighthly, It is clear, out of Scripture, that the first Christians were so fully possessed with the belief of the infallibility of the Church, that they would believe nothing but what they knew conformable to her doctrine. St. Paul was a Scripture-writer, and so great an apostle, and yet he saith of himself, Gal. ii. 1, " Then after fourteen years I went to Jerusalem again [not merely to satisfy a vain fancy of some particular men, but] I went up according to revelation, and conferred with them the gospel, which I preach among the Gentiles. But [I conferred] severally (or apart) with them that seemed to be some-

thing, lest perhaps I should run, or had run, in vain." So that he thought all his *fourteen years'* preaching, and also his future preaching, might come to be *in vain*, unless even his doctrine were made known to be approved by the Church, as wholly conformable to the Church. So much, in these golden days, were the first Christians taught to rely upon the Church, which had been imprudence if she had been fallible. Yet we must not think that then they did apprehend that the approbation of the Church did add any degree of truth to his doctrine, as it doth not add any degree of truth to the Scripture, or pretend to have power to change or correct true Scripture. And so St. Paul saith, ver. 6: "For to me, they that seemed to be something, added nothing." For as the touchstone adds no value to the gold, but only evidently manifesteth which is true gold, which not: so the Church, as then, did only manifest infallibly the truth of what he had preached. So also the Church, as now, doth only manifest to us that such and such books be the true word of God, such and such be not; such be true copies, such not, &c. But the word of God hath its true worth from itself, and not from the Church, as the gold hath its being true gold from itself, and not from the touchstone. So when Catholics say with St. Augustin, *Cont. Epist. Fundam*, chap. v., "I would not believe the gospel unless the authority of the Church moved me;" they do not mean that the Church can add, or take away from the truth of any true Scripture; but they mean that, by her definition as by a sure touchstone, it is now manifestly assured unto them that such a book is true Scripture, and such not. And as the oral preaching (even of such an apostle as had been a Scripture-writer) might have been *in vain* without this approbation, so also might his writings have been in vain. Whence we see that his epistle unto the Hebrews was not known or acknowledged as God's word until the Church approved it. If the Scripture-writer himself teacheth *in vain* without this approbation, much more will his writings teach in vain.

8. Ninthly, The Church is to be followed by us as an assured approver or reprover of spirits, and consequently as infallible. John i. 4, "My dearest, believe not every spirit, but prove the spirits if they be of God." Then, ver. 6, "We are of God; he that knows God, hears us [pastors of the Church]; he that is not of God, hears us not. In this we know the spirit of truth and the spirit of error." Here St. John expressly means to give to posterity a *standing rule* to know a true spirit from a false one. To wit, *by the hearing of us, or not hearing of us.* This could not be a rule to us, who live after the apostles, if by *hearing us* he only meant the apostles, and not their successors. Yea, he could not mean only the apostles; for the other apostles were all dead when he wrote this. Wherefore the true sense of St. John is: "In this we know the spirit of truth and the spirit of error, if they hear us,"—pastors and governors of the Church. Not that each one of these pastors and governors apart can say to any one, *hear me,* unless he teach that which all the rest are sufficiently known to teach; but they in a general council may most truly say, *hear us.* He that knoweth God heareth us.

9. Tenthly, In declaring the true meaning of the true Scriptures, the practice and doctrine of the Church is necessary to be followed as a certain guide. For example, when Christ said, "Do this in remembrance of me," he did impose, saith the Church, a true command to do so. Yet, though Christ no less clearly said, John xiii. 14, "That we ought to wash one another's feet; for I have given you an example, that as I have done, so you also should do;" he did not impose, saith the Church, any command obliging us to wash one another's feet. For though he said, "We ought to wash one another's feet," yet by the practice and doctrine of the Church it is assuredly declared to

us that these words of Christ contain no precept, though the former do.

10. Eleventhly, The same apostle, in his first Epistle, ii. 19, after that, concerning heretics, he had said, "They went out from us," he turns his speech to those who still remained in the Church, subject and obedient to it; and of them he saith, "But you have the unction from the Holy One, and know all things." To wit, the spirit of truth, residing in the Church, to teach her all truth, maketh you, who are guided by the Church, to know all things necessary for your information and instruction.

11. Twelfthly, It is grounded in this infallibility of the Church, that her prelates may exact obedience of her children in captivating their understanding to the faith, which she (by commission from Christ) delivereth unto them, 2 Cor. x. 4, "For the weapons of our warfare are not carnal, but mighty, through God, casting down imaginations or reasonings, and every thing that exalts itself against the knowledge, and bringing into captivity all understanding unto the obedience of Christ, and having in a readiness to revenge all disobedience." So St. Paul. But it is most irrational to say, God should empower his Church to force men to follow a Church, which not being infallible must needs confess that she may deceive you, and enforce you to follow errors. Yet this, in a Church having the infallible assistance of the Holy Ghost, is most rational. For there you are, to your apparent good, enforced to follow truth in place of such error as might be most hurtful to you.

Thirteenthly, The same St. Paul tells us that God, out of an express intention which he had to keep us from all wavering and unsettlement in faith, resolved so to assist the governors of his Church that we might rely securely upon them. For, Ephes. iv. 11, "He gave some apostles, and some prophets, and other some evangelists, and other some pastors and teachers; for the perfecting of the saints, for the work of the ministry; for the edifying of the body of Christ, until we all come into the unity of faith; [to what end all this? to the end] that we henceforth be no more children, tossed to and fro, and carried about with every wind of doctrine, by the sleight of men and cunning craftiness," from which his providence had not thus secured us, unless these our teachers had been infallible, when defining in a lawful council, or proposing what is universally taught by them.

12. *The second sort of texts*, proving the infallibility of the Church, contains such glorious titles given her, or such admirable things spoke by God's own mouth of her, as must needs be vain, empty, and truthless words, if the Church ever prove to be a mistress of errors, obtruding them on her children for divine verities. First, Psalm cxxxii. 13, " Our Lord hath chosen Sion; he hath chosen it for an habitation unto himself. This is my rest for ever and ever; here will I dwell, because I have chosen it." Now Christ's dwelling-place, as St. Paul tells us, is his visible Church, 1 Tim. iii. 15, "That thou mayest know how to converse in the house of God, the Church of the living God." He could not be taught how to converse in an invisible Church: he speaks, then, of the Church visible. Far be it from this house to be a store-house of errors. For how then could it be Christ's desirable *habitation*, and his *rest for ever and ever?*

13. Again, Isaias liv. 4, "Fear not, for thou shalt not be ashamed: neither be thou confounded, for thou shalt not be put to shame." What greater shame or confusion to a Church, which should be the pillar and ground of truth, to see herself grown now to profess open superstition, idolatry, and other pernicious errors in whole swarms? How, then, is that true which follows?

14. Thirdly, Isaias lx. 15, " I will make thee an eternal excellency, a joy of many generations." Fourthly, ver. 18, "Thou shalt call thy walls Sal-

vation; our Lord shall be unto thee an everlasting light. Thy sun shall go down no more, and thy moon shall be no more diminished, because our Lord shall be thine everlasting light." Words manifestly spoken, not of the elect, but of the visible Church on earth, even from the beginning of the chapter; for ver. 10, he tells how "kings should minister to her, and how he had struck her [when she was the synagogue] in his indignation." Which words cannot be understood of the elect, or the invisible Church. And so he still goes on speaking.

15. Fifthly, In the like sense, lxii. 3, "Thou shalt be a crown of glory, thou shalt be no more called forsaken [as thou wert when thou wert the synagogue], but thou shalt be called my delight in her." And, sixthly, to secure her from all error contrary to his will, he adds, ver. 6, "Upon thy walls, Jerusalem, I have appointed watchmen [and how careless soever they be by their own nature, yet by my continual assistance] all the day, and all the night for ever, they shall not hold their peace." To wit, by crying down errors. For they had better have held their peace that preached publicly errors every where. And, ver. 12, "Thou shalt be called a city sought for, and not forsaken." And yet Protestants say they did laudably *forsake* every visible Church upon earth, by adhering to Luther and his followers, who did separate themselves from all Churches visible in the whole world, openly professing that as then there was no one Church on earth worth *seeking for;* and so they did not join themselves in communion with any Church then upon earth, but pretended to return to the primitive Church as it was above a thousand years before; which is to say, that, for this whole last thousand years, the Church was a city *forsaken*, and that (for so long) her communion *was not to be sought for.*

16. Seventhly, There is a very convincing text, to prove the Church to be by divine Providence assuredly provided of faithful pastors and governors. Jerem.

xxxiii. 25, "If I have not put my covenant to night and day, and laws to the heaven and earth; then will I cast away the seed of Jacob, and David my servant, that I do not take from his seed princes to be rulers over the seed of Abraham, Isaac, and Jacob." So that we shall be as sure not to fail of faithful princes and governors in the Church (for none but such as are truly faithful can be truly said to be the *true sons of Jacob and David*) as we are sure to have night and day, the heaven turning over us, and the earth standing still under us.

17. Eighthly, The prophet Ezech. xxxiv. 22, "I will save my flock, and it shall be no more into spoil." But what spoil would that scab of error make over all Christ's flock, if it so infected it all, as Protestants say it did; yea, they will have even idolatry itself (the most deadly murrain) to have infected the whole Church this last thousand years and more.

18. *The third and last sort of texts*, to prove this infallibility, contains such as plainly say that God will still direct his Church to follow truth, or that it shall not revolt from the truth, but be a most direct way to the truth: that the spirit of truth shall be, as it were, entailed upon the doctrine of the Church, with which Church this spirit shall ever abide, teaching her all truth. So, first, Isaias lxi. 8, "I will direct their work in truth, and I will make an everlasting covenant with them," of preserving this never-failing truth. Secondly, Behold how plain and direct a way to truth is promised the Church of Christ: Isaias xxxv. 5, "Then shall the eyes of the blind be opened, &c. And a highway shall be there, and it shall be called the way of holiness [the Holy Catholic Church]; the wayfaring men, though fools, shall not err therein." It is therefore a way infallibly leading to truth. Thirdly, The same prophet, lix. 20, "There shall come a redeemer to Sion, and to them that shall return from iniquity in Jacob, saith our Lord. As for me, this is my covenant with them: my spirit

that is in thee, and my words that I have put in thy mouth, shall not depart out of thy mouth, nor out of the mouth of thy seed, nor out of the mouth of thy seed's seed, from this present and for ever." With what clearer words could the spirit of truth be entailed upon the Church present in each age, or be more clearly said to reside ever *in her mouth*, with which she delivers all her doctrine?

19. Fourthly, Most clearly, Jer. xxxii. 39, "I will give them one heart and one way, that they may fear me for ever: I will make an everlasting covenant with them, that I will not turn away from them; but will put my fear in their hearts, that they shall not depart from me." Note, I pray, these words, "I will put my fear in their hearts, that they shall not depart from me." Wherefore they did not revolt from him; they did not depart from him. Fifthly, No less fully speaks the prophet Ezekiel, xxxvii. 24, "My servant David king over them, and there shall be one shepherd over them all. They shall walk in my judgment, and observe my statutes, and do them. Moreover, I will make a covenant of peace with them: it shall be an everlasting covenant with them; and I will set my sanctuary in the midst of them for evermore." How fully is all this spoken of a visible Church, having one *shepherd over all!* Yea, the very heathens shall know who they be, as there is said. Sixthly, That, according to the prophet Micah, iv. 5, "All people will walk every one in the name of his God, and we will walk in the name of our Lord God for ever and ever." Which they do not who walk in a labyrinth of gross errors for a thousand years together. It followeth, "I will make her who was cast off a strong nation, and the Lord shall reign over thee from henceforth and for ever."

20. Seventhly, Matt. xvi. 18, "The gates of hell shall not prevail against it." If hell could ever come to make the Church a mistress of errors, so as to hold them forth for divine verities so many ages together,

the gates of hell should highly prevail against her. Now, I pray, note that for many ages there were no Christians which were not either manifest heretics (and held so by the Protestants themselves) or which did not (as all Roman Catholics now do) worship and adore Christ, as much under the shape of bread in the Eucharist as they worship him sitting at the right hand of his Father. If this be idolatry, the gates of hell have prevailed against the Roman Church; yea, and against the Churches in Greece, in Armenia, in Ethiopia, &c., who all, ever since they were Christians, have held this our doctrine, and do still hold it, though they add a world of other errors. Where, then, shall the Protestants find Christ a Church against which the gates of hell have not a vast long time together prevailed? They must either be forced to make Christ false in this his doctrine, or to confess our doctrine true. If it be not, how was this *covenant everlasting*, as hath been so often said in the now-cited texts; and also in the text following, in which Christ made the *everlasting covenant*, formerly promised to be made?

21. Eighthly, St. John xiv. 16, "And he will give you another Paraclete, that may abide with you for ever, the spirit of truth, whom the world knows not; but you know him, because he dwells with you, and shall be in you." Now the Apostles, not being to be *for ever*, and the spirit of truth being promised *for ever*, we cannot but say that the promise of this *spirit of truth* is made also to the successors of the Apostles, the governors of Christ's Church, to "abide in them and be in them, as the spirit of truth," directly opposite to the spirit of error. So, ninthly, John xvi. 12, "Many things I have to say unto you, but you cannot bear them now [hence appears how weighty those things were]; but when the spirit of truth cometh, he will guide you into all truth." To private persons the Holy Ghost is given as the spirit of sanctification; but to the Church he is given as the "spirit of truth,

guiding her into all truth," and so directly excluding all error from her.

22. Tenthly, That convincing place of St. Paul shall end all these texts, 1 Tim. iii. 15, where, speaking of the visible Church, in which he teacheth Timothy how to converse, he speaks thus: "That thou mayest know how to behave thyself in the house of God, which is the Church of the living God, the pillar and ground of truth." Can I lean more assuredly than upon the pillar of truth? Can I even wish to have a surer ground than the *ground of truth?* And yet such a ground is the Church acknowledged in this text, if it be not perverted by such interpretations as be the inventions of men, but of men unable to confirm their interpretation by any text clearer than this. Here then, behold, we have produced no fewer than *thirty texts* for the infallibility of the Church; whereas not half so many, nor half so convincing, texts can be alleged against it. And yet grant this, and you must grant all. Note, that besides these thirty texts here alleged I have also all those numerous and most full texts related at large, Point III. For whatsoever proves that the true Church cannot fail to be a true Church proves also her infallibility. For truth of doctrine is essential to a true Church. If therefore, by being fallible and erring, the whole Church could recede from the true doctrine of Christ, it manifestly follows that the whole Church could fail to be a true Church, contrary to these most express Scriptures there plentifully alleged.

23. Most impertinent is the distinction which our adversaries use to avoid the force of these texts. They say that the Church may be taken in two ways. First, for the visible Church, containing all believers, as well reprobate as elect; and this Church, they say, may err. Secondly, for the invisible Church, which only contains the elect; and this, they say, cannot err. But this is a palpable contradiction, if well noted. For this invisible Church of the elect, which, as you say, cannot

err, is contained in the visible Church, in which, as you say, both reprobate and elect are contained; which visible Church, you also say, may wholly err. But if the whole visible Church wholly err, then also the elect contained in it may err; or if they cannot err, then many in the visible Church cannot err. And yet you cannot find many in any Church visible upon earth whom you can show on the one side to have differed from the belief of the Roman Church, and on the other to have been guarded from error, as those who make the true Church must be. Again, I have showed that many texts here by me cited speak clearly of the visible Church.

POINT VI.

THAT THE ROMAN CHURCH IS THIS INFALLIBLE CHURCH, AND OUR JUDGE IN ALL POINTS OF CONTROVERSY.

1. THOUGH this question seems to import as much as the certain decision of all our controversies, yet having been so long in the former point, we are able to give in a word full satisfaction in this. For no man will deny the Church which is proved to be infallible to be the most commodious decider of all controversies. For what can a man wish more to the right decision of his controversy than a clear sentence, delivered therein by an infallible authority?

2. All that can be imagined against what hath been said is this, that we have not as yet proved the Roman Church to be infallible. We have indeed proved the true Church to be so; but there seems a vast labour to remain to prove the Roman Church to be this infallible true Church, and consequently the decider of all controversies. I most earnestly therefore beg of my reader to note well this one short de-

monstration, and he will see how evidently convincing it is to prove home our full intent, even in a word.

3. My demonstration is this: no Church can be the true infallible Church, and decider of all controversies, which teacheth herself to be fallible. For if any Church be infallible in all that she teacheth, she is infallible also in teaching herself to be fallible. And hence it followeth that infallibly such a Church is fallible; but every Church in the world but the Roman teacheth herself to be fallible; whereof, by evident demonstration, no other Church upon earth can be infallible. But the true Church is infallible, as has been proved by no fewer than *thirty texts;* therefore by evident consequence the Roman Church, by all those texts, is proved the only true Church, and our judge in all our controversies.

POINT VII.

THAT THE CHIEF PASTOR OF THIS CHURCH IS THE SUCCESSOR OF ST. PETER.

1. THE Old Testament helps us thus far in this point that it teacheth, first, that amongst the priests of the old law one was chosen successively to be the highest and chief priest, Num. iii. 32, "The prince of princes of the Levites, Eleazar, the son of Aaron, the priest." And, Num. xxvii. 21, "If any thing be to be done, for Joshua their governor, Eleazar the priest shall consult our Lord. At his words shall he (Joshua) go out and go in, and all the rest of the children of Israel with him." By *going in* and *going out*, all the principal actions are usually understood in Scripture. In those actions, therefore, God would have Joshua and all the people to depend on the high-priest. When, then, we read, Joshua iii. 8, that Joshua did command the priests, and that, chap. v., he ap-

pointed circumcision to be ministered, and that, chap. xxiv., he renewed God's covenant, &c., he is to be supposed therein, as in all his principal actions, to have proceeded according to the above-cited text, only executing that which God, by Eleazar the priest, had ordained him to do. For example : To command the priests to go with the ark into Jordan, to administer circumcision, to renew the covenant with God, &c. Again, when princes are also prophets (as Joshua, David, Solomon, and some others were), they might have some extraordinary commission to do, and order several things, which belong not to the orderly jurisdiction of temporal princes. So, Kings ii. 27, "Solomon cast out Abiather, that he should not be the priest of our Lord : yet this was done that the word of our Lord might be fulfilled which he spake concerning the house of Helie." Solomon, also as a prophet, by extraordinary commission, ver. 35, placed Sadoc the priest for Abiather.

2. Secondly, We have clearly in the Old Testament the distinction of the chief ecclesiastical and chief secular power. 2 Chron. xix. 11, "And behold Amariath, the chief-priest, is over you in all matters of the Lord," that is, " ecclesiastical affairs." Then for temporal, or secular affairs, Zebediah, the ruler of the house of Judah, for all the king's matters; whence it is clear that the former causes are not *matters which appertain to the kings*.

3. Thirdly, We have the old law, Deut. xvii. 8, commanding all such causes, as are ecclesiastical causes, to be brought to the tribunal of the high-priest, and his sentence to be obeyed even under pain of death. I call them ecclesiastical causes, because the former text saith, they *be matters of the Lord*, and distinct from *matters of the king*.

4. Fourthly, We have out of the New Testament this unanswerable text concerning the high-priests even of the old law, Matt. xxiii. 2, "Upon the chair of Moses have sitten the Scribes and Pharisees; all

therefore whatsoever they shall say unto you, observe and do it." No wickedness of the high-priest's person shall excuse your obedience, if he sit upon the chair of Moses. Moses was not only a secular prince, but also the first high-priest amongst the Jews, "Moses and Aaron amongst his priests," Psalm xcix. 6. Now those who succeeded Moses, as he was high-priest, are said *to sit upon the chair of Moses;* for as he was the secular prince of the people, Joshua in that dignity did succeed him. But he had but *part of his glory;* so, Num. xxvii. 18, "Take Joshua, the son of Nun, a man in whom is the spirit, and put thy hand upon him, who shall stand before Eleazar the priest, and thou, O Moses, shalt put some of thine honour upon him." Now the one part of Moses' honour was to be a secular prince and commander-in-chief. In this dignity Joshua did succeed him. But in Levit. viii. God commanded Moses to invest Aaron with the other part of his dignity, which was to be high-priest. But when Aaron now came to die, God said to Moses, Num. xx. 26, "Take Aaron, and his son with him; and when thou hast divested the father of his vesture, thou shalt revest therewith Eleazar his son: Moses did as our Lord commanded him." And thus successively God provided his Church of high-priests. Neither, for the wickedness of any of them did he cease to govern his Church by them, even by heavenly and supernatural assistance. As bad as Caiphas was, yet, because he was the high-priest, he did prophesy, John xi. 51, "He said not this of himself, but being the high-priest of that year, he prophesied that Jesus should die for the nation."

5. The old law being now transferred to the new, it was necessary that the priesthood also should be transferred, these two going together, Heb. vii. 12, whereof the new law being the lady, the old the handmaid, as St. Paul speaks; the new law also, according to him, being "established upon better promises," Heb. viii. 6, we may, with all ground in Scripture,

expect to see Christ's Church ever provided of such high-priests as shall, by his bounty, have many advantages above the high-priests of the old law. Christ, then, intending to build this new Church, he called to him, even among the first of his Apostles, Simon, and presently changed his name into Cephas, which is interpreted Peter, a rock, John i. 42. To this Simon, Matt. xvi. 18, he saith, "Thou art Peter," which, in that language which Christ spoke, is as much as to say, "Thou art a rock, and upon this rock I will build my Church." The wisest of men designs a sure rock for the everlasting building of his Church in the midst of all winds and waves; and if any one say that Christ himself is a rock, so as not to communicate this rock-like firmity of his also to St. Peter, he flatly contradicts Christ's saying, "Thou art a rock, and upon this rock I will build my Church." If any man should take a fair stone in his hand, and say, "Thou art a fair goodly solid stone, and upon this stone I intend to raise a chapel," who would conceive this man, in the last part of his speech, to point at any other stone than that which he had in his hand? True it is, that Christ is the foundation; yet without any dishonour to him (nay, to the increase of his honour), he communicateth that very title of foundation to others. So, Eph. ii. 20, we are said, "Built upon the foundation of the apostles and prophets—Jesus Christ being the chief corner-stone." Christ, then, is the chief rock of an everlasting perpetuity, and this by his own virtue. St. Peter is a rock standing firm everlastingly, not by his virtue, but by the virtue of Christ, and made thus, not for his own sake, but for Christ's Church's sake,—Christ intending that his Church should stand for ever: as I proved, Point III. Whence Christ adds, "Upon this rock I will build my Church." We willingly grant that the Church was to be built —not upon the shoulders of St. Peter, but upon his faith; yet his faith must not be taken as separated from his person, but it must be taken as the thing chiefly regarded in his person; for which, to him personally, this dignity was given; yet given chiefly for the perpetual good of the Church to be built upon him. Wherefore, lest the building should be shattered at his death, this firm perpetuity of a rock—that is, this "faith of his, which Christ prayed should never fail," Luke xxii. 32—was to be derived to his lawful successors; as the chair of Moses ever had the successors of Moses sitting in it; for no well-ordered commonwealth is destitute of sufficient means still to provide her of her lawful heads and governors appointed her successively. And as it is not enough to say, *Christ is King of kings and Lord of lords*, therefore the civil commonwealth needs no other king or lord; so it seems far greater nonsense to say, that because Christ is the chief head and priest of the Church, therefore we, upon earth, need no other head to govern such a commonwealth as the Church is, containing so many several people, of so many nations, natures, customs, and dispositions as be found from the rising of the sun to the going down of the same, though this so far-spread commonwealth were intended, from the beginning, to last as long as the sun and moon. It was, then, for this his Church's sake that some one was ever to be first and chief in it.

6. "Now," saith St. Matthew, numbering the apostles (princes of the Church), "the names of the twelve apostles be these: the first, Simon, who is called Peter," Matt. x. 2. And so in all places where the apostles are counted, as Judas is always the last, so St. Peter is counted first; and as it was said of Eleazar, "That he was the prince of princes of the Levites," Num. iii. 32, so amongst the spiritual princes of Christ's Church St. Matthew doth not only count him first, but plainly says he was *the first:* "The first, Simon, who is called Peter." He was neither *the first* in order of calling to the apostleship, nor in

age, for his brother Andrew was before him in both these, John i. Again, to signify that he was the head and chief in ordinary, Christ said to him, Matt. xvi. 19, "And to thee will I give the keys of the kingdom of heaven." For though the power of loosing and binding was afterwards given to the other apostles, John xx. 23, yet the *keys of the kingdom of heaven* are never, in Scripture, said to be given to any but to St. Peter. The giving of the keys is well known to signify naturally the supreme rule in a city or family. Hence the keys of a city are offered to the chief governors at their entrance. So, also, *the key of the house of David* is given to Christ, *being to reign in the house of David for ever*. Here Christ giveth the keys to St. Peter as to his successor in the "house of God, which is the Church of the living God," 1 Tim. iii. 15. By these keys is signified the plenitude of highest power.

7. Again, John xxi. 15, "Simon of John, lovest thou me more than these? Feed my lambs." And yet again, ver. 17, "Feed my sheep." Note that he would not have required *greater love* in Peter rather than in any of the rest, nor have said, "lovest thou me more than these?" if he had not here intended to give him higher dignity in pastorship than to the rest. If every one of the other apostles be sheep of Christ, St. Peter is here made pastor to every one of them, for he is commanded *to feed them*. Note again, and principally, that the whole flock of Christ, *his lambs, his sheep*, his subjects and their rulers, did not consist of those only men who then lived, but much more of all such faithful men as were to be of the flock and Church of Christ, even from his days to the end of the world. Wherefore this high pastorship being, as we said, chiefly instituted by Christ, out of his love and care to his flock, and not merely out of the desire of honouring St. Peter, was by ordinary course of succession to be devolved to all posterity.

8. And that no man should say that this succession shall ever fail, thus saith our Lord, Jer. xxxiii. 17, "David shall never want a man to sit upon the throne of the house of Israel, and of the priests and Levites there shall not fail a man," &c. And he adds, "That his covenant should sooner be made void with the day and the night, than his covenant should be made void with David his servant. That there be not of him a son to reign in his throne, and Levites and priests his ministers." And the prophet Isaias, in his last chapter, tells us that in the new law these Levites shall not be born Levites of the tribe of Levi, or any particular tribe or nation, but by election; they shall be chosen to be Levites out of several nations, particularly of Italians, Grecians, Africans, and the islands afar off; though the English Bible doth not translate these names; "I will take, saith he, of them to be priests and Levites." But shall there not still be one chief pastor of these never-decaying races of priests and Levites? Yes, there shall. "And they shall have one shepherd or pastor over them all," Ezech. xxxvii. 24.

POINT VIII.

THAT THIS OUR CHIEF PASTOR OR POPE IS NOT ANTICHRIST.

1. BECAUSE there is never a pulpit in England in which the Pope hath not been preached, by all our ministers, to be not only Antichrist, but also *the Antichrist* who is so much spoken of and detested in Scripture, I thought fit to make my dear countrymen see with their own eyes how unconscionably these their ministers so universally deal with them in this point, in which they cannot but see (if, indeed,

they read and will understand) how flatly and point-blank this doctrine is against most manifest Scripture.

2. First, The Scripture teacheth clearly that Antichrist is one particular determinate man, and not any rank of several distinct men successively living one after the other, as Popes do. Hence, 2 Thess. ii. 3, Antichrist is called "that man of sin, the son of perdition; the adversary." And, Apoc. xiii. 14, an image shall be made of this particular person, whereas no such image can represent those hundreds of popes who have sat in St. Peter's chair. Again, there it followeth, that this particular man shall have a special name, and such a peculiar number shall express this name: "For it is the number of a man." A man, I say, and not many men succeeding one another, as popes are; whence it followeth, "The number of him is six hundred sixty-six." Of that *him* whom Christ also insinuated to be one particular *man*, when he said, John v. 41, "If another shall come in his name, him you will receive." Whereas no one of the popes was yet received by the Jews. Wherefore, of the Pope it is false to say the *Jews have received him*. And this is the second reason why the Pope, according to Scripture, is not Antichrist.

3. Thirdly, This one particular man shall not come until we be close bordering upon the very last end of the world, Mark xiii. 25, "But in those days, after that tribulation [of Antichrist], the sun shall be darkened." Popes have been ever since St. Peter's days; and that which you all call Popery hath been (as you confess) above these thousand years, and yet the sun shines upon the world as clearly as ever.

4. Fourthly, This one special man shall reign but a short time; whereas these popes (upholders of confessed Popery) have reigned these many ages. Antichrist shall reign but three years and a half, "a time, and times, and half a time," Dan. vii. 25 and

Apoc. xii. 14. Hence, Dan. xii. 11, this time is further expounded to be "a thousand two hundred and ninety days." And the Church, a little after this persecution begins, shall fly into the wilderness "for a thousand two hundred and sixty days." And for this time of "one thousand two hundred and sixty days, the two witnesses shall prophesy," Apoc. xi. 3. For the persecution of Antichrist shall last but two-and-forty months, as is there expressly said. And, Apoc. xiii. 5, "Power was given (to the beast) to continue two-and-forty months." The time, therefore, of Antichrist's reign shall be short. "For the elect, the days shall be shortened," Matt. xxiv. 22. So, Apoc. xx. 3, it is said, that the devil shall be let loose for the short time of Antichrist's reign : "After these things he must be loosed a little time." That is, after Christ hath bound up the devil, during the long time of the New Testament (described there by the complete and perfect number of a thousand years), he shall be let loose for the short time of the reign of Antichrist.

5. Fifthly, All the ministers in England, or out of England, can never be able to show that the Pope did ever kill two such witnesses as Antichrist is clearly said to kill, Apoc. xi. 6. That is, "two witnesses who shall prophesy one thousand two hundred and sixty days, clothed in sackcloth; who shall have power to shut the heavens, that it may not rain in the days of their prophecy; and power of the waters to turn them into blood, and to strike the earth with all plagues as often as they will." If your ministers will prove the Pope to be Antichrist, they must not only prove that he did kill two such witnesses as they are (for the true Antichrist must do this), but also that they must prove that the Pope did kill two such witnesses in Jerusalem, leaving their bodies lying in the streets thereof. For this, also, the true Antichrist must do ; because it followeth, ver. 7, "the beast shall kill them, and their bodies shall lie

in the streets where the Lord was crucified," that is, in Jerusalem.

6. Sixthly, Hence appears that the chief seat of Antichrist shall be at Jerusalem, where he shall most show his power and glory, whence it was also said before that the Jews should receive him; and the holy fathers commonly say, he shall be born a Jew of the tribe of Dan, which is the cause why that tribe was not numbered with the rest, Apoc. vii.; neither could the Jews receive him if he were not born a Jew. None of these things agree to the Pope, and yet they all agree to Antichrist.

7. Seventhly, The beast which shall set up the power of Antichrist " shall make fire come down from heaven to earth in the sight of men," Apoc. xiii. 13. Tell me what setter-up of the Pope's power did ever do this?

8. Eighthly, There also, ver. 17, it is said, that he also shall effect " that no man shall buy or sell, but he that hath the character or name of the beast, or number of his name." In what Pope's days was this verified?

9. Ninthly, and lastly, 2 Thess. ii. 4, "That one special man (who is called *that man of sin*) is extolled above all that is called God, or (all) that is worshiped." Now, whosoever is extolled above "all that is God," is not only extolled above judges and kings, sometimes called gods, as all just men are, but "to be extolled above all that is called God," he must be extolled above God himself, who (in the very first place) is called God. So he that is extolled above (all) that is worshiped must be extolled not only above princes and kings, but above saints and angels, and God himself. Now, neither doth the Pope extol himself, nor is extolled by any of his adherents, above the apostles or angels, and much less above God himself, showing himself that he is God, as their said Antichrist shall do.

POINT IX.

OF THE SACRAMENTS OF THE CHURCH, AND OF THE CEREMONIES WHICH THE CHURCH USETH IN ADMINISTERING THESE SACRAMENTS, AS ALSO IN OTHER OCCASIONS.

1. HAVING treated of the Church, and her chief Pastor, it followeth to treat of the Sacraments of this Church. And because our Church useth several ceremonies in the administration of these sacraments (and especially in sacrifice of the Mass), as also in other several occasions (a thing much scoffed at by our adversaries), we will here also treat of these ceremonies.

2. First, then, concerning the sacraments in general, before we come to treat of every particular sacrament, to prevent mistakes, I define a sacrament to be *an outward sign, instituted by Christ, signifying the inward grace which it confers when duly received.* And here it must be exactly noted, that every such outward sign or holy ceremony (by the applying of which, inward grace is infallibly conferred, when it is duly received) must needs be a sign or ceremony instituted by Christ. For nobody but Christ could annex the infallible gift of inward grace to the applying of such an outward sign.

3. Now if any one will stand contending to prove that a sacrament is something else, and ought to be defined otherwise, all that I need to say in confutation of him is, that I will find in Scripture seven such holy signs or ceremonies, to the due application of which the gift of inward grace is infallibly annexed. And for this reason, I say, that these are either seven true sacraments, or else seven things much better than those which your definition will allow to be sacraments. For by these seven that divine quality of heavenly grace is conferred; by yours it is not. But before I come to show our seven sacraments in parti-

cular to be such holy signs or ceremonies instituted by Christ (from whom all grace is derived), I will, in the second place, treat of the ceremonies of the Church which Protestants are pleased to account foolish, childish, apish, comical, &c.

4. I say, then, that the light of reason teaches us in all actions (which we desire to raise above the rank of vulgar actions) to devise some ceremonies to set that action forth in such a manner that all shall, by the very sight of it, be stirred up to apprehend such an action to be far surpassing ordinary things. So, in the solemn inauguration of great princes, in the coronation of kings, in their going to sit in Parliament, yea, in their carrying to their graves and interment, great choice is made of exquisite ceremonies to set forth these actions, so that they may be raised much above the strain of vulgar actions. Wherefore, seeing no actions deserve more esteem, or to be raised to a higher degree of reverence and veneration amongst the Christian people, than the chief actions of our religion, it was consistent that the administration of the sacraments (being the chief of these actions) should, chiefly of all other actions, be graced and set forth with some kind of ceremonies, such as the Church should think most suitable, that so all the vulgar, by the very sight of those actions, may be excited to conceive a sacred esteem of those actions, set forth so mystically, in a manner quite different from ordinary and vulgar actions. By this argument, and not by any text of Scripture, you must justify your ministers' surplice.

The law of nature (which was before the ceremonial law) did teach the holiest men of that law thus, to raise the most pious actions they solemnly performed by addition of certain ceremonies. So, holy Jacob, Gen. xxviii. 18, "Arising in the morning, took the stone that he had laid under his head, and erected it for a title (or monument) and poured out oil upon the top of it." A ceremony so far from being supersti-

F

tious, that (Gen. xxxi. 13) God approves this fact, appearing to Jacob, and saying, "I am the God of Bethel, where thou didst anoint the stone, and didst vow thy vow to me."

5. And because our adversaries scoff at ceremonies as if they were ridiculous things, we desire them to reflect, whether a heathen may not as well scoff at the Jewish ceremonies, appointed by God himself; as indeed the Jews, both by the Greeks and the old Romans, were held for the most superstitious people of the world upon that account. And though the Jewish ceremonies appointed by God do now cease, yet it is now blasphemy to say any of them were foolish, apish, comical gestures. Yet looked upon with carnal eyes, they may (to the full) as much appear to have been so, as the ceremonies of the Church appear to you. For example, what a mimical action would you account it in us, if we should, in the consecration of the Pope, appoint that *the tip of his right ear, and the thumb and great toe of his right hand and right foot*, should be the parts particularly anointed; and yet God himself commanded (Exod. xxix. 20) that in the consecration of Aaron and his sons, "Thou shalt take the blood of a ram, and put it upon the tip of the right ear of Aaron and of his sons, and upon the thumbs and great toes of their right hand and foot." A number of as strange ceremonies as these are both in this book of Exodus, and particularly in Leviticus, and yet all set down by God's own appointment. And it is now blasphemy to say they were ridiculous.

6. But let us pass to the new law: though in this all Jewish ceremonies are abolished, yet is it nowhere said that we should serve God without ceremonies, which no nation under heaven ever did, as those who are skilled in antiquity know. Yea, Christ himself was pleased to set forth some more mystical cures, which he did, with such ceremonies as you would scoff at them if our Church (in far more mystical ac-

tions) had made use of them. So, Mark vii. 32, in the cure of a deaf and dumb man. First, *He took him from the multitude apart*. Secondly, *He put his fingers into his ears*. Thirdly, *Spitting, he touched his tongue*. Fourthly, *He looked up to heaven*. Fifthly, *He groaned*. Sixthly, *He used a word deserving special interpretation*, saying *Ephphetha*, that is, *Be opened*. So also, John viii. 6, in pardoning the adulteress, he, twice *bowing himself, wrote in the earth*, God knows what. And in the 9th chapter, curing a man blind from his nativity, ver. 6, "He spit on the ground, and made clod of his spittle; then he spread the clay upon his eyes." Lastly, "He said unto him, Go, wash in the pool of Siloe, which is interpreted, Sent." Thus teaching his Church to use ceremonies in such mysterious actions as are ordained to cure our spiritual deafness, spiritual dumbness, spiritual blindness. So we shall see it to be Scripture, that sprinkling of water must be used in baptism, imposition of hands in confirmation and ordination, anointing with oil in extreme unction. Before our Lord gave the eucharist to his disciples, he (Mark xiv.) made choice of a room very spacious and adorned. He first *washed his disciples' feet*, then sitting down, *he took bread, gave thanks, blessed it, brake it*, &c. When he gave his disciples power to absolve, and to administer the sacrament of confession (John xx. 22), he first said to them, "As my Father sent me, so I send you;" when he had said this, he breathed upon them, and he said to them, "Receive the Holy Ghost; whose sins ye shall forgive, are forgiven," &c. When the pastors of our Church use the insufflation or breathing upon any, for the like mystical signification, you cry aloud, Superstition, superstition, an apish, mimical action, &c.

7. There is also one very great commodity in the Church's prescribing such and such particular ceremonies in such and such actions, that hence it ensues that all her priests perform all these sacred rites in

administering sacraments, offering sacrifice, &c. after just one and the self-same manner all the world over, which is a most comely and orderly thing, and could not have happened had not such and such peculiar rites been prescribed to all.

8. But now, if after that we have proved ceremonies to be reasonable, you ask why the Church did prescribe just these particular ceremonies, and no other, — first, I answer, that either these particular ceremonies are more proper and becoming, and, as it were, more connatural to such an action; or secondly, they are best adapted to express some mystical signification. Lastly, I say, that our unsatisfied adversaries would have asked the self-same question of any other particular ceremonies, if the Church had peculiarly appointed them. Even as some men will curiously be asking, why did God make the world just at such a particular time, and not sooner or later? For, as St. Augustine wittily answers, had God made choice of any other time to make the world, you would still have been asking the very self-same wise question, *Why just now, and not sooner, or later?* Even so you would as wisely have been saying, *Why just such a ceremony, and not as well such or such a one?* Let this suffice for the justification of our ceremonies.

POINT X.

OF BAPTISM, WHICH IS THE FIRST SACRAMENT.

1. I WILL first show Baptism to be a holy sign or ceremony, signifying and causing grace in those who duly receive it. Ezech. xxxvi. 25, "And I will pour upon you clean water, and you shall be cleansed from all your contaminations." Behold, an outward pouring of water, cleansing inwardly from all contaminations. The baptism of St. John was an outward pouring of

water, with a solemn profession of doing penance towards the cleansing of the soul; but no grace was given by it to cleanse the soul. So, Matt. iii. 11, saith St. John Baptist, "I have baptized you with water, but he (Christ) shall baptize you with the Holy Ghost." His baptism shall give this soul-cleansing grace. Again, Acts ii. 38, "Be every one of you baptized for remission of your sins, and you shall receive the Holy Ghost." Again, Acts xxii. 16, "Rise up, and be baptized, and wash away thy sins." Nothing can cleanse from contamination, give remission of sins, wash away sins, but that which gives grace. Again, Gal. iii. 27, "As many of you as are baptized in Christ have put on Christ." Hence baptism is called, Tit. iii. 5, "the washing of regeneration," and by it man is born of the spirit. Whence, John iii. 5, "Unless a man be born again, of water and the Holy Ghost, he cannot enter into the kingdom of God." That is to say, baptism so breeds our spiritual birth in God, as our carnal birth causes our life into the world.

Wherefore, even the children of the just need baptism. For, Rom. v. 12, "Unto all men death did pass, in whom all sinned." Whence, David, Ps. li. 5, "And in sin did my mother conceive me." And therefore "unless such a one be born again, of water and the Holy Ghost, he shall not enter into the kingdom of God." For of every one it is said, Eph. ii. 3, "We were by nature children of wrath, as also the rest."

POINT XI.

OF CONFIRMATION.

1. CONFIRMATION is proved to be a sacrament causing inward grace, from Acts viii. 14, "And when the apostles that were in Jerusalem had heard that Sa-

maria had received the word of God, they sent unto them Peter and John, who, when they were come, prayed for them that they might receive the Holy Ghost. For he was not come upon any of them, but they were only baptized in the name of our Lord Jesus. Then did they impose their hands upon them (*behold the outward sign*), and they received the Holy Ghost." Behold the inward grace, given to those who, though they had been baptized, yet they had not received this particular strength, and *confirmation* of special grace, which the coming of the Holy Ghost in this sacrament did bring unto them. It is also most agreeable to Scripture that this sacrament be given not by inferior priests, but by bishops. Whence Bede excellently remarks, that it was not Philip the apostle who is here said to have converted Samaria, but Philip, one of the seven deacons. And though he could baptize them, yet he could not give them this sacrament, and therefore the apostles sent Peter and John to Samaria; not to baptize them again, but to confirm them. And though here is no mention of oil, yet it does not follow that oil is not to be used in this sacrament. For so in the Scripture there is no mention of water in that very text which mentions the institution of baptism, as Matthew, the last, "Teach all nations, baptizing them in the name of the Father, the Son, and Holy Ghost." Yet the practice of the Church, testified by all antiquity, sufficiently teaches the use of oil, or holy chrism, in this sacrament. See the Rhemish Testament upon the place of the Acts now cited. There also you shall find this memorable note, "That none ever but known heretics condemned this sacrament of chrism." Again, Acts xix. 5, "They were baptized; and when Paul had imposed hands on them, the Holy Ghost came upon them." And whereas some say the text I alleged for this sacrament proves only the gift of the Holy Ghost in order to speak several languages, I remit them to St. Austin, Tract vi. in Ep. John, "Is there any man (saith he) of so perverse a heart as to deny these children, on whom we now imposed hands, to have received the Holy Ghost, because they speak not with tongues?" Out of which words also you may observe how anciently they then *imposed hands and confirmed* children when they were of years of discretion, and could speak wisely, though not in any tongue but their own. This is still our practice.

POINT XII.

OF THE HOLY EUCHARIST.

1. FIRST, this holy sacrament, under visible signs of bread and wine, signifying nourishment, doth invisibly contain the body and blood of our Lord, which nourishes up our souls with his grace to life everlasting; Joh. vi. 48, "I am the bread of life; your fathers did eat manna in the desert, and they died. This is the bread that descendeth from heaven, that if any man eat of it he die not. I am the living bread that came down from heaven. If any man eat of this bread, he shall live for ever." Behold here the invisible grace. "And the bread which I will give you is my flesh, the life of the world." Behold the outward visible sign truly containing his person who gives the grace. And tell me not that it is said of his flesh, "the flesh profits nothing." For it is blasphemy to say so of his flesh, which he saith here, "My flesh is the life of the world." A carnal gross manner of understanding, that his flesh was, to this effect, to be eaten in its own kind (like flesh in the shambles), doth indeed put upon us a sense in which it is true "that his flesh profits nothing." Neither doth his flesh taken as they took it, that is as the flesh of one who was only man, profit any thing. But these his words are "spirit and life." For they should raise us in spirit

to believe this flesh to be joined to the divinity, which is so able to give this flesh to be eaten, that, by really feeding upon it, they may be nourished to eternal life.

2. Here then, secondly, comes in our belief of the *real presence* of Christ in the sacrament, which we all profess to be his true body, and consequently not to be bread, but living bread, as St. John calls it; whence followeth *transubstantiation*, or change of the substance of dead bread into the true body of Christ, which we all say to be as truly in the sacrament as he is in heaven at the right hand of his Father. And therefore adoration is no less due to him here in the sacrament than there in heaven, as reason persuades, if we can show that the self-same body is really present in the sacrament. Let the first proof hereof be taken from the clear and so often-repeated words (even word for word) in the Gospel of St. Matthew, St. Mark, St. Luke, and St. Paul, 1 Cor. ii. 24, "This is my body, this is my blood;" and in St. John, in the words now cited. If I can show that these places be not to be taken figuratively, but literally, my business is at an end. I think I can make this evident by this demonstration.

If these texts be to be understood figuratively (as you Protestants say), then questionless the apostles and their successors did tell the first Christians that it was so; and together with their first faith they received that doctrine, and they with that faith delivered it to their successors. And thus all believed for some time. But then you must come to some other time, in which some one man began first to teach that those texts are to be understood literally, as they found, and that one man taught that Christ was really present in the sacrament, and being so, was also to be adored. Now when this one man began this doctrine first (for some one man must have been at first the beginner), it could not but seem new, as being never heard before; it could not but seem suspected of falsity, as being notoriously then contrary to what all true believers in the world believed. It could not but be manifestly accounted of all understanding men to be idolatrous, as teaching that to be adored for God, which all (instructed by the apostles and their successors) taught to be nothing else but bread and wine. It could not but be accounted a doctrine incredible, which must needs teach the great body of a man to be wholly contained in a small quantity of a little piece of bread. And which must needs teach, one and the self-same body to be really present at a thousand several places, and to be eaten there, and yet to be still present here; which also must needs teach that there should not be bread and wine where our own senses tell us there was nothing else but bread and wine, yea, where (as then) faith itself told them the self-same thing. This being so, I ask this unanswerable question, How could this one man (who must first begin to broach this new doctrine) be able to set it forth so plausibly, it being a doctrine so against all reason, all sense, all experience, and all faith of all men (at that time), and also a thing so hard to persuade men of piety and of understanding for fear of open idolatry, and plain innovation in religion,—so hard to persuade bad and weak understanding persons, who, for no kind of gain or benefit, were to be made go directly not only against their ancient faith, but to go flatly against their own understanding and common sense? How could, I say, this one man be able to persuade this strange, new, unprofitable, hard doctrine, not to one town only, or city, or to one country or nation only, but to the whole multitude of Christians, from the rising of the sun even to the going down thereof? And this so, that no one is known to have, either by word of mouth, or writing, opposed his doctrine, but all to have so readily, and so peaceably, and so unanimously embraced it, that no kind of mention should be made in any history of the least stop it had, or of the least contradiction made any where against it, or of the least taxing it either of novelty, or of strangeness; yea, no mention is made in any one country (though there be so many countries in Christianity) when or where or by whom this strange new doctrine was begun. But behold on the sudden all Christianity (for so it was, as all learned men know), all Christianity, I say, both in the East and in the West,—both amongst those who hold with the Roman Church, and those who stood in defiance of it, either amongst the "Grecians, Georgians, Abyssines, Ethiopians,—all, I say again, all of them (who would be called Christians) every where firmly believing, every where professing and confessing the real presence of Christ in the sacrament, and falling on their knees to adore him. Is it possible, that in a point so hard as this is, so many, so differing in customs, languages, manners, educations, interests, opinions, and beliefs, so distant from one another in place and affections, in dictamens and practices, should all be found at once (and nobody can tell at what time first) to consent most unanimously? Could so great a thing as this be done upon the persuasion of one man, and done so silently, that no one single writer should be found to record who that omnipotent man was, or by what means he could possibly effect a thing so incredible all Christianity over, without finding any where, amongst good or bad, learned or unlearned, any considerable opposition? This seems to me a thing so incredible, that all you can say against our faith in this point is nothing so hard to believe as this alone. Wherefore if this cannot be so, as surely it cannot, you must all be forced to confess, that when the faith was first preached by the apostles and their successors, they did not teach your doctrine concerning this sacrament, but they taught and delivered our doctrine. And then you will soon understand that all the difficulties here mentioned be easy to be answered. For hence you will easily understand how no other beginning than that of our first Christendom could be found of this doctrine, because such a doctrine as this is, found so universally spread over all Christendom, and never recorded to have been accounted new, or to have had any particular author or opposer, could not possibly have had any other beginning; or if it had, more notice would have been taken of it. But coming in with first Christianity, you cannot wonder to see all Christianity found embracing it. And though it be a doctrine containing so many difficulties, yet being proposed as a part of that Christian doctrine, with all those powerful motives (which first moved all Christians to be Christians), you cannot wonder to see those who received Christianity, to receive also this Christian belief. Whereas, if they all had at first received the contrary belief, surely at the first proposing of this known novelty, somebody or other, in some one place of Christianity or other, would have opened his mouth, and said, "We cannot adore that for God which the whole torrent of antiquity, from Christ to us, hath taught to be bread, as also our senses tell us. Had it been to be adored, the apostles, and those who were taught by them, would have taught us so, or at least somewhere somebody or other would have heard some news of this doctrine before now. But that which you say is too new to be true, it is too contrary to all people's faith, to all practice, to all reason and common sense." Can any man imagine that in all Christianity there was neither grace nor wit enough to say this? And certainly, at that time, the very saying of this must needs have quite overthrown that new paradox, or at least have withdrawn thousands in all nations from following of it with so great facility. For against a novelty so notorious and so absurd, so much would have been said, so much would have been written, so much would have been acted in councils, either general or national or provincial,—that some small mention of all this would have come to notice of posterity, as we see things of a thousand times lesser concernment have done. Even by your own backwardness to believe transubstantiation, and by your great wondering at us for believing it, and by the many and great difficulties which you still object against us, you may clearly see how evidently true all that is which I have here so fully set down, because it imports so much.

3. Let us go on now. When (Joh. vi.) Christ said, "I am the bread of life;" ver. 48 and ver. 51, "The bread which I will give you is my flesh, for the life of the world;" the Jews therefore strove amongst themselves, saying (as you Protestants say), "How can this man give us his flesh to eat? Jesus therefore said unto them, Amen, Amen, I say to you, Unless you eat the flesh of the Son of man, and drink his blood, you shall not have life in you. My flesh is meat indeed, and my blood is drink indeed. These things he said, teaching in the synagogue." And he was so far from declaring himself to speak figuratively, that by all he was conceived so manifestly to mean literally, that many of his disciples, and not only ill-affected persons, hearing, said, "This saying is hard, and who can believe it?" And all this happened, though even then he told them, that "the words he spoke to them were spirit and life." Because, as I said, these words ought to have raised up their spirits to believe this flesh of his not to be mere man's flesh, but to be joined with the Divinity, which was able (by virtue of its omnipotency) to give them his flesh to eat like bread, and his blood to drink like wine; yet there being not faith enough for this high point, "from that time many even of his disciples went back, and walked no more with him," ver. 67. That you may evidently see how hard this doctrine would have sounded at first broaching of it in the Church if Christ had not delivered it, seeing that, at that very time when it came first, even *from his mouth*, it found so small acceptance even amongst many of his disciples, "Jesus therefore said to the twelve, Will

you also depart? Peter answered, We believe and know thou art the Son of God;" and so art able by that thy Divinity, to which thy flesh is joined, to give us thy flesh to eat like bread. Now to what end had either this been said, or Christ, the lover of souls, permitted all those *many disciples to go back* to their ruin, and now *to walk no more with him?* to what end this, if he might have saved them all by declaring in a word, that he only intended to give a sign or figure of his body to eat? This one word would have saved both them, and would also have saved those millions and millions which afterwards believed these words to be literally meant, as I expounded them; and St. Peter seems to have understood them, when, to make them appear credible, he said, "We believe, and know thou art the Son of God;" and consequently that thou canst make good thy word, which had been a very easy matter if he only spoke of giving his flesh to be eaten in a mere sign or figure of it; had St. Peter thought this, I dare say he would have pulled the other disciples back, saying, "Our Master only speaks of giving a sign of his body." Had this been so, then also undoubtedly the other Evangelists, when they had come to write of this mystery (which had scandalised so many before their writing), would not have increased the scandal by writing so unanimously of this sacrament, in words sounding so loud a literal sense as these do, "This is my body, this is my blood." But they would rather have lessened the difficulty by declaring it only to be a figure, which they might have done in a word. St. Paul was so far from declaring it to be so, that (1 Cor. xi. 27) he flatly saith, "Therefore whosoever shall eat this bread, and drink the chalice of our Lord unworthily, he shall be guilty of the body and blood of our Lord." Which could not be, unless he received the body and blood truly, and not in a figure only. To eat a paper-picture of Christ makes no such heinous guilt, though it be done by a sinner, and it be also a figure of his body.

4. St. Luke also had been particularly to blame in increasing the scandal by expressing so clearly a literal sense, chap. xxii. ver. 19, "This is my body, which is given for you. This cup is the new testament in my blood, which chalice shall be shed for you." I say, *which chalice*, that is, *that which is contained in the chalice*, shall be shed for you. Now wine was not shed for us, but his true blood. His true blood, therefore, was the thing contained in the chalice. For though by the Latin or English words we cannot tell whether Christ said, his blood should be shed for them, or the chalice or cup; yet St. Luke, writing in Greek, makes it evident to all who know that language that he said, the *chalice should be shed for us;* for he speaks in the nominative case, by a word which cannot agree with the blood, which in Greek is the dative. Now thus having proved that Christ literally said, *This is my body;* I have proved also that *this is not bread, for it is his body;* which is as good a consequence as this, *this is a stone*, therefore *it is not bread;* or, this *is not bread, for it is a stone.*

5. Coming now out of Scripture to answer the chief objections, I begin with one which doth afford me a new strong argument. They object, then, idolatry to us for adoring that which is bread. I answer, that according to Scripture, idolatry cannot be found in the only visible Church of Christ, for Scripture saith clearly of this Church, Isa. ii. 18, "And idols shall be utterly abolished." Again, Ezech. xxxvi. 25, "And I will pour upon you clean water, &c., and from all your idols will I cleanse you." And in the next chap. ver. 23, "Neither shall they defile themselves any more in their idols." Again, Micha v. 12, "Thou shalt no more adore the works of thy hands." Again, Zachar. xiii. 1, "In that day shall be a fountain lying open to the house of David. And it shall be in that day, saith the Lord of Hosts, I will cast off the names of idols out of the land, and they shall be

remembered no more." Hence I argue thus: in the whole visible Church there continued, and doth still continue, adoration of the sacrament, but idolatry did not continue in the whole Church visible; therefore adoration of the holy sacrament is not idolatry. Moreover, if worshiping this holy sacrament were idolatry, all Christianity (for many ages practising this adoration) had committed idolatry, and Christ's Church (for so many ages) had quite failed, as is clear out of the third and fourth points. For Christ had no other Church for many ages, but that which every where practised this idolatry, as you miscall it. Or, tell me if you can, what other visible Church Christ had upon earth different from the Roman in faith and worship, for the thousand years before Luther. If this be the only visible Church Christ had upon earth, then I have proved it could not be guilty of idolatry.

6. Against such a torrent of Scripture as we have for us, you ground yourselves not in the Scripture, but in philosophy, which, tried by Scripture, will be found to fail you in all your objections. First, then, you object that an accident cannot be without a substance. We answer out of Gen. i. 3, "God said, Be light made; and light was made." Light is a quality or accident. Yet hence St. Basil, St. Greg. Naz., and Theodoret, are of opinion that light was without any substance at all; for the Scripture specifies no substance in which it was put. Whence follows that at least they must needs think it possible that light should be without a substance. Secondly, you object that the same body of Christ cannot be multiplied so often over. We answer again out of Gen. ii. 21, " Our Lord God cast a dead sleep upon Adam, and when he was fast asleep he took one of his ribs, and filled up flesh for it. And our Lord God built the rib which he took of Adam into a woman." I ask, how many times over must this one rib be multiplied before a whole woman (of a comely proper stature)

could be made up of it? After the same manner God can of one ordinary brick make a pillar of many feet high, by multiplying that one brick. In the like manner our Saviour multiplied those five "barley loaves with which he fed above five thousand," John vi. For if he made new loaves, he did not feed them with those five, but with those many hundred new loaves which he made; and yet the Scripture saith, ver. 12, 13, "After they were filled, they gathered the remnants, and filled twelve baskets with the fragments of the five barley loaves," and not of any new loaves created by Christ; so that the bread which was eaten remained still to be eaten. And it is worth our noting, that our Saviour did this miracle immediately before he did first declare this strange doctrine of giving his flesh to be eaten like bread by every one, that so when he should presently declare this strange doctrine, they should have no reason to disbelieve the possibility thereof. For his disciples, seeing that he had done that most prodigious miracle so very lately, ought not presently to have said, ".This is hard, and who can bear it?" Neither ought they so soon "to have walked apart from him," as there St. John saith they did; but rather they ought to have said with St. Peter, "We believe and know thou art the Son of God, able to make thy words good, as thou wert able so to multiply so few loaves."

7. Hence appears a solution of that which also they still object,—one body cannot be in two places at once. For if whole Eve were made of one rib of Adam (as the Scripture testifieth), surely the whole substance of that one rib must have been in many places, or else Eve would have been a very little woman, or Adam must have had very great ribs. Again, our Protestants commonly read thus, Acts iii. 21, "Whom the heavens truly must contain" (we read, receive) "until the time of restitution of all things." Hence they infer, that after Christ's ascension the heavens at all times must contain his body. There-

fore (say they) after his ascension his body cannot be on earth. This their own text shall refute them thus. The heavens must, at all times, after his ascension, contain his body. But after his ascension, the earth also did contain his body; therefore his body can be contained in two distant places. And if in two, why not in three, and more? Make the Scripture judge of this point, and it will clearly cast you; for did not Christ, after his ascension, appear in his true body to St. Paul? Acts ix. "Who said, Who art thou, Lord? And he answered, I am Jesus," v. 5 and v. 17. Ananias saith to him, "The Lord, even Jesus that appeared unto thee in the way that thou camest." That he appeared in his own true body, I prove by evident Scripture; for by reason of this his apparition, St. Paul numbers himself amongst those who with their own eyes had seen Christ, risen again in his true body. For labouring to prove Christ's resurrection in a true, and not in a fantastical, body (as some heretics will have it), he proves it by eye-witnesses, who all must have seen Christ now risen in his true body, or else their testimony is vainly brought to prove a true resurrection of the flesh; he then bringing eye-witnesses, who had seen Christ now risen in his true body, makes himself as true an eye-witness of this as any other. For thus he speaks, 1 Cor. xv. 4, &c., "He rose again, and was seen of Cephas, after that of the eleven. Then he was seen of more than five hundred brethren together; moreover he was seen of James, then of all the apostles. And lastly of all, he was seen also of me." To wit, in his true body, or else all others may be said to have seen him in a fantastical body; and also because any other manner of seeing him had been to no purpose to prove the true resurrection of dead bodies, which is here his drift. Where, supposing himself (by these eye-witnesses) to have proved this, he presently saith, ver. 12, "How do certain amongst you say that there is no resurrection of the dead?" Yet again,

Acts xxii. 14, "But he (Ananias) said to St. Paul, The God of our fathers had preordained thee, that thou shouldst know his will, and see that Just One, and hear the voice of his mouth." Therefore he appeared in a true body which had a *voice* and a *mouth* of flesh. But as Christ saith, Luke xxiv. 39, "A spirit hath no flesh and bones, as you see me have." Yet again, Acts xxiii. 10, St. Paul seeth Christ on earth; for when there was made a great dissension, the tribune, "fearing lest Paul should be torn in pieces by them, commanded the soldiers to go down and take him out of the midst of them, and to bring him into the castle. And the night following, the Lord stood by him, and said: "Be constant; for as thou hast testified of me in Jerusalem, so must thou testify of me at Rome also." Here we have that very Lord of whom St. Paul did testify, *standing by him* in the castle far distant from heaven; by which is evident in how distant places Christ's body may be. To disprove so many clear texts, give me but one (if you can) that St. Paul did not see Christ after his ascension, in his true body upon our earth; if you cannot do this, you are cast by Scripture in this point, which proveth that one body can be at the same time in two distant places.

8. Lastly, they object that so great a body as Christ's body is, cannot be in so small a compass as a little bit of bread. We still answer out of Scripture. First, Matt. xix. 26, where speech is of making the great body of a camel pass through a needle's eye, Christ saith, "with men this is impossible." Where note that Christ here, according to the three Evangelists, speaks of such a passage through a needle's eye as is *impossible with men;* so that though with men there is no such thing possible as penetration of several parts of the same great camel's body, brought into so small a compass as is a needle's eye, yet not so with God: *with God all things are possible.* Secondly, God can put two different bodies so as to take

up only the place of one body; therefore he can put all the parts of one body so as to take up only the room of the least part, with which he can penetrate all the rest. Thus, John xx. 19, "When the doors were shut, where the disciples were gathered together, for fear of the Jews, Jesus came and stood in the middle." So that, as at his birth his body penetrated through his mother's womb, at his resurrection through the great stone of his monument, and as at his ascension he did not make a hole through the body of the heavens, but his body was penetrated with those heavenly bodies, so here it penetrated through the shut door or wall; and so two bodies were in one place at once; by which also we prove that one body may as easily, by his power, be in two places at once. Wherefore it is to you (who against Scripture thus stand still alleging philosophy) that we must say with St. Paul, Col. ii. 8, "Beware lest any man deceive you by philosophy and vain fallacy, according to the tradition of men, and the elements of the world, and not according to Christ," against whom you cite Aristotle.

POINT XIII.

OF COMMUNION UNDER ONE KIND.

PROTESTANTS complain we take half of the sacrament from them. We complain they have taken five sacraments from us, and grace from all seven. And as for this sacrament, they have taken both the body and blood of our Saviour from it, and left only bread and wine. If we had taken wine away, no great hurt—wine being nothing but wine. To the purpose we have a full, complete, and perfect sacrament, when we have such an outward sign as signifieth and containeth invisible grace. The consecrated bread alone doth this; in this, therefore, we have a full, complete, and perfect sacrament. Christ speaks this clearly, John vi. 48, "I am the bread of life; your fathers did eat manna in the desert, and they died. This is the bread that descendeth from heaven, that if any man eat of it, he die not. I am the living bread, that came down from heaven. If any man eat of this bread, he shall live for ever." Behold as full an effect of the sacrament as is any where promised to both kinds. And he being living bread, you have all him in it, and so you are deprived of nothing. He gave us his body, not his carcass without blood. In his body we have all, both body and blood. You take both from us; we give both. Agreeable to this saith St. Paul, 1 Cor. xi. 27, "Therefore, whosoever shall eat this bread, or drink this chalice of our Lord unworthily, he is guilty of the body and blood of our Lord;" which he could not be, if he did not receive both *body and blood;* so that by either *eating* or *drinking* both are received. Again, Luke xxiv. 30, "And it came to pass while he sat at table with them (the two disciples in *Emmaus*), he took bread, and blessed, and brake, and did reach to them." Twice Christ with his own hands gave the communion. First, at the last supper, under both kinds. Secondly, here at Emmaus, under one kind only. For many holy Fathers (without ever scrupulising at the giving only one kind) absolutely say, Christ here gave them the communion. And the text insinuates as much, by the use of those sacramental words, of *taking, blessing, breaking, reaching*, with the ensuing effect of *opening their eyes to know him* to be the same Christ, who at his last supper had done the same action. So that it is the more probable that he did administer the communion under one kind than that he did not. How, then, dare you absolutely condemn this? They object, *Drink ye all of this*, Matt. xxvi. But this command was only given to all then present, and was fulfilled; *and they all drank of it*, Mark xiv. 23. So when he commanded, *Do this*, he did not command laymen to do what he did. Their other objections are excellently answered by the Scriptures alleged in the Council of Trent, sess. xxi. c. i., in these notable words: He that saith, "Unless you eat the flesh of the Son of Man, and drink his blood, you shall not have life in you," hath also said, "If any one eat of this bread he shall live for ever." And he that said, "He that eateth my flesh, and drinketh my blood, hath life everlasting," hath also said, "The bread which I shall give you is my flesh, for the life of the world." He that said, "Whoso eateth my flesh, and drinketh my blood, dwelleth in me, and I in him," hath likewise said, "He that eateth this bread shall live for ever." What need we more than to live for ever?

POINT XIV.

OF THE MASS, OR OF THE HOLY EUCHARIST, AS IT IS A SACRIFICE.

1. CHRIST, in his last supper, said, Luke xxii. 19, "Do this in remembrance of me." We must see, then, what Christ did, that we may know what is commanded here to be done. If he did offer his body and blood then in sacrifice, the Church also is bound to have some ministers *doing that in remembrance of him*. We say, then, that Christ did then offer his body and blood in sacrifice; and we say, that the doing this is the very essence of our Mass. I know, as soon as Protestants hear the word *remembrance*, they will object, that Christ cannot be really offered there where the offering is done to his remembrance. I answer, that St. Paul tell us, what it is to do this in remembrance of Christ, 1 Cor. ii. 24, 26, "This do ye in remembrance of me; for as often as ye shall eat this bread, and drink this chalice, you shall show

the death of our Lord until he come." Christ here is remembered by us to have died for us, yet he doth not here really die again bloodily, but this unbloody sacrifice is done in remembrance of his real bloody death. It is not only in "remembrance" of him that we do this, but we do this in remembrance of him dying for us a bloody death upon the cross. Now his being truly present maketh the *remembrance* not less, but more lively and perfect. For if a prince, who had gained a great battle with much loss of his blood, would have yearly some action or representation exhibited in remembrance of it—would in person be present with his wounds acting his own part—the representation would not cease to be a *remembrance*, but it would rather be a far more lively *remembrance*, as often as the king should act his own part. And the year he should not do this, the remembrance would be less lively and less representative: so, &c. How perfectly in this sacrifice is Christ's death represented, whilst by the force of these words, "this is my body," only his body is put in shape of bread in one place wholly different from that other place in which, by force of those words, "this is my blood," his blood in a liquid shape of wine, like blood lately shed, is put in the chalice apart from his body!

2. Now I will show, that Christ did truly sacrifice and offer up his body and blood under the forms of bread and wine. First, out of the Old Testament, Psalm c. 5, it is said of Christ, "Our Lord swore, and it shall not repent him, Thou art a priest for ever of the order of Melchisedeck;" which words St. Paul, Heb. v. 10, saith to have been spoke of Christ, and of this his priesthood. "We have great speech (saith he) and inexplicable to utter, because you are weak to hear." You must look therefore for a mystery, not easily understood by new Christians. The famous priesthood in the old law was settled in Aaron and his sons, Levit. viii.; they offered bloody sacrifices; and yet our Saviour is not said a priest according to

the order of Aaron, but of Melchisedeck, who was not so much as a Jew. "He whose descent is not counted from them, took tithe of Abraham, and blessed him that had the promises," Heb. vii. 6; which shows he was a priest of higher degree than Abraham, as St. Paul here proves. Let us see now all that the Old Testament relates of Melchisedeck and his priesthood; and you shall find it to be only that which is written, Gen. xiv. 18, "But Melchisedeck, king of Salem, bringeth forth bread and wine. And he was the priest of the most high God. And he blessed him (Abraham), and he gave him tithes of all." So unanimous is the consent of all the holy Fathers (who did write either upon this text of Genesis, or on that of St. Paul, or that of the Psalm), that the priesthood of Melchisedeck did consist in offering bread and wine by way of sacrifice to God, and that Christ being a priest according to his order did consist in his offering up and sacrificing his body and his blood for us, under the forms of bread and wine, that to deny this is to cross all antiquity. See the Rhemists upon these two last texts. Now because Christ to the end of the world offers still this sacrifice, by his vicars' or ministers' hands, in the sacrifice of the Mass, he is said "to be a priest for ever, according to the order of Melchisedeck." For by force of these words, "this is my body," his body is put under the species of bread; and then, in a place apart from that body of his, he, by force of these words, "this is my blood," doth put his blood in the chalice, under the shape of wine like blood, poured forth and separated from the body.

3. Again, Jeremy xxxiii. 18, "There shall not fail of David a man to sit upon the throne of the house of Israel. And of the priests and Levites there shall not fail from before my face a man to offer offerings, and to kindle meat-offerings, and to do sacrifice continually." By such sacrifices as then were known, God expressed the continuance of true sacrifice in his

Church; there must not, then, fail now priests and Levites offering a true sacrifice.

4. Now, God speaks thus expressly to the priests of the old law, "I have no will in you, saith the Lord of hosts; and an offering I will not receive of your hands," Malac. i. 10. So that the former text must needs be understood of priests offering continually sacrifices in the New Testament. But now a clean sacrifice, not a bloody one; therefore, here in the next verse it followeth, "For from the rising of the sun, even to the going down, great is my name among the Gentiles. And in every place incense shall be offered to my name, and a pure offering;" to wit, the pure offering and clean oblation of Christ's body under the sweet and lovely shape of bread and wine, into which all those holocausts, burnt-offerings, and killing of victims, were turned; though Jeremy used these terms because they, as then, knew no other sacrifices, as they knew no other priests and Levites, but such as were killers of victims in a bloody manner. But it is very observable that the same prophet, Malachy, speaking in the third chapter, of the coming of the Messias (and *the Lord whom ye seek*, ver. 1), doth also tell us clearly this, "then shall the offerings of Judah and Jerusalem be pleasant unto the Lord," ver. 4; although before he had so flatly said to the priests of Judah and Jerusalem, "I have no will in you, and offerings I will not receive at your hand." Whence it is evident that, by the pleasing sacrifice of Judah and Jerusalem, he meaneth not the carnal, but the spiritual, Judah and Jerusalem, that is, Christ's Church, where sacrifice is to be done continually, as we did now say out of Jeremy.

5. In the very last years of the world, Antichrist, knowing the chief worship of God to consist in this sacrifice, shall so mightily labour to abolish it, that he shall seem (for a very short time) to have prevailed, Dan. ix. 27. "And in the half of the week shall the host and the sacrifice fail, and there shall

be in the temple abomination of desolation." Which last words our Saviour himself expoundeth to be understood of the end of the world, Matt. xxiv., "What sign of thy coming, and of the consummation of the world? said the apostles to him," ver. 3. Our Lord, telling many other signs, at last saith, ver. 14, "This Gospel shall be preached in the whole world, and then shall come the consummation thereof; therefore, when you shall see the abomination of desolation which is spoken of by Daniel the prophet," &c. This, then, shall not happen until the world is even come to the end, and the Gospel shall have been preached every where.

6. According, therefore, to the practice of the law of nature in the time of Melchisedeck, and according to the practice and manifest prophecies in the written law, exterior sacrifice (which from the beginning of the world was ever held the chief and peculiar worship due to God) is also to be found in the Church of Christ, from the rising of the sun to the going down, even till the world's end, when Antichrist for a short time shall in great part abolish it. Let us, then, see the sacrifice that Christ (a priest for ever, according to the order of Melchisedeck) did institute in his Church, Luke xxii. 19, "This is my body, which is given for you." Now given in this very present time, and now by me offered in an unbloody manner; he saith not *to you*, but *for you*, that is, for your sins; which body presently after I will offer in a bloody sacrifice upon the cross. Behold here a sacrifice, and a propitiatory sacrifice: for what is offered *for us*, and offered *for remission of sins*, is a propitiatory offering, applying plentifully the satisfaction of Christ's passion to us; not derogating from that sacrifice, but deriving the fruits thereof to us. Thus his body is properly said, *given for us;* but when it is given in the sacrament, it is said, given *to us*, not *for us*. This sacrifice the apostles were offering to our Lord, Acts xiii. 2, when they are said to have been ministering to our Lord. Had

they been ministering the word of God, or ministering the sacrament, they had ministered *to the people*. But they had not been *ministering to our Lord*, that is, offering something to him. In the Greek text it is, "they being offering sacrifice to our Lord." And so Erasmus translates it.

7. This sacrifice is plainly insinuated in St. Paul, 1 Cor. x., if his discourse be well noted. He there discoursing on Jewish and heathenish sacrifice doth conclude, that all such persons as will be partakers of these sacrifices cannot be made partakers of the Christian sacrifice of the body and blood of our Saviour. First, then, ver. 14, he bids them *fly from serving idols*, by either sacrificing to them, or eating of that which hath been sacrificed to them. If they will do this, he tells them of a far better sacrifice, of which they may be made partakers at our altars. For, saith he, ver. 16, "the chalice of benediction which we do bless, is it not the communication of the blood of Christ? And the bread which we break, is it not the participation of the body of our Lord?" And having thus taught them that, by virtue of the priest's benediction or consecration, the true body and blood of Christ are made communicable upon our altars under the shapes of bread and wine, he goeth on to tell them they cannot be partakers of this sacrifice if they will continue still to partake of either Jewish or heathenish sacrifices, of which they truly make themselves partakers if they will still eat of that which is sacrificed by them. "For behold Israel," saith he, ver. 18, "they that eat of the sacrificed hosts, are they not partakers of the altar?" For by thus doing they communicate with those that sacrifice. And having thus spoken of the Jewish sacrifices, he speaks to them of the Gentile sacrifices. "But the things which heathens do sacrifice, to devils they sacrifice, and not to God. And I will not have you have fellowship with the devils," as you will, if you eat or partake of what is immolated to them, and will drink

the libations offered out of their cup. "For," saith he, "you cannot be partakers of the table of our Lord, and of the table of the devils." The reason why we cite and expound this place so fully is because we desire exceedingly to have it noted, how that here "our chalice, our bread, our table, and altar, the participation of our host, and oblation," are, point by point, in all conditions, effects, and proprieties, compared to the altar, hosts, sacrifices, and oblations of the Jews and Gentiles; and as he calls their chalice the *chalice of the devils,* for no other reason but because it contains liquor sacrificed to them, so he must be said to call *our chalice* the *chalice of our Lord,* because it contains the liquor of Christ's blood sacrificed *to our Lord.* For by force of these words, *this is my blood,* his blood, under a liquid species, is put in the chalice, as it were, apart from that body, which before he had put under the shape of bread. All which discourse had been very ineffectual if this had not been the proper sacrifice among the Christians, as those others were the known sacrifices of the Jews and Gentiles.

8. Again, the same St. Paul saith, Heb. xiii. 10, "We have an altar, of which they have no right to eat who serve the tabernacle;" still pressing the Jews that they cannot partake of the sacrifice of our *altar,* if they will stick fast to their old sacrifices. And note that which he called before *the table of our Lord,* he now calleth an altar, truly and properly ordained for sacrifice, and so he terms it *thysiasterion,* that is, *sacrificatorium,* an *altar to sacrifice upon.* And by that word always the altars of the Jews, ordained for sacrifice, are still out of the Hebrew interpreted in Greek. Well, then, *we have an altar* built purposely to offer sacrifice upon, therefore we have a true sacrifice, not of bread and wine (for in no man's opinion we sacrifice these), but of the body and blood of our Saviour, under the shape of bread and wine. And this was the reason, why, in the primitive Church, the

heathens would sometimes say we worshiped *Bacchus*, the god of wine, and *Ceres*, the goddess of corn. Sometimes they traduced us as *feeders on man's flesh*, for eating the flesh of our Saviour in this sacrifice.

9. I conclude, that had not this manner of sacrificing in the Mass been delivered us with our first faith from the apostles, it could never (without notice being taken of the first author, and of the time, &c.) have been universally received without opposition of any, or without being ever taxed by any one of novelty, yea, and be received also so universally, that if before Luther's days you look into all parishes of Christianity (where confessed heretics did not domineer) you will in every parish thereof find no other common service used publicly in that parish, but the saying and celebrating Mass, with offering that which they all adored for the true body and blood of Christ under the shape of bread and wine. A proof unanswerable. See what we said before, Point XII. No. 2.

POINT XV.

OF SAYING MASSES, AND OTHER PUBLIC PRAYERS, IN THE LATIN TONGUE.

1. In St. Matthew i. 17, "All the generations, from the transmigration of Babylon unto Christ, fourteen generations," a very long time. And yet all this time the Jewish Church (the only true Church in the world) had all her Scriptures, and all her public service and prayer (which was all taken out of the Psalms, the law, and the Prophets), in that very language in which they were written, to wit, in old Hebrew; that is, in a language well known indeed to the common people of the Jews before their transmigration into *Babylon;* but in their captivity at *Babylon* they lost the knowledge of their old Hebrew language (in

which all their Scriptures were written), and did not perfectly learn the Chaldean or Babylonian language; whence they made a mixture of both those languages, which was called the Syriac language. The very letters and characters of this language differ as much as the Greek letters differ from the Latin: so that those who can perfectly read the one, cannot so much as read the other. Neither do they understand one another, more than the Italians can understand Latin, which was their ancient native tongue. The Scriptures were not at this time (but some good time after Christ) translated into Syriac, as your great doctors (who have set forth the Bible of so many languages) do profess in their preface to their Bible. And, by the way, they also (in the same preface) plainly and openly confess, that in no parish in Christendom they could in any of those nations (which they have caused to be searched for old copies) find so much as one ancient service-book written in a language understood by the vulgar or common people of the place. A testimony to their own condemnation and confusion. The knowledge, then, of the old Hebrew tongue, in which all the Scriptures were written, being so much lost in the captivity of *Babylon*, they had all their Scriptures and public service (which was taken out of the law and the Prophets, and Psalms) read in a language unknown to all the common people, and this was done *for fourteen generations*.

2. Hence, presently, after their captivity, when they first returned into their country, *Esdras* was forced by himself and others to interpret the law for them, Nehem. viii. 13. So when our Saviour upon the cross did, in the old Hebrew words of the Psalm, say as it was first written, "Eli, Eli, lamasabacthani" (Matt. xxvii. 46), St. Matthew, who did write his Gospel in that new kind of Hebrew or Syriac (which was vulgarly spoken by the Jews in Christ's days), is forced to interpret these words, saying, *which is interpreted, My God, my God, why hast thou forsaken*

me? For this reason, also, he interpreted several other Hebrew words. A manifest sign they could not be understood by the Jews (in whose language he did write) without interpretation. And as he who writes English should ridiculously interpret English, so, if those words of the Psalm had been written by David in the same language in which St. Matthew did write, it had been ridiculous for him to add their interpretation. Josephus the Jew tells you what a world of schools there were in *Jerusalem* for children to learn the law and Prophets, they being written in a language otherwise unknown. Well, then, as those who have not been now at our Latin schools understand not our Latin Bible and service, so then the vulgar sort understood not their Scriptures, nor their common service taken out of them, and read in their synagogue before their sermons and exhortations, which St. Paul calls "the lesson of the law and Prophets," Acts xiii. 5. Neither after the captivity did the vulgar understand the words of "Moses, who of old times hath in every city those who preach him in the synagogue, where he is read every Sabbath," Acts xv. 21. Read, I say, but not as then understood by the vulgar. This practice was practised before the eyes of Christ and his apostles, and they never did the least reprehend it, or give order to have the Bible turned into the Syriac language, that the vulgar might understand it. Why, then, must we be blamed for using either Scriptures, or divine service, in a language not understood by the people?

3. Secondly, I ask what you say to that place of Levit. xv. 17, "Let no man be in the tabernacle when the high-priest goeth into the sanctuary to pray for himself and his house, and for the whole assembly of Israel, until he come forth." See you not here public prayer made expressly *for the whole assembly,* and yet no one of the assembly permitted to hear or see what there was done by the priest to God for them, even then, when the priest made an atone-

ment for himself, for his household, and for all the congregation of Israel? Again, Luke i. 10, "All the multitude of the people was praying without at the hour of incense." The priest was doing his duty within (where he could neither be seen nor heard by the people without), yet they assisting at the priest's function, done for them, were not less partakers of the benefit thereof, though they could neither see him nor hear him: so, prayer made and offered up for the people in a low voice, or in an unknown language, is available to them who know not the particular meaning of the words said for them. It is sufficient when they know they contain a particular praise of God, and a special worship of him, and a peculiar recommending of our necessities unto him; and that they are, as most pious prayers, approved by the Church, and recommended by all the learned men thereof, who very well understand them. Now a petition well made, even when it is presented by a petitioner who understands not the language in which the petition is made, obtains of the king, or emperor (who understands it), as much as if the petitioner had perfectly understood every word of it. When the children, Matt. xxi. 16, cried in the temple, "Hosanna to the Son of David," though they knew not what they said, yet Christ called it a *perfect praise*, saying, "that out of the mouth of infants and sucklings thou hast perfected praise." A rich jewel in the hands of an infant who knows not to penetrate the value of it doth not, for that cause, cease to be truly of as great value as when it is in the hands of a jeweller. So Latin prayers in the mouths of the vulgar be as precious in the sight of God (when they be said with equal devotion) as when they are in the mouths of great scholars. You who scorned to use Latin service soon came to see your *English* service with all scornful contempt banished out of almost all your churches. And your people did soon grow to like no service at all, since they misliked the Latin service.

4. I will now examine our adversaries' chief ground in Scripture, which is out of 1 Cor. xiv., where I would have the reader to note, that until ver. 14, St. Paul only speaks of using an unknown language in preaching, exhorting, interpreting, and teaching, in all which exercises we still use the vulgar tongue; so that hitherto he hath nothing against us. From the 14th verse he begins indeed to speak of praying, but not of public divine service, but of such extempore prayer as is made before all, that all may join with it; and he speaks there, not of the use of any set form of prayer, practised by the Church (as the Liturgy is), but he manifestly speaks only against the use of an unknown and barbarous tongue, in the making of such hymns and canticles and prayers as many then did use to make by divine inspiration, in the presence of the whole congregation, to edify the brethren assembled, and to excite them to love, to honour, and praise God; not intending chiefly to pray to God for the people, as we do in our Liturgy, of which kind of set form of prayer St. Paul cannot be said to speak. For it is apparent that among the *Corinthians* (to whom he wrote) there was no use at all of an unknown or barbarous language in the Liturgy or divine service; wherefore of this St. Paul could not complain, for their Liturgy was undoubtedly in Greek, which was the known language among them, and in which he did write this very Epistle to them; also in which they had their set forms of prayer. Now, then, St. Paul speaks not at all against the use of an unknown tongue in either the Liturgy or in any other usual set form of public prayer, for there was no abuse at all in that kind; but he only speaks against that use practised by some in those extempore canticles, prayers, and hymns (which then divers used); yet of such kind of prayers also (though made in unknown and barbarous tongues) he saith, ver. 14, "If I pray in an unknown tongue, my spirit prayeth," and this great good I have by my prayer, *but my understanding*

is without fruit; that is, without the fruit of instruction or edifying others. A fruit which ought to be sought for by those to whom God had so particularly given that miraculous gift of speaking in several tongues, purposely that they might excite and stir up the people of several tongues and nations to the knowledge, praise, honour, and love of God; and therefore he addeth, "I will pray in spirit, I will pray also in understanding," that in those prayers I may not deprive the standers-by of that fruit. But you must know that neither the Mass, nor the set forms of prayer in our liturgy, are ordained for this end of instructing others. Because, for this, we have other exercises of catechising, expounding, exhorting, preaching, &c. But chiefly those prayers are appointed to the priest (who well understands them), to offer them up to God for the people. The Epistles and Gospels which contain instructions are interpreted and fully declared to the people in our churches upon those days on which they are bound to assemble and to resort to Mass. The other chief parts of the Mass are in all Masses the same. And being so often used (and therefore upon occasions so often declared to the people), they must indeed be very *idiots* if they know not when to say *Amen,* when to kneel, to adore, to knock their breasts, when to arise, when to stand, or to do any thing else that concerns them, or is proper for them to do. Therefore it cannot be said against our Mass what is objected from ver. 16, "Else when thou shalt bless with the spirit, how shall he that occupieth the room of the unlearned say Amen at thy giving of thanks, seeing he understands not what thou sayest?" This, as I said, cannot be said of our so well-known set form of prayer and service, which we all knowing to be approved by the Church, and to be understood and so highly esteemed by our learnedest men, fear not to say *Amen,* or to join our intention with any part of it; neither doth its approbation depend on our *Amen.* I answer, therefore,

H

that St. Paul spoke of those extemporary blessings, canticles, and lauds, or such-like inspired prayers of private persons, which he recommends to be said in the vulgar language, yet the contrary is not ill, though it be less perfect. For even to him who doth the contrary it is said, v. 17, "Thou verily givest thanks well," and not foolishly or superstitiously: "but the other is not edified," which fruit and end thou shouldest chiefly have intended, God having to this end given thee this gift. And therefore in such exercises of devotion "I will speak five words with my understanding, rather than ten thousand words in a tongue," that is, a barbarous tongue,—strange to the hearers,—because the chief end of these exercises is to edify and excite the people to praise God; whereas, the chief end of the liturgy is to pray to God for the people.

5. I also note that St. Paul doth not so much as mean here to exclude the use of such well-known tongues as the Greek and Latin were; that is, such as were the languages well known to all the better-bred sort of most nations; so that here is nothing against the Mass said in Latin through the Latin Churches, or in all those western parts where all knowing and understanding men very commonly know this language. I prove this manifestly: for if St. Paul should call this praying in a tongue (your Bible puts in a different letter the word *unknown*) so as to make such a tongue as this unfit for public service in these countries, he himself had notably transgressed in this matter, for he writes to the *Romans* in Greek, knowing well that they spoke Latin only, and that the vulgar knew no other language. Yet he did thus write to them a very large epistle in Greek, now divided into sixteen chapters. And although he did write this chiefly for their instruction and edification, behold, this was done even by him who said before, "I had rather speak five words with my understanding, that my voice might teach others, than ten thousand words in an unknown tongue." You must not

then call speaking in *an unknown tongue* the speaking in such languages as are well known to the more learned of those people to whom you speak. Wherefore you must not say he spoke in a tongue, or *an unknown tongue* to the *Romans*, when he wrote in the Greek tongue to them, though he was not understood by the vulgar of them, but only by the more learned sort. Now then, as he cannot be said to have spoken in an unknown tongue to the *Romans* when he wrote this epistle to them in Greek, because Greek is not a barbarous tongue, wholly *unknown* to the better sort, so a *Roman* priest saying mass in Latin in the western parts doth not say mass *or speak in a tongue* that is a tongue wholly unknown to the better sort. Wherefore, as the Greek tongue was not judged a tongue unfit for St. Paul writing to the *Romans*, even when their instruction was chiefly to be regarded, so it is not unfit when not instruction, but making prayer for the people to God, is chiefly intended, as in the Mass. Read the *Rhemish* Testament, handling this chapter very well.

6. And observe also that the service of the Catholic or universal Church is best celebrated by a Catholic or universal tongue, such as Greek is in the East, Latin in the West; tongues not subject to such alterations and peril of changes in substantial words as vulgar languages are, and therefore less fit for the everlasting perpetuity and universality of the Church. If at our conversion we had had our Mass in the old British or old English language, who would now have understood it? Yea, who doth not laugh at all English he reads which is much above an hundred years standing? It was most unfit the liturgy should be so often chopped and changed as vulgar languages alter, or that it should usually be so often turned into several tongues not understood by the Church representative, so that she could not pass her judgment whether there were any gross corruptions crept into this most divine service. Therefore, in respect of universality, both of

all ages (for which the Church was to last) and of universality of all nations (through which she was to be spread), no language is more fit for her public constant service than Hebrew, Greek, and Latin. God regarded unity in worship so much that he would have the whole nation of the Jews (for a thousand and six hundred years) only to sacrifice in one place; though it might be objected that this much hindered the many and frequent sacrifices which would otherwise have been offered if in any place they might sacrifice. To keep unity in religion, it is most rationally ordered that sacrifice should be celebrated with prayers in one and the same language over one and the same Church. Moreover, it is well known that a distance from what is ordinary and vulgar produces respect and reverence. And on the other hand, it was found that public service in *English* was soon vilified and contemned by the vulgar *English*, and at last, with all expressions of contempt and derision, quite exploded and abolished. Cast pearls before swine, and the Scripture tells you how they will behave themselves towards them.

7. Lastly, show me but one service-book in all the fifteen hundred years before *Luther* in any one vulgar tongue which agreeth with your service-book, and for that one book's sake we will all come to your service.

POINT XVI.

OF THE SACRAMENT OF PENANCE, OR CONFESSION.

1. EVEN in the old law some particular confession of particular sins was, under precept, appointed to the Jews, Num. v. 6: "Speak to the children of Israel, man or woman, when they shall do any of all the sins that are wont to chance to men, and by negligence have transgressed the commandment of their Lord,

and have offended, they shall confess their sin. And (if their sin were in point of wronging their neighbour) they shall restore the principal itself, and the fifth parth part over, to him against whom they sinned." Behold confession, behold restitution; and for satisfaction, *the fifth part* over and above to be given. And besides that, sacrifice to be offered to God, so to repair the dishonour done him.

2. The new law perfecting the old, confession was elevated by Christ to a sacrament, giving grace, John xx. 23 : "He said to them, Receive the Holy Ghost; whose sins you forgive, they are forgiven; and whose sins you retain, they are retained. But Thomas was not with them when Jesus came;" yet no man can deny that this power was also given to *Thomas*. Whence appears that it was not given only to those who then were present, as a grant given merely for their sakes, and to increase their authority, but this grace was given for the sake of all belonging to Christ's flock, of which flock the far greater number lived after the times of the Apostles.

3. That this text is literally to be understood (as I have interpreted it) may be demonstratively proved by the same argument by which we proved that text, *this is my body*, to be literally understood, Point XII. n. 2. For if the Apostles with the first faith did not deliver this literal sense, but only taught this power to end with them, and that no man after their days either had power to forgive sins or stood obliged to confess them, then you must say that in some after age some one man began first (for always one begins at first) to vent abroad these two strange things: first, "that all priests had power to forgive sins; secondly, that all Christians guilty of sin were bound, under pain of damnation, to confess their sins to the priests, though they were ever so foul or ever so secret." But shall any one man make me believe that this single man's doctrine, so new and so hard, could presently, without contradiction, grow to be so gene-

rally received and practised, not in one, but in all parts of Catholic Christianity, and that no history should tell us who this man was, where or when he broached this doctrine? or how he could so bewitch all that no man should contradict him, or that no one should have grace or wit to say, "If priests had this power, or if all Christians had this strict obligation, surely the Apostles and their successors would have made this known, and they would have made both priests and Christians to do their duty in this kind? For their only saying this would have (then) been enough to have stopped this man's mouth." Neither is the doctrine of confession or the practice of it so easy to be brought in that it could possibly be thus silently and speedily entertained; yea, and entertained all the Christian world over without contradiction or opposition even so much as in any one single place; for we nowhere hear of any such contradiction.

4. I know, after confession was every where practised, that the Novatian heretics did oppose it, saying that "it was a dishonour to God that man should forgive sins." But all Catholics hold this to be a heresy in them. And St. Ambrose saith to them, Luke i. 7, "Why should it be more a dishonour to God, or be more inconvenient, that man should forgive sins by penance than by baptism, seeing it is the Holy Ghost who in both cases doth it by the ministry of the priests?" So he. In baptism the priest says, *I baptize thee;* that is, *I wash thee.* I ask, from what? Surely from sin; according to that, Acts xxii. 16, "Rise up and be baptized, and wash away thy sins." I ask again, can your priests or ministers wash sin away? You will answer that they can administer the sacrament, which washeth sin away; and so they wash away sin, not by their own power, but as ministers of Christ's sacraments. Just so each priest saith, *I absolve thee.* Yet our priests absolve not by their own power; but as ministers of Christ they administer the sacrament of absolution, which cancels all sins. Lastly, I observe

that when Christ did forgive the paralytic his sins, Matt. ix., the multitude was so far from saying this was a dishonour to God, that "the multitude glorified God, who gave such power unto men," ver. 6.

POINT XVII.

OF THE SACRAMENT OF EXTREME UNCTION.

THE very name of this sacrament has become even unknown to us here in England, who boast so much of the word of God. And yet, according to the word of God, there is not any sacrament at all which can be more manifestly proved a true sacrament than this, both in regard of the outward or visible sign, or in regard of the invisible grace. This visible sign is proved evidently by our Saviour, because nobody but he could annex the gift of invisible grace to this visible sign; to which sign most clear Scripture doth testify this grace to be annexed. For so we read, Jam. v. 14, "Is any man sick among you? Let him bring in the priests of the Church, and let them pray over him, anointing him with oil in the name of our Lord." (Behold the visible outward sign of this sacrament.) And in the next words behold the invisible grace annexed thereto: "And if he be in sins, they shall be remitted him." Now, good Protestant, give me leave to ask thee this one question, Is there any time in which it more imports a man to have so good a warrant as God's word is for the remission of his sins than in the time of his departure out of the world? Behold then here a means to obtain this remission even at this very time, and this means warranted by the very word of God. And yet, without any ground at all in God's word, you have rejected a thing so important to all Christians, though you found the practice of all Christianity to be conformable to the words as they sound. How doth this stand with your pretence of reforming our errors by the rule of Scripture? You go so flatly contrary to clear Scripture, even in a point of abolishing a sacrament which was used by all the Catholic Church before your reformation, and having so clear a text for it and no one single text against it.

2. To take away the force of this text; first, in place of *priests* you are pleased, against all antiquity, to read *elders*, because the Greek word that signifieth *priests*, in vulgar use signifieth *elders*. Now this is as ridiculous, as if one would say, *the bigger of the city*, in place of saying, *the major* (mayor) *of the city*, because the word *major* signifieth the *bigger;* or as if, for the like cause, you would call a *doctor of physic*, a *teacher of physic*, whereas a *doctor* is well known to signify such a degree. As also a *major* (mayor) is notoriously known to signify a secular office, or dignity in a city: so the name put in Greek for a priest, *presbyteros*, is as notoriously known to signify a *priest* endued with a priestly order, office, and function in the Church of God. Whence this name is improperly translated *elder*, when Church affairs are manifestly referred to, as in this instance St. James speaks of some ministry or other, by which sins are forgiven.

3. I know that those who grant that here is a command (for councils you will have none) to anoint the sick with true oil, pretend that this was commanded to be done only for obtaining a miraculous cure. A doctrine full of absurdities. The *first* of which is novelty. The *second* is flat contradiction to the text, expressing the chief effect to be sought for (not to be the health of the body, but of the soul), "and if he be in sins, they shall be forgiven him." The *third* absurdity is to say, there was in the Church (for a time) a command to any one sick among us, to seek for a miraculous cure. The *fourth* is to say, that any priest or elder whatsoever might be called in to work

this miraculous cure. Upon what authority of Scripture or history is this said? Give me leave, in the last place, to ask, if ever you did read or hear, that at the use of any element, which was not sacramental, sins were promised to be forgiven by any one, even of Christ's apostles?

4. Other of your doctors will have this anointing with oil to be only the oil of devout prayers, or charity. But first, where have you that, at your elders' or priests' prayer, it will follow, that "if the sick man be in sins, they shall be forgiven him"? Do you not scoff at priests' forgiving sins, and will you allow a sure warrant, attested by God's own word, that at the priests' prayer, yea, at the elders', the sick man's sins shall be forgiven? Again, this free license of interpreting *oil* to be prayer or charity, opens a gap to interpret all that is said of applying water in baptism, to be understood only of applying the clear and cleansing streams of heavenly doctrine, teaching them to believe in the name of the Father, Son, and Holy Ghost, without ever casting water on them. Again, did ever any holy Father thus interpret this place of St. James? Shall I, upon your hitherto unheard-of interpretation, go and forsake a remedy taught me by the practice of all the Church, and by so clear a text, upon which remedy the forgiveness of my sins at the hour of my death, and consequently my eternal salvation, may depend? God give me my wits, and I will never do it.

POINT XVIII.

OF THE SACRAMENT OF HOLY ORDER.

1. HERE also Scripture teacheth an outward visible sign, to which the giving of inward grace is annexed. 1 Tim. iv. 14, "Neglect not the gift which is in thee." (Here you have the inward grace given.)

"With the laying on of the hands of the presbyters." Here you have the outward sign by which it is given. Again, 2 Tim. i. 6, "I put thee in remembrance, that thou stir up the gift of God which is in thee." Behold the inward grace. "By the putting on of my hands." Behold the outward sign, at the putting on of which that inward grace was conferred. Note, that though St. Paul were called from heaven, and had received the true Spirit of God, yet he was ordained by the imposition of hands, Acts xiii. 3.

2. Now I pray you, where have you one text in Scripture to prove Holy Order not to be a sacrament? And so I say of Matrimony, Confirmation, Penance, Extreme Unction.

POINT XIX.

OF THE SACRAMENT OF MATRIMONY.

1. WHEN (Gen. ii. 22) our Lord "had built the rib which he took of Adam into a woman, and brought her to Adam, Adam said, This now is the flesh of my flesh: wherefore man shall leave his father and mother, and shall cleave to his wife; and they shall be one flesh." In the New Testament (Matt. xix. 5 ; Mar. x. 7) our Saviour repeats those words, and hence infers, "Therefore they are not two, but one flesh." Then of himself he adds, "That therefore which God hath joined together, let no man separate." Now St. Paul repeating part of our Saviour's words here cited, saith, "This is a great mystery" (we read sacrament); "but I speak in Christ, and in the Church," Eph. v. 31. Although St. Paul applies here the very name of sacrament to Matrimony (which name is not once in all Scripture applied to any of the other sacraments), yet it is not from hence we infer Matrimony to be a sacrament; for by that word, in this place, we know he only means a mystery; yet

a sacramental mystery. But we infer out of his discourse, that this mystery is now elevated by Christ to be a sacrament, because St. Paul cited the words of Christ spoken (as we have seen out of St. Matthew) when he did abrogate the law of Moses (which law permitted, in several cases, husband and wife to be separated), and spoken also when he declared expressly that he would have this contract made hereafter inseparable; saying, "That which God hath joined together, let no man separate." Christ then marrying to his Church for ever, would elevate this chief contract, that is in mankind (which he made from that time to be an inseparable contract), to signify this most sacred mystery, and therefore he saith, "This is a great sacrament or mystery," so much and so nearly " concerning Christ and the Church," as St. Paul tells us.

2. We may here note their impiety, who knowing by St. Paul that Christ thus inseparably had wedded his Church, do notwithstanding presume to call this his beloved spouse a whore and a harlot, falsely accusing her of superstition and idolatry. But to proceed, Marriage being elevated by Christ to be a great sacrament, or sacred mystery, and to signify the inseparable conjunction between him and his Church, a signification so far beyond its own nature (which was only to be a civil contract), he made it a fit ceremony, to which now he might annex his grace given, to the parties joined by this sacrament, to observe matrimonial continency. "That every one may know to possess his vessel in sanctification and honour, and not in the passion of lust, as Gentiles," 1 Thess. iv. 4. They therefore having this grace, given to this end, are thereby enabled more fitly to express in their mutual fidelity and affection the mutual fidelity and affection which should be for ever between Christ and his Church. This is the proper effect of the grace given in Matrimony.

3. By this our doctrine of Matrimony, let any im-

partial man judge whether we or our adversaries honour it more; they having taken this chief honour of being a sacrament from it, which we allow to it, are now come to celebrate it in profane houses, before justices, and this only for civil ends intended by the commonwealth. Neither have they one text of Scripture to prove that their ministers ought always to join others in Matrimony.

POINT XX.

OF THE SINGLE LIFE OF PRIESTS.

1. MATRIMONY being a sacrament, and giving grace, it may seem to some that all should do better to make themselves partakers of this grace. I answer, that the want of this one grace is more than abundantly recompensed by those many great and often received graces, of which a single life makes us far more capable, as of receiving more frequently and worthily the sacrament of sacraments, the body and blood of our Lord, which priests daily do, with great increase of greater graces; very singular graces also are obtained by prayer, to which chastity doth exceedingly conduce, as Scriptures teach.

2. Let us hear the Scripture: Luke i. 23, "And it came to pass that after the days of his office were expired, he (Zacharias the priest) departed into his house: and after these days Elizabeth his wife conceived." Hence it appears to be true which St. Jerome saith, contra Jovian, l. i. c. xix., and Ep. 1. c. 3, that, even in the old law, the priests, who offered the holy Host for the people, did not so much as stay in their own houses; but were purified, and so separated, for that time, from their wives. Whence the Scripture saith, "After the days of his office, he departed into his house; and after those days his wife

conceived." Our priests of the new law being to offer daily sacrifice, are daily to observe virginal purity.

3. Again, even in married laymen, St. Paul approves abstaining from their wives, "for a time, that they may give themselves to prayer," 1 Cor. vii. 35. "And this (saith he) I speak to your profit, not to cast a snare upon you, but for that which is comely. And that you may attend upon the Lord without distraction." Priests, therefore, who daily should be attending upon our Lord, and praying for themselves and the people, and so often also sacrificing, should daily abstain from woman, as St. Jerome argues, lib. i. c. xix. contra Jovian.

4. Thirdly, 1 Cor. vii. 32, "He that is without a wife is careful of the things that pertain to our Lord, how to please God; but he that is with a wife, is careful of the things that pertain to the world." Priests should still be in a state most capable of being "careful of things that pertain to God, and how to please him." Therefore they should not have wives; "for he that is with a wife is careful of things that pertain to the world," which priests should not be. But if any men, surely priests chiefly should be the men, "who make themselves eunuchs for the kingdom of heaven's sake," Matt. xix. 12.

5. Fourthly, "No man being a soldier to God entangleth himself in the affairs of this life, that he may please him who hath chosen him to be a soldier," 2 Tim. ii. 4. Of all men, clergymen should take care to please him, who hath chosen them to be soldiers to him; and therefore they, of all men, should not "entangle themselves with secular businesses" and worldly affairs. And yet if they be married, necessity enforceth them to entangle themselves in them above all other married men. For the greater part of other married men have a settled estate left them to leave their children. But the greater part of clergymen live wholly on the benefices which they

can get. And being well bred, and made fit company for the chief of the parish, they also, and their wives, and their children, look high, and must be highly maintained. To maintain them thus, only by the benefit of a benefice (enjoyable at the furthest during life, and perhaps to be taken away far sooner), there is a kind of necessity for them to make hay apace while the sun shines, they not knowing how little while that may be, and knowing that it cannot be long. But let us proceed.

6. Fifthly, "It behoveth therefore a bishop to be the husband of one wife," 1 Tim. iii. 3. In the first birth of Christianity virginity was so rare both among Jews and Gentiles, that it was not possible to find men endued therewith who were both of the sufficient maturity in years and knowledge and experience in affairs that is requisite in bishops and priests. Yet even then the apostles would have this at least observed, that no man who married a second wife should be made a bishop; no, nor a deacon; and therefore not a priest. And thus this place is understood by the councils and fathers unanimously. See the Rhemish Testament on this place. But as for marrying after priesthood received, it is a thing wholly unheard of in God's Church. "Neither is there one authentic example thereof in the whole world," as the same Rhemists say. St. Paul adds yet further: "Let the deacons be the husbands of one wife," ver. 12.

7. Ridiculous is the interpretation of those who say St. Paul would only have such made deacons, priests, bishops, who have but one wife at once. For this is to require no more than he requires of all Christians. If you say, he yet requires of them that they never had at one and the same time more wives than one before their conversion, this is showed evidently not to express the meaning of these words; for he useth just the same words, and the like expression, when he could have no such meaning. For (chap. v.) where he speaketh of choosing a widow

(for the end there intended), he in like manner saith, "She should be a widow, having been the wife of one man," ver. 9. How ridiculous is it to say that here (where there is just the same expression) the meaning is, that only such should be chosen to be widows (for the end here appointed) who had had but one husband at one time before her conversion! For neither Jews nor Gentiles did ever permit women to have more husbands than one at once. It had been therefore ridiculous to require that which could not but be.

8. Your chief objection against all this, as also against vowed virginity, is that you conceive St. Paul, 1 Tim. iv. 3, to teach that this is "the doctrine of devils forbidding to marry." I answer that St. Paul speaks only against the doctrine of heretics (cited by the Rhemists here, to which add the Manicheans and others), who taught that the use of marriage came from a bad god, or devil. As for us, we honour marriage more than you; for we hold it to be a sacrament, which you do not. Neither can you say that we absolutely forbid marriage, because we forbid, or rather declare marriage to be by God forbidden to those persons only who cautiously and willingly have either vowed virginity, when they might have married, if they pleased, or who cautiously and willingly (when they might as freely have married) undertook holy orders, to which state they knew none were admitted but such as would voluntarily and freely profess virginity. For the Church now, abounding with very sufficient choice of worthy persons, who will voluntarily make such vows, and undertake freely such a profession, will admit no others to holy orders, because she is taught (in all the texts I cited in the beginning) that these are the fittest. With us, therefore, there is no man or woman who might not have married if they would; and therefore we cannot be said to forbid marriage, unless you will say that St. Paul did forbid marriage when he for-

bad bishops, deacons, and vowed widows to pass to second marriage. This is only to forbid breaking of vows to such as voluntarily would make them when they might freely have married.

9. Your other objections are foul corruptions of Scripture. The first of them is this, 1 Cor. ix. 5, "Have we not power to lead about a woman, a sister, as also the rest of the apostles, and our Lord's brother, and Cephas?" Here in place of a woman your Bibles read a wife, making the Holy Ghost restrain the word *gynaika* to a wife, though it is known that this word is usually put for a woman, whether wife or not wife. Here the Rhemist Testament shows how antiquity ever expounded this place of leading about such devout women as followed Christ "to minister to him," Matt. xxvii. 55. I could thus have maintained myself, saith St. Paul, by partaking of your temporal goods, to whom I give spiritual goods. But to burden nobody, I (being a tradesman) have made it my glory to maintain myself by the labour of my own hands. Yea, your own Bible but two chapters before translated the self-same Greek word for such a woman as could not be a wife. 1 Cor. vii. 1, "It is good for a man not to touch a woman." Translate (if you dare) "It is good for a man not to touch a wife," *gynaika*.

10. The second corrupt text you object is Heb. xiii. 4. For where we read word for word out of the Greek, "marriage honourable in all," you read, "marriage is honourable in all men," adding the verb *is* and the noun *men;* yet your best Bibles have not this noun (men), and they print this verb (is) in a different letter. As also in the former text they did print the word woman in the margin. This juggling, the vulgar do not perceive. And the Bibles used it to make them take for the true text that which is but their interpretation of it. But if a man would presume to add a verb, which should come as near as may be to the mind of the apostle, then he

should put the verb in the imperative mood thus: "Let marriage be honourable in all." For St. Paul uses this mood in the first verse, "Let brotherly love continue;" and in the second, "Be not unmindful," &c.; and in the third verse, "Remember them in bonds." The fourth verse, being the one we speak of, should be likewise expressed by a verb in that mood, especially seeing he still goes on in that mood in the fifth verse, "Let your conversation be without covetousness." The apostle's sense, then, seems clearly to be, "Let marriage be honourable in all;" that is, let no man dishonour his marriage-bed with either unfaithfulness to his spouse, or with unnatural or brutish lust: and so his next words very fitly are, "For God will judge fornicators and adulterers." But your Bible by a double imposture makes a quite different sense. The first is to put the verb in the indicative mood, "Marriage is honourable:" and because this alone helped not much, you used a second imposture in the words following, which in Greek are *en pasi*, in Latin, *in omnibus*. And in both languages all scholars see that there is doubt whether this should signify in all men (taking the adjective in the masculine gender), or in all things, taking it in the neuter gender. Our Bibles leave it as they find it in all. But your Bible undertakes absolutely to determine the sense of the Holy Ghost, and makes him say roundly, "Marriage is honourable among all men." Thus your Bible (anno 1577). Yea, "*Inter quosvis*," saith Beza (1565); that is, "Marriage is honourable among any kind of persons." Out of which new Scripture the people easily infer, marriage is honourable among those who have received holy orders, or have made vows of virginity; and the text being thus stretched, they might add, "Among brothers and sisters, father and daughter." But we shall (in the next Point, No. 5.) show how flatly this consequence is contrary to St. Paul, who plainly denounceth damnation to such as have married after they had vowed chastity. Your objection is sufficiently answered by having showed a double corruption in the text alleged, as many of you do allege it.

POINT XXI.

OF THE SINGLE LIFE OF SUCH AS HAVE VOWED PERPETUAL CHASTITY.

1. How commendable works of supererogation are (by which we voluntarily do what we are not commanded, and observe that which is of counsel, and not of precept), we shall see in the next Point. Yet here we cannot but speak something, to show how much the vowing of chastity is counselled and recommended; and show also how strictly those who vow chastity are obliged to keep their vows, which voluntarily they made. Num. xxx. 3, "If any man make a vow to our Lord, to bind himself by an oath, he shall not make his word frustrate, but all that he promised he shall fulfil." Whence St. Aug., Q. lvi. *in Num.*: "He that voweth abstinence from a thing lawful, maketh it unlawful to himself by his vow." Now that you may evidently see that the Scripture speaketh here of vows made in matters not commanded, it followeth, "if a woman vow any thing, and bind herself with an oath, she that is in her father's house, and as yet in maiden's age; if her father know the vow she promised, and the oath wherewith she bound her soul, and held his peace, she shall be bound to the vow; whatsoever she promised and swear, she shall fulfil indeed. But if immediately as he hears it, her father doth gainsay it, both her vows and her oath shall be frustrate, neither shall she be bound to the promise." The same he saith of the vows of a wife, that they shall hold, if her husband hold his peace; "but if he gainsay it,

he shall make her vow frustrate." Who sees not that it could not be either in the power of the father to make his daughter's vows void, or of the husband to frustrate and annul the vows of his wife, if they had vowed things which they stood obliged to perform by commandments from God? For example, if she should vow to fast in the feast of expiation, her husband could not have made void her vow by gainsaying it. For the law obligeth her, saying, Levit. xxiii. 29, "Every soul that is not afflicted,"—that is, which fasteth not this day,—"shall perish out of his people." By this you see, that the Scripture here speaketh of vows made to do that to which they were not otherwise obliged. But after the vow, they stand now obliged to fulfil in deed what they promised by word.

2. Take a further evident proof of this: Deut. xxiii. 21, "When thou hast vowed a vow to our Lord thy God, thou shalt not slack to pay it, because our Lord thy God will require it; and if thou delay, it shall be imputed unto thee for sin. If thou wilt not promise, thou shalt be without sin. But that which is once gone out of thy lips thou shalt observe, and shalt do as thou hast promised to our Lord thy God, and hast spoken with thy own will and thy own mouth." What could be said more manifest to prove, that where there was no kind of sin or breach of obligation before, now there is a sin by the breach of a most strait obligation arising from this vow? Again, Eccles. v. 4, "Whatsoever thou hast vowed, pay it. And it is much better not to vow, than after a vow not to perform the thing promised." For this is a sin, as hath been proved by the former unanswerable text.

3. As for the particular vow of chastity, we have our Saviour's own words: Matt. xix. 12, "And there be eunuchs, who have made themselves eunuchs for the kingdom of heaven." "Those make themselves eunuchs for the kingdom of heaven, who vow chastity," saith St. Aug., de Virg. c. xxvii. For by vow they make

themselves, as it were, impotent for marriage. And the doing this *for the kingdom of heaven* is a clear proof that this state doth much further towards obtaining heaven. Again, both voluntary poverty and chastity are particularly rewarded by our Lord, Luke xviii. 29, "There is no man who hath left either house, parents, or wife, for the kingdom of God" (note still how chastity furthers towards the kingdom of God), "who shall not receive manifold more at this present time, and in the world to come life everlasting." Here I find a reward for leaving a wife; show me a reward for marrying one.

4. St. Paul is most clear: 1 Cor. vii. 25, "As concerning virgins, a command of our Lord I have not, yet I give my judgment or counsel" (can you give better counsel or judgment? which is) "Art thou loosed from a wife, seek not a wife." Why so? It follows, ver. 32, "He that is without a wife is careful of the things that pertain to our Lord, how he may please God" (note still how chastity conduces to the gaining heaven); "but he that is with a wife, is careful of the things that pertain to the world. The virgin thinketh of things that pertain to the Lord, that she may be holy both in body and spirit. But she that is married, thinketh of things that pertain to the world." And, ver. 38, "He that joineth not his virgin in matrimony doth better." And, ver. 40, "But she is happier, if she so abide, after my judgment."

5. Again, 1 Tim. v. 9, "Let a widow be chosen, which hath been the wife of one husband." Here he speaks of the choice of such widows as then were deputed to the service of the Church, in assisting to prepare women catechumens to baptism, as also to serve the sick, to administer to the poor, especially of their own sex. And this they did, living under the charge of the deacons, whence they were called *diaconissæ*. St. Paul here saith he would have none chosen, or taken to this kind of state, who had been

married more than to *one man.* Neither doth he permit them (after they have once undertaken this state) to marry again. That hence you may see evidently how far he was from permitting priests to marry again after the state of priesthood undertaken, hear his discourse (C. v. n. 11): "Younger widows avoid" in this choice; "for when they have begun to wax wanton again" (that is, well fed by Church goods offered to Christ, as those widows were), "they will marry, having damnation; because they have cast off their first faith." Behold here their marriage and their damnation joined together; and the reason given why they have incurred *krima,* damnation, or judgment to their condemnation, to wit, because they have cast off their *first faith.* This first faith is their vow of keeping perpetual widowhood, according to all Fathers, Greek and Latin, whoever did write upon this place, saith the Rhemish Testament, here citing also St. Augustine, who, together with two hundred and fifteen fathers in the fourth council of Carthage, speaketh thus: "If any widows have vowed themselves to God, and left their laical habit, and, under the testimony of the bishop or Church, have appeared in religious weed, and afterwards go any more to secular marriage, they shall, according to the apostle, have damnation; because they were so bold as to make void the faith or promise of chastity, which they vowed to our Lord. And as St. Augustine saith, Heres. 82: "Jovinian the heretic was the first who induced vowed virgins to marry." And, lib. iii. Retr. c. 22, for this his new doctrine he calls him a *monster.*

6. Let us go on with St. Paul, vers. 14, 15, "I will therefore the younger to marry" (such as be frail), "to give no occasion to the adversaries to speak evil; for some are already turned aside after Satan." Whence it is evident that breach of vows is damnable, even in these younger widows, who (by reason of that breach) are said to have "turned aside, or gone after Satan," thus making their first faith void.

7. I end with that praise given to virgins, Apoc. xiv. 4, "These are they which follow the Lamb whithersoever he goeth."

POINT XXII.

OF THE WORKS OF COUNSEL AND SUPEREROGATION.

1. PROTESTANTS deny all works of supererogation, that is, works which we of our ownselves superadd to our bounden duty; and consequently they will have no good work to be only counselled unto us, but they say we are commanded to do all the good we can. Against this error be almost all the texts in the former Point, and particularly the text I there cited (No. 1) out of the book of *Numbers*, and what I cited (No. 4) out of St. Paul, flatly saying, "Concerning virgins, a command of our Lord I have not, but counsel I give." And again, "Art thou loosed from a wife? Seek not a wife." Is this a command? Woe, then, to ministers marrying when they were free men. If it be no command, what can it be but a counsel? And again, "He that joineth not his virgin in matrimony, doth better;" to wit, by doing something which you dare not say he is commanded, but which St. Paul once before told you she was only counselled. And he tells you also once more that it is only a counsel: "More happy (saith he) shall she be, if she remain so, according to my judgment or counsel." Is thine better?

To the proof of this point make all those manifold texts, which in the next Point we shall bring, to prove how commendable voluntary austerities be, for none of those austerities are by any precept commanded, but only commended to us; and so they be not of precept, but of counsel, superadded to what we are commanded, and therefore they are works of supererogation. See all those texts, for they are most convincing.

2. In the law of nature, I find Jacob freely, without being commanded, vowing to build a house for God, Gen. xxviii. 20, "And he vowed a vow, saying, If God shall keep me in the way, and I shall be returned prosperously to my father's house, this stone which I have set for a pillar shall be God's house." Which he being safely returned did fulfil, xxxv. 6, "Jacob came to Luz, surnamed Bethel, and he built there an altar, and called that place the house of God."

3. In the law of Moses God himself giveth a rule, Num. vi. 2, "To man and woman who shall separate themselves to vow a vow, to separate themselves to our Lord." For those, I say, who shall separate or consecrate themselves; which manner of speech showeth that they were obliged by no precept; but as long as they would be separated or consecrated, God obligeth them not to drink wine, nor eat grape or raisin. Yea, Jerem. xxxv. 6, Jonadab the son of Rechab most commendably (though he were not commanded) did give these laws to himself and his sons, "You shall not drink wine, you and your children for ever" (though wine were as common drink with that nation as beer with us); "and you shall not build houses, and you shall not sow seed, and you shall not plant vineyards, nor have any. But you shall dwell in tabernacles all your days. We obeyed the voice of Jonadab our father." Wherefore to them by Jeremias, ver. 18, "Thus saith the Lord, For that you have obeyed the commandment of Jonadab your father, and have done all things that he commanded you; therefore thus saith the Lord, There shall not want a man of the stock of Jonadab the son of Rechab standing in my sight, all days, or to stand before me for ever." As your Bibles have it. This is true; for the sons of promise (though not the sons of flesh) to the Rechabites are our religious, of which from the time of the Apostles to the last day there shall not fail to be many devout men still standing in God's

sight. Let Protestants show any such amongst them, who can be esteemed of the stock of Jonadab, or a Rechabite. They are so far from this, that they rail at us for being followers of superstitious inventions of men, when we follow the giver of so holy rules as Jonadab gave to his son, so praised and so rewarded by God for following them. Let them tell us (if they can) how amongst them it is true, "there shall not want a man of the stock of Jonadab."

4. Suppose the book of Judith, if you please, to be only a true history, which you do not deny, from thence then we have a true relation how piously Judith lived without any precept, who, viii. 3, having but lived three years and a half with her husband, he dying, " she in the higher part of her house, made herself a secret chamber, in which she abode, shut up with her maids; and having cloth of hair upon her loins, she fasted all the days of her life, but sabbaths, and the feasts of the house of Israel;" and this though " her husband left her much riches, and a great family." And, xvi. 26, " There was also chastity joined to her virtue, so that she knew not man all the days of her life, after that Manasses her husband was dead. And she abode in her husband's house an hundred and five years;" so that she, so fair and so rich, lived a widow about *sixty-nine years* in chastity, in prayer, in a perpetual fast, and hair-cloth. Who commanded her this, or who required it at her hands? Love of serving God more perfectly.

5. Wherefore, in the Gospel, to the young man whom our Saviour loved, because he truly (for he loves not lying boasters) did say "that he had kept the commandments from his youth," Mark x. 20, Christ notwithstanding said, "One thing thou lackest: Go thy way, go sell whatsoever thou hast, and thou shalt have a treasure in heaven." This one thing was not wanting to any duty, which he was bound to perform, to be saved. For to *enter into life*, Christ did only bid him *keep the commandments*, Matt. xix.

17; but, saith our Lord, ver. 21, "If thou wilt be perfect, go sell the things thou hast, and give to the poor, and thou shalt have treasure in heaven, and come and follow me." This, then, is that one thing which thou lackest,—I say, thou lackest this one thing, not to the state of salvation (for keeping the commandment doth suffice to the state of salvation), but thou lackest this to the state of perfection, if thou wilt be perfect. For this one thing contains all the three evangelical counsels. First, poverty, to "sell all and give to the poor." Secondly, chastity; for him whom he counselleth to sell all, and give to the poor, he must needs counsel not to take a wife with charge of family and children, for else something were to be kept for them. Thirdly, obedience; "come and follow me," under the obedience of those whom I shall place over thee in lawful authority; for our Saviour in person was not to live but a very short time after this. See all that followeth in the next Point.

POINT XXIII.

OF VOLUNTARY AUSTERITY OF LIFE.

1. I HANDLE this point apart, because there being such daily practice of these kinds of works in our religion, and so little in our adversaries (they scoffing at all we do or suffer, in this point), we will show whether they scoff not at the practice of virtue, recommended by Scripture.

2. First, then, observe all that hath been said in the last Point doth recommend austerity of life, by counselling a chaste life, which cannot be maintained unless the flesh be tamed by some austerities; neither is chastity itself a small austerity. Note also that they who in the old law, Num. vi., "had a will to separate themselves to God," had also a will to

choose an austere life, abstaining from wine, the usual drink of that country. How great and voluntary was the austerity of the Rechabites, or sons of Jonadab, who "neither did drink wine, nor build houses" (but lodged abroad in tabernacles), "nor possessed vineyards, nor sowed corn or any seed"! And yet how doth God praise and reward them for it? Jer. xxxv. 18. How great and how voluntary was the austerity of Judith, living *sixty-nine years in chastity*, in upper rooms retired from the world, almost in continual fast, continual hair-cloth, most frequent prayer, she being so rich, and, when she began this course, so young and so beautiful! Christ also counselled no small voluntary austerity to him whom he advised, for greater perfection, to *sell all;* for money being the price of all commodities, the want of it brings all incommodities. He was advised also to follow him, "who had not a hole to shroud his head in." What austerity is here counselled!

3. Much like this was the voluntary austerity of the first Christians, forsaking money, the price both of all delights and also of all convenient accommodation; and yet, Acts iv. 34, "As many as were owners of lands, or houses, sold, and brought the prices of those things which they sold, and carried them before the feet of the apostles." Who commanded this? Love of serving God more perfectly; for if we speak of any obligation, they had no other than we have. Hence St. Peter to Ananias, ch. v. 4, "Whiles it remained, was it not thine own? and after it was sold, in thine own power?" That is, thou *hadst power* to keep it wholly to thyself, or to vow it wholly to God; after which vow thou hadst no further power to keep it, according to what we proved fully out of Scripture, Point XXI. Nos. 1, 2.

4. But to speak more particularly of that which we call austerity of life,—such as that of Judith was, both great and voluntary, as also that of the Rechabites, or sons of Jonadab,—how great and voluntary

was the austerity of holy David, though a king! "His knees were weak through fasting," Psalm cix. 24; "I am weary with my groaning. All the night make I my bed to swim. I water my couch with my tears," Psalm vi. 6; "By reason of the voice of my groaning, my bones have cleaved to my skin," Psalm cii. 5; "I have eaten ashes like bread, and mingled my drink with weeping," ver. 9. His prayers also far exceeded any command given him, Psalm cxix. 148, "Mine eyes have prevented the night watches, that I might meditate thy word. I prevented the dawning of the morning, and cried." And, ver. 62, "At midnight I will rise to give thanks to thee." And ver. 97, "Thy law is my meditation all day." And ver. 164, "Seven times a day I do praise thee." Daniel, ix. 3, of himself saith, "I did put my face to my Lord God, to beseech and pray him in fastings, sackcloth, and ashes." And, Nehemiah ix. 1, "The children of Israel came together in fasting and sackcloths, and earth upon them." What the Ninevites did is well known. Of Jacob, as wealthy as he was, the Scripture tells us how, sleeping on the ground, "he used a stone for his pillow," and so was favoured with that heavenly vision, Gen. xxviii. 11; so to all Israel is said, Joel ii. 12, "Turn ye to me with all your heart, with fasting, with weeping, and with mourning."

5. Now in the New Testament, Christ's doctrine would have made the great sinners of Tyre and Sidon do penance in sackcloth and ashes, Matt. xi. 12. He saith to all, "He that will come after me, let him take up his cross." Great and voluntary was the austerity of St. John Baptist: "He shall be great before our Lord. Wine and cider, or strong drink, he shall not drink," Luke i. 15. "The child grew, and waxed in spirit, and was in the desert until the day of his manifestation, or showing in Israel," ver. 80. That is, from his childhood until he was above thirty years old. "He was clothed with camel's hair,

and a girdle of skin about his loins, and he did eat locusts and wild honey," Mark i. 6. And he did eat so sparingly, that of him Christ saith, "John came neither eating nor drinking," Matt. xi. 18. Of his disciples' *often fasting* we read, Matt. ix. 14. And they were instructed by him, of whom Christ said, "Amongst the children of women there hath not risen a greater than John Baptist." Christ also promised there, that his disciples should do as John's did, that is, *fast often*, when "the bridegroom should be taken from them."

6. They did but what St. Paul taught, 2 Cor. vi. 4, " In all things approving ourselves as the ministers of God, in much patience, in tribulations, in necessities, in distresses, in stripes, in prisons, in seditions." To these (which all perhaps were not voluntary) he exhorts us voluntarily to add, " In labours, in watchings, in fasting, in pureness or chastity. For as we shall be partakers of his sufferings, so shall we be of his consolation," 2 Cor. iii. 7. "Mortify your members which be upon earth," Col. iii. 5. But before I pass hence, I must observe what is said of holy Anne, Luke ii. 37, " She was a widow until eighty and four years" (living even until that age); " she departed not from the temple, by fasting and prayers serving God night and day." Behold by what exercises God is served. Who commanded her this? The desire of serving God more perfectly.

7. Hear St. Paul of himself, 1 Cor. ix. 27, " I keep under my body, and bring it into subjection, lest perhaps, whilst I preach to others, myself may become a castaway, or reprobate." Who commanded him? Desire of securing his salvation. Again, Col. i. 24, "I Paul, who now rejoice in suffering for you, and do accomplish, or fill up that which is behind, or those things that are wanting, of the affliction of Christ in my flesh, for his body, which is the Church." Behold another reason, which was to suffer, thereby to satisfy for the sins of others, of which text more

when we shall speak of satisfactory good works in the next Point, No. 6.

8. St. Timothy, disciple to St. Paul, having great weakness of stomach, and frequent infirmities in the midst of so great labours, did notwithstanding so continually drink water at all his meals, that St. Paul thought it necessary to write to him thus, 1 Tim. v. 23, "Drink not yet water, but use a little wine for thy stomach, and thy often infirmities." So that you see, that before he did not so much as drink a *little wine*, though it were the common drink of that country, and though he were so weakened by sickness and labour; thus voluntarily abstaining from wine, so good a creature of God. Who commanded him this abstinence? Love of perfection.

POINT XXIV.

OF SATISFACTORY GOOD WORKS.

1. THESE voluntary austerities, of which we spoke in the former Point, and all such painful and laborious good works, when they are performed in a state of grace, are held by us Catholics to have a great satisfactory virtue, by which the pain due to our sin is forgiven, and is more or less cancelled, as the works are more or less perfect. For we teach that, after the sin itself is forgiven, by our true repentance and humble confession, there yet remains the guilt of temporal pain, to which that sin makes us still liable, as I shall prove in the next Point, which, if you please, you may read before this. Protestants think they much magnify the passion of our Saviour by saying, "that by the virtue of that alone all sins, and all pain due to all sins, are quite forgiven." But, first, I ask them if nothing else be required on our parts. They are forced to confess that something

else is required: for they are constrained to acknowledge, *First*, That we must be baptized. *Secondly*, That we must lay hold of the passion of Christ by the hand of faith. *Thirdly*, That besides this faith, we must have true repentance. *Fourthly*, They must needs say, that also you must have a will to receive the body and blood of Christ: "Unless you eat the flesh of the Son of Man, and drink his blood, you shall not have life in you," John vi. 53. *Fifthly*, They must needs also say, that either the observation of the Commandments is necessary (as we shall show, Point XXXVI.), or at least a good will and serious endeavour to keep them. "He was made to all that obey him the cause of eternal salvation," Heb. v. 9. So that *obeying him* is required on our parts to have him be effectual to us,—"the cause of eternal salvation."

2. By this discourse it is evident, that though the passion of Christ in itself be of a sufficient worth and value to satisfy for all the sins of the world, yea of a million of worlds, and also for all the pain that is, or can be, due to those sins, yet Christ, out of his prudence and justice, thought fit to order so, that this full fruit of his passion should not be applied to any, but such as should perform several things which he requires at their hands for this effect. Not that there is need of this to supply any want of value in his passion, but there is need to do all this, to fulfil, on our parts, the covenant and conditions upon which this benefit is granted. As you must say of all those five several things which you yourselves require to be superadded by us on our part, that we may enjoy the full fruit of his passion. To these five things we Roman Catholics add a sixth, and we have Scripture for this sixth, as well as you have for the other five. That sixth thing is, that Christ requires of us several penal and laborious works, which though in themselves, and as they merely proceed from us, they have no sufficient proportion to cancel the pains due unto

our sins, as also you must confess all that is done by us in baptism, or in believing, or in repenting, or in receiving his body, or in endeavouring to keep his law, hath also no such proportion, yet each of them have virtue to this effect: but this virtue is merely from the virtue of the passion of our Saviour, which is communicated to us by the performance of these things. For we so magnify the virtue of our Saviour's passion, that we say a most satisfactory virtue, or a special efficacy to cancel pain due to sins, is not only communicated by it to faith, but the like efficacy, in order to this effect, is by the same passion communicated to our painful and laborious works of fasting, hair-cloth, watching, praying, alms-deeds; and therefore this our doctrine is so far from derogating to our Saviour's passion, that it honoureth more than yours, which doth deny the passion of our Saviour this praise, of being sufficient to elevate and raise our poor endeavours of satisfying to any ability of making real satisfaction.

3. The force and virtue of these actions was well known to holy David, who did practise them so much, as I showed in the last Point, No. 4. His knees were weakened with fasting; he laboured in sighing; he every night washed his bed, and watered his couch with his tears. The voice of his perpetual groaning for his sins, with other austerities joined therewith, made his bones cleave to his skin, he being merely skin and bones; for he did eat ashes as bread, and mingled his drink with his most frequent tears. He gave himself to prayer night and day; every night washing his bed with tears, rising at midnight to confess to our Lord, and then preventing the dawning of the day by the cry of his morning prayers. Seven times in the day he said praise to God; all this he did, being a king. Alms-deeds may seem less wonderful in a royal person; yet his bountiful alms, considering the charge of so continual wars, were even incredible. Towards the building of the temple, 1

Chron. xxii. 14, "Behold (saith he) I, in my trouble, prepared the charges of the house of our Lord. Of gold a hundred thousand talents, and of silver a thousand thousand talents, and of brass and of iron without weight, for the number is surpassed by the greatness: timber and stones I have prepared to all the charges." To all this in chap. xxix. 3, "Above all these things which I have offered into the house of my God, I give of my own peculiar goods gold and silver unto the temple of my God, besides those things which I have prepared for the holy house. Three thousand talents of the gold of Ophir, and seven thousand talents of most approved silver." Thus he excelled in fasting, prayer, and alms-deeds, to which three all other satisfactory works are reduced. Who commanded David this? The excellency of his charity to God.

4. In like manner Job of himself, "I abhor myself, and repent in dust and ashes," Job xlii. 6. And as for alms, chap. xxxi. 17, "If I have eaten my morsels alone, and the fatherless hath not eaten with me. If his sides have not blessed me; and he was not warmed with the fleeces of my sheep. The stranger tarried not without; my door was open to the wayfaring man. If I have been afraid of a very great multitude." In another place, "He was an eye to the blind, a staff to the lame," &c. Of holy Judith's actions we spoke in the former Point. Hear what is said to that wicked king by Daniel, iv. 27, "Wherefore, O king, let my counsel be acceptable to thee, break off thy sins by righteousness, and thy iniquities by showing mercy to the poor." Behold the sins even of Nebuchadnezzar might be cancelled by alms. For, Prov. xvi. 6, "By mercy and truth iniquity is purged." Joel ii. 12, "Turn to me with all your heart in fasting, and in weeping, and in mourning, and rend your hearts and not your garments." Jonas iii. 5, "The men of Nineveh proclaimed a fast, and were clothed with sackcloth," &c.

"And God saw their works, and had mercy," &c. Why? "He saw their works."

5. In the New Testament we are exhorted to approve ourselves ministers of God in labours, in watching, in fasting, in chastity, 2 Cor. vi. 4. We have St. John Baptist neither eating nor drinking, Matt. xi. 18. His disciples fasting often; Christ promising that, after his death, his also should fast as St. John's did, that is, should fast often, Matt. ix. 14. We have St. Anne by fasting and prayers serving night and day, Luke ii. 37. St. Paul chastising his body; his disciple Timothy drinking still water. And as for alms, after so many woes denounced to the most unclean Scribes and Pharisees, Christ himself saith, "But yet what remaineth, give alms, and behold all things are cleansed unto you," Luke xi. 41. So that to cleanse them by his blood, he would have their alms joined with the virtue of his blood, which blood gave this cleansing power to their alms. And St. Paul promiseth us, Rom. viii. 17, "That we may be heirs of God, and joint heirs with Christ, if so be we suffer with him, that we may also be glorified with him." Note the condition, if so be that we suffer: though Christ's suffering of its own self be more than enough, yet he will have ours joined. Upon these terms he covenants to communicate the full fruit of his passion to us; and therefore unless this be done on our part, something is said to be wanting to the passion of Christ in order to its full effect.

6. This is clear out of Col. i. 24, "I Paul, who now rejoice in suffering for you, and do fill up what is behind of the afflictions of Christ in my flesh, for his body which is the Church." Notwithstanding Christ's passion (as I declared in Nos. 1 and 2) some scores are left behind, so that some things are wanting; not wanting on Christ's part, but Christ requires them to be done on our part, for they be our scores which be thus behind, until we shall have done all that he hath ordained that we should do, to be

partakers of the full fruit of his passion, in order to
the cancelling of pains due for our sins. And we
must either by ourselves fill up what is behind, or
accomplish these things which want of the passion of
Christ to this effect, or our charitable brothers must,
by their suffering for us, help us out; as St. Paul
here saith, "He did help out of the Colossians by his
suffering for them." So that if we be fellows in his
passion, we shall be fellows in his resurrection and
glory.

7. The obtaining of this remission of all sins, and
of all pains due to these sins, which are committed
after baptism, is not done with that facility and easi-
ness with which all this was done in baptism, but it
is a thing which requires much labour and pain.
Heb. x. 26, "For, if we sin willingly after the knowledge of truth received, there is not left an host for
sins." Wherefore though it be most true which was
there said, ver. 14, "By one oblation he hath perfected for ever them that are sanctified;" yet the true
meaning of that text is, that he hath done this in
that manner which he, in his prudence and justice,
hath thought fit; that is, he hath, by that one oblation, so perfected them for ever, that they, to be partakers of this consummated perfection, completed on
his part, must do all things which he exacts to be
done on their parts; that is, believe, repent, resolve
to keep, or endeavour to keep, the commandments.
If thus disposed, they superadd baptism, all is perfected, wholly supposing their perseverance. But if we
sin after this baptism, in which we profess the knowledge of the truth received, there is now not an host
for sin; that is, the host of Christ crucified, which is
the oblation consummating them for ever, is not left;
to wit, it is not left to cancel and cleanse our sins so
easily as before. For none can again be baptized in
cold water, but we must be re-baptized in the hot
water of our tears, in the baptism of penance,—for so
the Scripture calls penance,—in fasting, sackcloth,

watching, praying, alms-deeds; or else we must smart in purgatory, as by Scripture we shall now prove.

POINT XXV.

OF PURGATORY AND PRAYER FOR THE DEAD.

1. SOME are so ignorant in the understanding of Scripture, that if they find not there the name of *purgatory* they presently conclude that, according to Scripture, there is no such thing as purgatory. This is as great simplicity as it would be to deny the most blessed Trinity because this name cannot be found in all the Scripture, Old or New. Such men are to be taught that any thing is sufficiently proved out of Scripture if the Scripture can be showed to contain such principles as cannot be true, unless it be true also that there is a purgatory.

2. I say, then, the Scripture holds forth unto us *three several principles;* all of which three must be false unless we grant a purgatory. For, first, if any Scripture teach that although our sins be forgiven us whensoever we truly repent, but yet that they are only forgiven so that all the pains due to them be not always forgiven them together with these sins, then that very Scripture teacheth us also that there is a purgatory; because it may often happen that he to whom all sins were forgiven did depart this life before that all the pains due to those his sins were remitted. These pains being due to divine justice, and not being cancelled by any satisfaction made for them in this world, it evidently follows that divine justice must exact the payment of them in the next world; but not in hell; because no man is condemned to hell who did truly repent for his sins. Therefore some other place or state must needs be granted, in which such a soul is to pay those temporal punishments which are yet due

to her by divine justice. This place or state is that which we call *purgatory*.

3. Secondly, If any Scripture teacheth us that we may live and die with such sins as be not damnable, but only deserve temporal punishment, and not eternal, that Scripture also must needs teach us purgatory, which is nothing else but a place in which souls departed suffer only for a time, and not for eternity.

4. Thirdly, If any Scripture teach us to pray for the dead, that very Scripture teacheth us a purgatory. For prayers for the dead are unnecessary to those who are in heaven, and unprofitable to such as are in hell. Those dead, then, who can receive help and relief by our prayers, must neither be in heaven nor in hell, but in a third place, which we call purgatory. My work then is done, if I can show *that these three principles be held forth unto us in holy Scripture.* Yet, fourthly, we shall add several other texts in proof of purgatory.

5. Let us now begin with the *first principle*, and let us show how the Scripture teacheth us that full often, after the sin itself is forgiven, there do remain some pains yet due even to that sin. We are all born in original sin. This sin is quite forgiven to many children, whether it be by the faith of their parents, as in the law of nature, or by circumcision, as in the old law, or by baptism, as in the new. And yet those very infants to whom this sin is forgiven do notwithstanding, for the self-same forgiven sin, suffer the punishment of death due unto them for no other cause but for that very original sin which was forgiven them. This is taught by St. Paul, Rom. v. 12, "As by one man sin entered into the world, and by sin death, so unto all death did pass;" yea, truly unto all did death pass, even to those innocent children who have not committed the least offence in the world.

6. In the book of Numbers, xiv. 20, the people grievously offended God by murmuring; but Moses praying earnestly for them, our Lord said, "I have

forgiven it according to my word. But yet all the men that have seen the signs that I have done in Egypt and in the wilderness, they shall not see the land for which I swore to their fathers. In this wilderness shall your carcasses lie (28, 32). Your carcasses shall be in the wilderness; your children shall wander in the desert forty years, and shall bear your fornication, until the carcasses of their fathers be consumed in the desert. And forty years shall you bear your iniquities. For as I have spoken, so will I do." Note here that God with his own mouth said *he had forgiven the sin;* and yet he, with the same mouth and breath (as I may say), tells them there shall be still a just punishment undergone for this very sin, *for which* (though forgiven) *they shall die in the wilderness, and for forty years their very children shall bear their fornication;* and they shall suffer all the incommodities of wandering in a wilderness.

Can, then, any man wonder if they themselves, who had their pardon on these terms, and then were slain the very next day by their enemies, should for a time, yea, perhaps for forty years, suffer some punishment after death? Eternal punishment (the old sin being forgiven) they could not suffer, if they did no new one; yet manifestly some punishment after death could not but be due to them, seeing that so great a punishment was so justly laid upon their children for their sake, for forty whole years.

7. Let us go on. 2 Sam. xii. 13, upon David's great repentance for his great sins of murder and adultery, God by the prophet Nathan told him, "Our Lord also hath taken away thy sin. Howbeit, because by this deed thou hast given great occasion to the enemies of the Lord to blaspheme, the child that is born unto thee shall surely die." Behold the sin taken away, and yet behold a punishment still due, even for this deed. "Yea, for this deed the sword shall not depart from thy house for ever. I will take thy wives and give them to thy neighbours; and

they shall sleep with thy wives in the sight of the sun," ver. 10, 11. All which great punishments, even after this *forgiven sin*, did befall David and his family. His son died, ver. 18; three more of his own sons were slain,—Ammon, in the next chapter; Absolom, chap. xviii.; Adonias, 1 Kings ii. 24. Yea, Absolom before his death did raise an army against David his father, and enforced him to fly; Jerusalem being taken, they pitched a tent for Absolom in the house-top (the leads of the place), "and he went to his father's concubines before all Israel," 2 Sam. xvi. 22; thus in the sight of the sun lying with his own father's wives, called here concubines, because they were not admitted to the title of queens.

8. Our Lord said to Moses and Aaron, Num. xx. 12, "Because you have not believed me, you shall not bring this people into the land which I will give them." And, ver. 24, "Aaron shall be gathered to his people (that is, shall die), for he shall not enter into the land which I have given to the children of Israel, because he rebelled against my word;" and, ver. 28, "Aaron died there on the top of the mountain;" and, chap. xxvii. 13, "God said to Moses, When thou hast seen it (the land of promise), thou also shalt be gathered unto thy people, as Aaron thy brother was gathered; for ye rebelled against my commandment." Thus you see these two great saints both punished with a most speedy death for that very sin of which they, being admonished by God himself, questionless did repent. Whence after this sin committed God did so familiarly converse with Moses from chap. xx. to xxvii. By all these, and a world of other such examples, it is made evident, that, upon the true repentance of the delinquent, though the pain of eternal death be always forgiven him, yet often the delinquent remains liable to suffer temporal punishments: even as in this world, though upon the repentance of a delinquent deserving death the punishment of death be forgiven him, yet

he is justly made liable to suffer imprisonment, or condemned to pay such a fine.

9. Out of this principle it clearly followeth that there is a purgatory: for seeing that a man may die before he hath suffered, or satisfied for the punishment due by divine justice unto him, it doth necessarily follow that this punishment, according to the same justice, must be given him in the world to come: not in hell, because the sin is forgiven him; but yet in the prison of purgatory, out of which he shall not go until he hath paid the last farthing, Matt. v. 26. It remains then proved, that this principle (so well grounded in Scripture) cannot be true unless it be also true that there is a purgatory.

10. I pass to the second principle, teaching, that some sins are only venial, deserving indeed some punishment, but not eternal. For, as he were a tyrant who would punish every offence (though it deserve but whipping) with a cruel death, so we should have too hard opinion of God's justice if we believed, that for every merry lie, for every idle word or passionate speech, for every trifling away of a small time unprofitably, for every vain or lazy action, he should punish the delinquent with death everlasting, and the endless and unspeakable torments of hell-fire if the person dieth without repentance, as thousands must needs do who die suddenly, or out of their senses, or in their sleep, &c.

11. That there be such venial sins or smaller offences as these are which be truly sins, yet not mortal or damnable, is clear out of Scripture, Exod. i. 17. But the midwives of Egypt feared God, and preserved the men-children, contrary to the command of the king; who, questioning them for breaking his commandment, they answered, "The Hebrew women are not as the Egyptian women, for they have the knowledge to play the midwife themselves, and before we come to them, they are delivered." God therefore did well to the midwives; and because they

feared God he built them houses. Here you see the midwives telling an officious lie, which is a sin; yet this sin did not take from them the love of God, or make God hate them: but they even then feared God, as the Scripture saith, and he for this their fear (exercised not in this lie, but in their charity and mercy) highly rewarded them. Yet this lying being a sin, divine justice could not but reserve some punishment for it, though not eternal.

12. Even so, Joshua ii. 1, the spies sent by Joshua entered the house of Rahab. "And it was told the king of Jericho. He sent to Rahab, saying, Bring forth the men that came to thee, for they be spies. And the woman taking the men hid them, and said, I confess they came to me when the gate was a shutting in the dark, and they withal went out; I know not whither they be gone; pursue quickly, and you shall overtake them. But she made the men go up to the roof of her house, and covered them with the stalks of flax which were there." Here you have another officious lie, but only a venial, not a damnable sin. By lying, she sinned venially; but by that act of charitably hiding the spies, she pleased God. For St. Paul saith, "By faith, Rahab perished not, receiving the spies with peace," Heb. xi. 31. And St. James, ii. 25, "Rahab, was she not justified by works, receiving the messengers, and putting them forth another way, after that she had first hid them?" Of these kind of venial sins the Scripture also saith, "Seven times shall the just fall and rise again," Prov. xxiv. 16. For these smaller sins cast us not out of God's favour; wherefore by his grace we soon get pardon again. And hence these sins are called venial, such as easily have pardon.

13. Whence our Saviour himself doth distinguish several sins, and affirms some of them to deserve punishment, but not hell-fire: Matt. v. 22, "Whosoever is angry (for so the Protestant Bibles read it) with his brother, shall be in danger of judgment:

and whosoever shall say to his brother, Raca, shall be in danger of council: and whosoever shall say, Thou fool, shall be in danger of hell-fire." Of which only eternal punishment, the two former sins did not endanger us, they being but venial. Hence it is evident, that there be some sins which God judgeth worthy of punishment, and yet not to deserve hell-fire; and he speaks of the punishment of the next life as of hell, &c. Again, Matt. xii. 36, "I say unto you, that every idle word that man shall speak, he shall render an account thereof in the day of judgment." The words of lesser anger deserved not hell-fire, as the former text taught us; yet they, being worse than mere idle words, some punishment is due to them. For here this text saith, some account must be rendered even for every idle word, but a lesser account than for angry words, and therefore they will not alone make us liable to hell-fire. Again, Matt. vii. 3, some sins be called *beams*, some only *motes;* which name Christ (hating deadly sin to death) would never give to any sin that were damnable. Neither would he (if these lesser sins were damnable) speak of them as he doth, Matt. xxiii. 23, "You tithe mint and anise, &c.; blind guides that strain at a gnat, and swallow a camel." Behold, some sins only like gnats, and the doing of them compared to the fault that would be in omitting to pay tithe for mint and anise. Yet because all venial sins do something pollute the soul, this stain must be purged or cleansed. Often this is not done in this world, for we see daily men continue in doing these sins to the last, losing all sense, and life also, before they repent them: some account, then, in judgment (following after death immediately) will be given of them; not in hell, for they deserve it not; therefore in purgatory.

14. Agreeable to this is that which our Saviour saith, Luke xii. 47, "That servant who knoweth the will of his lord, and doth not according to his will, shall be beaten with many stripes; but he that

knoweth it not, and doth things worthy of stripes, shall be beaten with few stripes." Hence it is evident, that there be some men who do things worthy of stripes, which they shall not escape, but yet they shall be beaten with few stripes. But if these stripes be to be laid on for all eternity (as all stripes be which are paid in hell), they will not be few; because, being everlasting, the number of them will be without number. Will, then, any one call these stripes few? Or can any man persuade himself that a God who is all mercy will, in this unmerciful manner, punish the speaking of one idle word? Yet Christ himself saith, "that we shall be accountable for every idle word we speak," Matt. xii. Wherefore we must be liable to some punishment for every idle word; so that, if a man of full age, converted from idolatry, be baptized, and by and by after be killed, before he commit any other sin than the speaking of any one idle word only, shall this man be tormented for ever and ever, so long as God shall be God? And shall the Father of mercies give this unmerciful sentence? Doubtless, if any man can do a thing worthy of stripes, and for doing it deserve only to be beaten with few stripes, this man may hope for this mercy. But for greater than this he cannot hope, seeing that Christ saith that some account is to be given for that idle word. Some punishment, therefore, he must suffer, but not eternal; and consequently not in hell, but in purgatory: for he must be beaten with few stripes, not with many or everlasting stripes. If this principle (so well grounded in Scripture) be true, then it cannot but be true that there is a purgatory.

15. The third principle, clearly also contained in Scripture, is, that prayer may profitably be made for the dead. This is proved as well out of the Old as New Testament. In the Old Testament, 2 Macc. xii. 43, where, after divers of the soldiers of Judas Maccabeus had been slain in the battle, "He, making a gathering, sent twelve thousand drachms of silver

to Jerusalem, to have sacrifice offered for the sins (of the dead), well and religiously thinking of the resurrection. For unless he hoped that they who were slain should rise again, it should seem superfluous and vain to pray for the dead. It is therefore a holy and healthful cogitation to pray for the dead, that they may be loosed from their sins." Your English Bibles so mangle the sense here that I would not follow them.

I know Protestants will say these books be not canonical, though in the third council of Carthage, held anno 397, can. 47, they be registered in the Canon. Yet not to dispute this matter, I take that which is granted without all dispute—that is, that these books be written by a true and faithful writer of the ancient church history; or else why do you place them in the Bible? And without dispute also they were written before our Saviour's time. So that by the most grave testimony of so ancient a writer of ecclesiastical history, we have, first, that Judas Maccabeus, who then was high-priest, and also chief commander of the Jews (God's only true people), did hold prayer for the dead to be laudable. Secondly, That this was not his private opinion, but a thing done conformably to the custom of the Jewish Church, which to this very day uses prayer for the dead. Thirdly, All the soldiers, being men who had devoted their lives for the defence of the true belief, concurred by contributing to this act of piety, *that sacrifice might be offered for the dead.* Fourthly, The priests of Jerusalem, who best knew their Church's custom in sacrifices for the dead (which were the same that were for sin), are never said to have scrupled at the matter. Fifthly, This most ancient historian recommends this custom as holy. All these things not being singular in those men alone, and happening not full two hundred years before Christ, and still lasting to this day among the Jews, there could not but be many who practised this (so common a thing) in his and his Apostles' times. And yet you never read the least reprehension given them for it.

16. Out of the New Testament we have two places. First, St. Paul, 1 Cor. xv. 29, "What shall they do who are baptized for the dead? If the dead do not rise at all, to what end are they baptized for them?" As if he could say, To what end do men do penance for the dead? To what end is this done, if there be no resurrection, and the soul do not still survive, expecting to be re-united to the body? St. Paul can speak here of no other baptism which can profit the dead but the baptism of penance; for so St. Mark and so St. Luke speak. And certain it is that St. Paul takes his argument from that, which with profit to the dead can be performed for them. Otherwise, when he presseth so hotly those words, "To what end are they baptized for them?" one might easily answer, To no end. True, then, it is that to a very good end we undertake this painful baptism of penance for the dead, so taking upon us part of their fiery baptism in purgatory. This is the language of holy Fathers expounding Scripture, as Bellarmin showeth (*l.* 1 de Purgatorio, cap. 4) out of St. Hierom, St. Basil, and Bede, all expounding those words, "He shall baptize you in the Holy Ghost and fire," Matt. iii. 11. That is, say they, with the Holy Ghost shall he baptize in this world, and with fire in the world to come. To the same effect he cites St. Gregory Nazianzen, calling purgatory's fire the last baptism.

17. The second text is, 1 John v. 16, "If any man see his brother to sin a sin not to death, let him ask, and life shall be given for them that sin not to death. There is a sin to death (committed by irrepentant sinners), I do not say that he shall pray for it." And so we never pray for those whom we know to die unrepentant. This is the true sense of this place, and hence it is clear that there be *sins to death, and sins not to death.* The meaning is not that there be

sins mortal and sins venial, neither according to our interpreters or according to yours, who deny all venial sins. As for us, we all hold prayer lawfully and fruitfully made for any sin whatsoever, during the life of the sinner. Wherefore a "sin to death is to leave faith, working by charity even to death," as St. Austin saith, de Correp. et Gra. c. 12. Whence it followeth contrariwise, that a "sin not to death" is that which a man committeth, but doth not persevere in it until he be dead. St. John therefore encourageth us with confidence to pray for any whom we do not know to be departed in deadly sin unrepented. For it is evident that St. John speaks here of praying for the dead. First, Because before the death of any sinner we may pray for pardon of his sins, whatsoever they may be, and our prayer may be heard. But St. John speaks of a sinner now placed in such a state that prayer for him will not be available, therefore he speaks of praying for sinners who are dead. And of those, some are dead in their sins without repentance; for these he bids us not pray. Others of them are dead after they duly repented of their sins; and for these he encourageth us to pray. I prove this, secondly, Because he speaks of their prayer, "who know their brother to sin not to death"—that is, to have given signs of true repentance. "For any such, let him ask, and life (of glory) shall be given him, sinning not to death." Now if this principle of praying for the dead be true, it cannot but be true that there is a purgatory, seeing that prayer brings no relief to any that are either in heaven or hell.

18. To these three principles we may yet add several texts to the same effect, as Apoc. xxi. 27, "There shall in no wise enter into it (heaven) any thing that defileth." Many die polluted with multitudes of venial sins unrepented. This pollution must be purged before they enter heaven. Many also die before they have fully satisfied for all pain due to

their mortal sins forgiven them. This full satisfaction must be made before they enter into heaven. But where? in that prison, of which it is said, Matt. v. 26, "Amen, I say unto you, thou shalt not go out from thence until thou payest the last farthing." Upon which place St. Jerome, "This is that which he saith, Thou shalt not go out of prison, until thou shalt pay even to thy little sins." And so St. Cyprian. Now that after the paying of the last farthing there is going out, and forgiveness in the world to come, Christ himself doth teach, Matt. xii. 32, saying, "It shall not be forgiven thee, neither in this world, nor in the world to come." For it is nonsense to say, "I will neither marry in this world, nor in the world to come;" because in that world there is no marrying. The like nonsense would be in Christ's words, if there were no forgiveness in the next world. I conclude with St. Paul, 1 Cor. iii. 15, "If any man's work shall be burnt, as wood, hay, and stubble will do (by which lesser sins are signified), he shall suffer loss; but he himself shall be saved, yet so as by fire." Which St. Ambrose, Serm. 20, in Psalm cxviii., expounds thus: "Whereas St. Paul saith, yet so as by fire, he showeth indeed that he shall be saved, but yet shall suffer the punishment of fire; that being purged by fire he may be saved, and not tormented for ever, as infidels are, by everlasting fire."

19. All these proofs we have out of Scripture, though they be so little noted by our adversaries, who daily read Scripture. Yet they are to know, that if they will do what they pretend, they should by clear Scripture, before they deny purgatory, show us manifestly "that there is no purgatory." For their prime pretence of just separation from us is, that they were enforced thereunto for such errors as they can manifestly, "by only Scripture," demonstrate to be damnable. Let them show this of purgatory, and we have done.

POINT XXVI.

OF INDULGENCES.

1. To understand this point well, which is misunderstood by a world of people, note, first, what we proved in the former Point, that full often, after that God hath pardoned the guilt of sin, he doth not pardon the guilt of all that pain to which the sinner, according to justice, is still liable for the sin forgiven. Note, secondly, that we are most grossly belied by our adversaries, who say that our doctrine is, *That the Pope can forgive us our sins by granting indulgences unto us.* Whereas no Catholic doctor can ever be showed to have taught this doctrine. We all unanimously teach, that *the Pope by no indulgence can forgive any one single mortal or venial sin.* For our faith tells us, that those sins are only forgiven us by true contrition, or due sorrow in the sacrament of confession, joined always with a sincere purpose of offending no more. That which is forgiven by an indulgence is not the guilt of any sin, either mortal or venial, but *it is only the pardoning of part, or of all that pain,* which yet, according to God's justice, we stand liable to pay for the sins already forgiven. Neither doth any Catholic doctor teach that the Pope can forgive any sinner this pain at his pleasure, by granting him a plenary indulgence. But, if our doctrine be truly understood, we all require more for gaining pardon, even of the least part of the pain still due to our very least sins, than Protestants require to the full forgiveness of all the greatest sins that are, or can be, taken altogether with all the pain which can be due unto them; which is a point exceedingly to be noted, it being evidently true.

2. For the first thing which we require to gain any part, even of the least indulgence, is to have true faith producing true repentance for our sin. This

alone with Protestants suffices to remit the guilt of all sins whatsoever, and all pains due to all sins of which any man can be guilty. Doth it do so with us? No, it is far from it. We say that after this, First, He must make a true entire confession. Secondly, He must moreover stand obliged to make perfect restitution of any thing to which he is bound. Thirdly, He stands obliged to perform the penance enjoined him. Fourthly, If this penance fall short of satisfying the divine justice for the pains yet due to the sins forgiven, the sinner stands still obliged to satisfy the divine justice by other penal works. Now all that we say is, that this pain may be pardoned him by indulgences; though not by indulgences granted merely at the Pope's pleasure; but by indulgences granted by him upon sufficient causes, which causes he must carefully examine. And after the grant of indulgences, upon due causes, you must not think any thing is done until we, on our parts, have done what is required. What is that? It is that, after such humble repentance, and after such an entire confession and restitution, as I said, we perform the things expressed in the grant of the indulgence. And when all is done, the most that we obtain is, to have pardon of the punishment due to such sins, the guilt of which is already forgiven by our repentance and confession. But the Protestants teach, that faith alone quite frees men for ever of all their sins, and of all the pain that was due for their sins, though never so many, or so great; for after this faith, God imputes their sins no longer to them.

3. Before I prove that the Pope hath power by indulgences, granted upon just cause, to pardon such as duly perform what is enjoined, I further note that the blood of Christ was of that infinite value, that the shedding of one drop thereof was able to satisfy divine justice for all the sins of the world, yea, of a million of worlds; and able to satisfy also for all the pain that could be due for all those sins. Wherefore,

seeing Christ did not shed his blood for us by drops, but by showers, hence it followeth evidently that the satisfactions of Christ alone are, in a most high degree, superabundant. Tell me now, is the most precious treasure of all this superabundance of satisfactions, in order to cancel the pain due to our sins, so wholly lost, that even the living members of Christ's body can receive no benefit by this superabundance? God forbid. They are not treasures wrapped up in a napkin. Wherefore there must be a power on earth to dispense this rich treasure; but yet to dispense it so as becomes a prudent dispenser of the mysteries of God. Now who is the highest and chiefest in this dignity of dispensing, but he whom we have proved to be the head and chief pastor of Christ's Church, to whom it was said, "To thee I will give the keys of the kingdom of heaven," Matt. xvi. 19; "Feed my sheep," John xxi. 16. See the seventh Point.

4. That such indulgences as here described may be granted, I prove first, because to give thus *the keys of the kingdom of heaven* to St. Peter, and to his successors, as is there proved, is to give power of removing any bar that may shut us out of heaven; whether this bar be the sin itself, which excludes us eternally if not removed, or whether it be the guilt of pain for our sins forgiven, which excludeth us only until such time as due satisfaction is made for that pain. Satisfaction may be made for this pain, either by ourselves performing sufficiently for this effect such satisfactory works as we spoke of, Point IX. No. 24, or which may be performed for us by others. For as I may pay my debts by myself, so I may pay them by a friend.

5. And the proof of this is a second proof of indulgences, out of Col. i. 24, "I, Paul, who now rejoice in suffering for you, and do accomplish those things which want of the passion of Christ in my flesh, for his body which is the Church." Of which text see what I have said, Point XXIV. No. 6, whence it

appears, that notwithstanding the fulness and superabundance of Christ's passion in itself, yet, in order to our being made completely partakers of the several fruits thereof, something may be, and often is, wanting on our part. What is this? It is the adjoining of those satisfactory works, which, in that point, we have at large showed Christ to expect at our hands. And until such works be performed, either by us in person, or for us in the person of some other, we stand liable to the pains due to our sins forgiven. Now, that another may offer such works for us is made evident by the texts we cited out of St. Paul, affirming that he rejoiced in doing this deed of charity, which consisted in suffering, that is, in doing a work most satisfactory, for them, and by it "to fill up, or to accomplish, in his flesh that which was yet behind, or as yet wanted of the passion of Christ;" that is, what was wanting, not on Christ's part, but on the part of his body, which is the Church. Now as St. Paul, as then confirmed in grace, had few sins, and many sufferings which he could well spare, and give away to pay his brother's debt, so had St. John Baptist, so had our Lady, so the Apostles, so the holy martyrs, and many others. But above all, Christ's sufferings alone had an inexhaustible superabundance; which sufferings, although Christ by his ordinary course of providence doth not apply to the full cleansing of our sins, and of the pain due to our sins, unless we do what is required on our part, yet he hath left power to his Vicar on earth, upon just causes, and with due circumspection, to impart, by way of special favour or indulgence, those superabundant satisfactions of Christ and his saints unto us, that by his superabundance our wants may be supplied, if we duly dispose ourselves by his grace to be partakers of that great favour.

6. A third proof of indulgences out of Scripture is to show St. Paul exercising, in the person of Christ, this special favour or indulgence towards the incestuous Corinthian, whom, in his first Epistle to the Co-

rinthians, he had given over to Satan by excommunication; yet afterwards, moved to be more favourable unto him by his great repentance, he doth not only absolve him from the sin, and from the excommunication, but having enjoined him a most severe public penance, which was to have lasted for a great time before the pains due to his enormous offence would have been fully cancelled, he notwithstanding, out of the plenitude of his apostolical power, graciously pardons the remnant of his penance. Now this pardon would have been no favour nor grace, unless at the same time he had pardoned the remnant of the pain still due according to divine justice. Therefore, he declares expressly that he doth it in the person of Christ; so he saith, 2 Cor. ii. 10, "To whom you forgive any thing, I forgive also in the person of Christ;" that is, by Christ's commission I give this pardon, Christ ratifying the pardon or indulgence which I give to one so well disposed, as I see this delinquent to be.

7. And hence comes in a fourth proof, John xx. 23, "Receive the Holy Ghost: whose sins you shall forgive, they are forgiven; and whose sins you shall retain, they are retained." Behold power in the Church not only to forgive the remnant of the pain due to the sins forgiven, which is all that is done by indulgences, but also behold a power to forgive the very sin itself, and consequently to take quite away the very eternity of pain which before was due to the sin. See Point XVI. Whence you cannot wonder to see power of taking away only temporal pain due to sin, when such conditions are fulfilled as we did express here, No. 2.

POINT XXVII.

THAT FAITH ALONE DOTH NOT JUSTIFY.

1. THIS is a point point-blank against the very prime point of Protestant religion, as their grand reformers call it, who define this faith to be an assured confidence that their sins are forgiven them wholly by Christ's passion; and yet in all Scripture they will not find one single text to prove that ever yet any one single man was justified by this special faith, as they call it; I say, by this special faith, which breeds in them an assured confidence that their sins in particular are pardoned them for Christ's sake. We ask only for one such text: and yet though the belief of this (the Protestant belief) be chiefly grounded in this point, they have not so much as one simple clear text, so groundless is their very ground. Look upon the faith of Abraham, who is called "the father of all that believe," and see what faith "was counted to him for his righteousness," Rom. iv. 3. And you shall find that verse taken out of Gen. xv. 6, where, when God hath told him "he would multiply his seed like the stars, Abraham believed God, and he counted it to him for righteousness." Why so? For his believing promptly that which God had revealed in a matter so hard to his understanding, as is expressly said, Rom. iv. 21, 22. Hence I argue thus: here is no mention of his assured confidence that his sins were forgiven him by Christ's passion, but here is mention of justifying faith, or of *faith counted or imputed to man for righteousness;* therefore justifying faith is no such matter as this special faith, or confidence. How this faith of Abraham came to justify, St. James tells us, "That it was by being a faith effective of good works." For he so firmly believed what God had said, that he feared not to see that saying made null and void, though he should offer upon the altar that very son of his, upon whom, by name, all God's

fair promises seemed grounded. "For was not Abraham our father justified by works, when he had offered Isaac his son upon the altar?" James ii. 21.

2. We say, then, that faith alone doth not justify, but that faith, working by charity, completes justification. Luke vii. 47, "Many sins are forgiven her, because she loved much." So Matt. xxii. 11, he that was called to the marriage-feast, and came to it, and entered in, and sat down, could not do this but by faith entering the Church, yet because he was *not attired in a wedding garment*, of charity, he was cast out, and for his sake it was said, "Many are called, but few are chosen."

3. St. Paul also inculcates this, 1 Cor. xiii. 2, "If I should have all faith, so that I could remove mountains, and have not charity, I am nothing." Note the words "all faith." Again, ver. 13, "The greater of these three is charity." And again, Col. iii. 14, "But above all things have charity, which is the bond of perfection." For, Matt xxii. 40, "On these two commandments (of charity) dependeth the whole law and the prophets." Yet again, Gal. v. 6, "Neither circumcision availeth any thing, nor uncircumcision, but faith which worketh by charity or love." Behold that very faith which our very doctrine requires, that is, "Faith working by charity," which also before he called, "Faith observing the commandments of God." Again, the Apostle saith, 1 Cor. vii. 19, "Circumcision is nothing, and uncircumcision is nothing, but the keeping of the commandments of God." Again, Gal. vi. 15, "Neither circumcision availeth any thing, nor uncircumcision, but a new creature," formed by charity, according to God's commandments. Again, Eph. i. 4, "He hath chosen us before the foundation of the world, that we should be holy, and without blame, before him in love, or charity." Note how that which makes us holy, and without blame before him, is charity. Again, Eph. iii. 17, "Christ dwells by faith in the heart rooted in

charity." Again, Heb. v. 9, "He became the author of eternal salvation to all that obey him." He was not made the author of this salvation to any but such as did obey him. For as is said, 1 John i. 7, "If we walk in the light (*Lex Lux*), the blood of Jesus Christ cleanseth us from all sin." Where read you that it doth so, "If we walk not in the light, or do not obey him"?

4. Note, that besides other texts, I have cited here *eight* out of St. Paul, because our adversaries chiefly ground themselves in those his words, Rom. iii. 28, "A man is justified by faith without the works of the law." Where his meaning only is, that neither the works *of the written law*, done by the Jew, nor the works *of the law of nature*, done by the Gentile, before either of them believe in Christ, can, without faith in Christ, justify any one. For neither Jew nor Gentile is justified by any one of those works; but they are justified by that faith which he told you in the former texts *to work by charity*, and to be a *faith observing the commandments of God, making us a new creature, rooted in charity, and obeying him*. Thus St. Paul is explicated by St. Augustine upon this place. Yea, he is explicated by St. James in many places of his second chapter, as ver. 14, "What doth it profit, though a man say he hath faith, and hath not works? can faith save him?" Note here, first, that St. James supposeth this may happen, that "a man may have faith but not works," and that, in this case, "his faith will not save him;" which is that which St. Paul also said before, "If I have all faith, but have not charity, I am nothing." St. James goes on, ver. 21, "Abraham, was he not justified by works, offering Isaac? Seest thou how faith wrought with his works, and by works faith was made perfect?" If this faith had justified before any works proceeded from it, it had been perfected before any such works. Yet it is said, "That by works this faith was made perfect." Whence followeth, ver. 24, "You see then how that

by works a man is justified, and not by faith only." This, then, is our demonstration: If faith justifieth alone, it justifieth without works: but St. James saith it doth not justify without works; therefore it doth not justify alone. "For by works, and not by faith alone, a man is justified." What more clear?

POINT XXVIII.

WHETHER OUR JUSTIFICATION BE ANY THING INHERENT IN US.

1. OUR adversaries' doctrine is, that we are only just because God is pleased to repute us so, in regard of Christ's justice imputed to us, and thus he doth only cover our sins, these sins still remaining in us; but God doth not impute them to us, because we having once laid hold of Christ's justice by the hands of faith, this justice is made ours, and by Christ's merits we shall undoubtedly be saved. Our doctrine, opposite in all points, shall be, point after point, proved out of Scripture.

2. First, then, we say our justice is a quality truly inherent in us: Ezech. xxxvi. 26, "A new heart also I will give you, and a new spirit I will put within you. And cause you to walk in my statutes. And ye shall keep my judgments, and do them." I need speak no clearer. So Rom. v. 5, "The charity of God is poured forth in our hearts by the Holy Ghost, which is given us;" by the infusion of his charity into us, in us is framed the "new creature," Gal. vi. 15. And this new "inward man" is said, Col. iii. 12, to be put on us by such virtues as are inherent; as by "the bowels of mercies, kindness, humbleness of mind, meekness." And, ver. 14, "Above all these by charity, which is the bond of perfection:" behold the parts of this inward new man, of which again he saith, Eph. iv. 23, "Be renewed in the spirit of your mind,

and put on the new man, which after God is created in righteousness and true holiness," which are qualities most inherent. And, Eph. i. 4, " He hath chosen us before the foundation of the world, that we should be holy and without blame in his sight in charity," which charity is an inward quality.

3. Secondly, We say that by this quality we are not only reputed just, but we are just verily and really. And because we verily are so, we truly are to be reputed so, we being "holy before him in charity." For, as was said in the former texts, we have in us " a new heart, a new spirit by charity, poured forth in our very hearts," transforming us inwardly into *new creatures* and new men, being truly *renewed in spirit*. Whence, 1 John iii. 1, " We are not only called the sons of God," but " now we are the sons of God." So when you read that Abraham's faith, working by charity, was "imputed to him to righteousness, and he was called the friend of God," James ii. 23, you shall note that he therefore was reputed just, and therefore called the friend of God, because truly he was just, and was truly *God's friend*, having faith quickened by charity in him. So, Luke i. 6, of Zachary and Elizabeth, "They were both righteous before God (whose eyes see what is the most covered), walking in all the commandments and ordinances of our Lord without blame." They therefore were just, even *before God's eyes*. And this true justice in the eyes of God is, in the same chapter, promised to us, by the grace of the Saviour there foretold, " that we may serve him in holiness, righteousness, and justice, before him all our days," ver. 75. Note this holiness *before him*, which is to be *holy in his sight*. Hence God to Noah, Gen. vii. 1, " I have seen thee righteous before me." Hence also, Col. i. 10, " That you may walk worthy of the Lord, unto all pleasing, being fruitful in every good work. Giving thanks to the Father who hath made us meet to be partakers of the inheritance of the saints." So, Apoc. iii. 4, "Thou

hast a few names in Sardis, which have not defiled their garments, and they shall walk with me in white, because they be worthy." And, 1 John iii. 7, "Little children, let no man deceive you: he that doth righteousness is righteous, even as He is righteous." Note these words, *even as He* (that is God) *is righteous*. For God is righteous, not by imputative, but true interior justice, of which inward justice Christ saith, Matt. v. 20, "I say unto you, unless your righteousness shall exceed that of the Scribes and Pharisees, you shall not enter into the kingdom of heaven." If there be not righteousness in us exceeding that of the Scribes and Pharisees, we shall be condemned, and no righteousness shall be imputed to us. For as it is said, Rom. ii. 2, "We are sure that the judgment of God is according to truth," it were not verity but falsity to repute him just, who in very truth is not just, but is still a sinner. Hence, Prov. xvii. 15, " He that justifieth the impious, and he that condemneth the just, both are abominable before God." Dare you say that God doth that which is abominable? He reputes things to be as they truly are in themselves. So Rom. ii. 9, "Wrath and indignation, tribulation and anguish, upon every soul of man that worketh evil." He imputes justice to no sinner until he leaves off to be so, by true returning to works of justice. Those whom he reputes clean, truly are clean. "And you are clean," John xiii. 10.

4. Thirdly, Hence we say that our sins are not only covered, but wholly taken away. For we, by virtue of God's inward grace given for Christ, are cleansed, made white, and glittering. For "Christ is the Lamb of God, who taketh away the sins of the world," John i. 29. He doth not only cover them, but takes them quite away. And so, Ps. xxxii. 2, when David saith, " Blessed is the man to whom the Lord doth not impute iniquity, and whose sins are covered," it followeth, "there is no guile in his spirit." And because there is no guile, therefore no

iniquity can be imputed to him. Protestants still cite the former words, but leave out these latter, which words teach us excellently, that what is covered from God's eyes must not be at all, and therefore his sin now not being at all, cannot now at all be seen. For as the same David tells you, Ps. ciii. 12, "As far as the east is distant from the west, so far hath he removed our transgressions from us." This expression, though it may be thought very full, yet really our sins forgiven are as far from us as that which is not now is distant from that which is now, which is a greater distance than east from west, though that be far enough to declare a true perfect remission by quite abolishing the sin forgiven by infused grace, according to Ezech. xxxvi. 25, "I will sprinkle clean water upon you, and ye shall be clean from all your filthiness." And, 1 John i. 7, "And the blood of Christ cleanseth us from all sin." So that by this his blood, "the body of sin is destroyed," Rom. vi. 6. And thus "he will cast all our sins into the depths of the sea," Mich. vii. 19.

POINT XXIX.

WHETHER OUR JUSTIFICATION MAY NOT BE LOST.

1. "THE heart is deceitful above all things; who can know it?" Jer. xvii. 9. Yet Protestants, placing justification in such a special faith as assures each man of his salvation by the merits of Christ, are hence enforced to teach two strange paradoxes. The first is, That this special faith breeds a full assurance, grounded in a real truth, wherefore we need not fear our salvation. The second, which is contained in the former, or thence clearly deduced, is, that this justification of ours cannot be lost; for else that assurance might have had a lie for its ground and sole foundation.

2. We teach, first, that no man, without a special revelation, is assured to be saved, and so all ought "to work their salvation with fear and trembling." St. Paul every where proveth our doctrine: "Thou by faith dost stand; be not high-minded, but fear," Rom. xi. 20. Again, 1 Cor. iv. 4, he saith, "I know nothing by myself (concerning any guilt), but I am not justified hereby. But he that judgeth me is the Lord:" I dare not "judge myself, though I know nothing by myself;" how, then, darest thou? Again, 1 Cor. ix. 27, "But I keep under my body, and bring it into subjection, lest by any means whilst I preach to others, I myself may become a castaway, or reprobate." Again, chap. x. 10, "Therefore he who thinketh himself to stand (as Protestants do), let him take heed lest he fall." Again, Phil. iii. 11, "If by any means I might attain to the resurrection of the dead." He found no security in that special faith you speak of: therefore he said, Phil. ii. 12, "Work out your own salvation with fear and trembling." Apoc. iii. 11, "Hold that fast which thou hast, that no man take thy crown." For, Luke viii. 13, "There be those who for a time believe, and in time of temptation fall away."

3. Secondly, Conformably to all the texts we say, that those who were just, may come finally to be damned. For, Exod. xxxii. 33, "Whosoever hath sinned against me, him will I blot out of my book." Those who are baptized, are "born again of water and the Holy Ghost," John iii. 5. Yet how many thousands of these once regenerated men sin afterwards, and never rise again! and truth saith of him who riseth not again, *whosoever hath sinned against me, him will I blot out of my book:* out of which he could not be dashed, unless his name had once been enrolled in it. Solomon's salvation is much doubted of by holy fathers, yet there could be no doubt thereof, if your opinion were true; for God himself saith he once was just, 1 Chron. xxviii. 7, "I will establish

his kingdom for ever, if he be constant to my commandments and judgments as at this day." At *that day*, then, he was in a state pleasing to God, and yet, you see, doubt of his perseverance is even here intimated. Yea, by and by David his father tells him, "But if you forsake him, he will cast thee off for ever," ver. 9. David did not judge Solomon to be at this time out of God's favour, yet his words show he feared that he might hereafter come to lose God's favour. What Solomon after did, the Scripture tells us, 1 Kings xi. 3, "Women turned away his heart. And when he was now old, his wives turned away his heart to other gods. He worshiped Astarthe, the goddess of the Sidonians, and Moloch, the idol of the Ammonites. He built a temple to Chamos, the idol of Moab, and in this manner he did to all his wives, who were strangers. Therefore the Lord was angry with Solomon, because his heart was turned from the Lord," ver. 9. Did he not cease to be just when *his heart was turned away from the Lord?* David saith, Ps. v. 7, "Thou hatest all workers of iniquity." God, then, *did hate* Solomon. I dispute not whether he repented or no, whether he were saved or no; but without all dispute, he once lost his former justice, his heart and mind being turned away from God, and our Lord therefore bearing wrath against him and hating him. Let us proceed.

4. The Apostles, Acts vi. 3, commanded seven men full of the Holy Ghost to be made deacons. "One of them was Nicholas, a stranger of Antioch. These they set in the presence of the Apostles, and praying, they imposed hands upon them." Yet this Nicholas did fall finally into heresy, and began the heresy of those who, from his name, are called Nicolaites, Apoc. ii. 6. St. Paul also, Heb. vii. 46, tells us the sad condition of those who were made partakers of the Holy Ghost, if they shall fall away, which is manifestly to suppose that even such men may fall away. So, "The foolish Galatians, having begun with the spirit, ended

with the flesh," Gal. iii. 3. It is therefore said to them, "You did run well: who hindered you not to obey the truth?" Gal. v. 7. Behold, they came not to obey the truth, who before did not only walk well, but also run well: hence also it is that the Scripture useth to speak thus fearfully and conditionally concerning our perseverance in justice: John xv. 6, "If a man abide not in me, he is cast forth." And, Rom. xi. 22, "If thou continue in his goodness, otherwise thou also shalt be cut off." And, 2 John 8, "Look to yourselves, that ye lose not these things which ye have wrought." Evident therefore is our doctrine thus delivered by Ezekiel, xxxiii. 12: "The righteousness of the righteous shall not deliver him in the day of his transgression. Neither shall the righteous be able to live for his righteousness in the day that he sinneth. All his righteousness shall not be remembered: but for his iniquity, which he hath committed, he shall die for it." He then may *die for iniquity* who was once just. Hence he taught his just Apostles to pray, "Lead us not into temptation," for fear of falling into it. Let us therefore, when we have faith, "Hold faith and a good conscience, which some having put away, concerning faith have made shipwreck," 1 Tim. i. 19.

POINT XXX.

TO JUSTIFICATION IT IS NECESSARY TO KEEP THE COMMANDMENTS. THIS IS POSSIBLE.

I SAY, first, that it is possible to keep the commandments by the help and assistance of God's grace, sufficiently afforded us to that end. Deut. v. 1, "Moses called all Israel, and said to them, Hear, Israel, the statutes which I speak in your ears this day, learn them and do them." And then, in the sixth verse, he begins to tell all the ten commandments, which God would have them "learn, and keep, and do." But God will exact of no man to keep and do that which is impossible; ergo, this by his grace is possible. "I will give my law in their bowels; and in their heart I will write it," Jer. xxxi. 33. "The law of God is in his heart, none of his steps shall slide," Ps. xxxvii. 31. And, Rom. viii. 4, "God sending his Son, &c. That the justification of the law might be fulfilled in us." All these texts prove that, by God's grace, we may fulfil his law. And therefore, as St. Leo excellently saith (*Serm.* 16, *De Passione*), "*Justè Deus instat præcepto, qui præcurrit auxilio.*" God justly presseth upon us the doing of that, to performance of which he offereth us his grace.

2. And because some Protestants say that *the commandment of loving God with all our heart and soul* is the commandment impossible to us all in this life, I will show this to be flatly against Scripture. For of David, 1 Kings xiv. 8, it is said, "He kept my commandments, and followed me in all his heart." So of Josias, 2 Kings xxiii. 25, "He returned to our Lord with all his heart, and with all his soul, and with all his might." What more is commanded any where? "With my whole heart have I sought thee," Ps. cxix. 10. He who hath commanded us to do this, hath promised grace enabling us to perform his command. Deut. xxx. 6, "Our Lord thy God will circumcise thy heart, and the heart of thy seed, to love our Lord thy God with all thy heart, and with all thy soul." And, ver. 11, "This commandment that I command thee this day, is not far off: it is not in heaven (where Protestants say it shall only be fulfilled), that thou mayest say, Which of us is able to ascend to heaven to bring it to us, that we may hear it and do it? (as God required in the first text); neither is it beyond the sea, that thou shouldst say, Who should go over the sea for us, and bring it unto us, that we may hear it and do it? But the word is very

nigh unto thee, in thy mouth, and in thy heart, that thou mayest do it;" do it, I say, by the help of my grace, making this possible even in the old law. So, Ps. cxix. 55, " I have kept thy law."

3. And this grace makes this really done and performed far more in the New Testament, God saying, Ezek. xxxvi. 26, "I will give you a new heart, and will put within you a new spirit, and cause you to walk in my statutes, and ye shall keep my judgments and do them." And, chap. xxxvii. 24, " They shall walk in my judgments, and observe my statutes, and do them." This, then, can be done. Likewise this was done by Zachary and Elizabeth, Luke i. ver. 6, "They were both righteous before God, walking in all the commandments and ordinances of our Lord blameless, or without blame." Also, Matt. xix. 20, " The young man saith to him (Christ), All these have I kept from my youth;" and, Mark x. 20, "All these things I have observed from my youth. And Jesus beholding him, loved him," which he would not have done if he had been a liar in what he said. This young man, then, was not a liar. But he "that saith he knoweth God, and keepeth not his commandments, he is a liar and the truth is not in him," 1 John ii. 4. For as it is said there, " Hereby we do know that we know him, if we keep his commandments." Again, John xvii. 6, "And they have kept thy word." And yet farther, 1 John iii. 22, "Whatsoever we shall ask, we shall receive of him, because we keep his commandments, and do those things which are pleasing in his sight." Again, Apoc. xiv. 12, "Here are they that keep the commandments of God." It is the saying of Christ himself, " If thou wilt enter into life, keep the commandments," Matt. xix. 17; Mark x. 20 ; Luke x. 28. And, John xiv. 15, " If ye love me, keep my commandments." And, ver. 21, "He that hath my commandments, and keepeth them, he it is that loveth me." They may therefore be kept. Yea, Christ himself saith,. Matt. xi. 30,

"My yoke is easy, and my burden is light." For, 1 John v. 3, "This is the love of God, that we keep his commandments: and his commandments are not grievous." Note also, that all the ensuing texts, which prove keeping of the commandments in those who are of age to be necessary to our justification, do prove also that they are possible to be kept; for no impossible thing can be necessary to our salvation.

4. Secondly, Then I say, To all, who have the use of reason, keeping of the commandments is necessary to salvation, and consequently to justification. This is taught in a number of texts which I cited (Point XXVII.) to prove that faith alone doth not justify, but chiefly requires charity. And St. John saith, 1 John v. 3, "This is the love of God, that we keep his commandments." And, Matt. xxii. 40, "On those two commandments (of Christ) hang all the law and prophets." Our justification, therefore, cannot but depend upon those two commandments.

5. Hence St. Paul, 1 Cor. vii. 19, "Circumcision is nothing, and uncircumcision is nothing, but the observation of the commandments of God." So that if this be nothing, or a thing impossible, all comes to be nothing. Again, what we cited in the 27th Point, No. 4, evidently proves works to be necessary to salvation. But no works are more necessary than those that are commanded; these, therefore, are chiefly necessary to justification.

POINT XXXI.

HOW STILL WE HAVE FREE WILL TO DO GOOD OR EVIL.

1. WE are foully slandered by those who make us to teach that it is in our power to do that which is able to advance us towards heaven; as if we said this without adding, or at least understanding, *that this is in our power only by the help of God first moving*

and exciting us; and then lending us his helping hand, even all the while that we are doing any work which can advance us towards heaven. By this help, we say, our free will is still enabled to do good or avoid evil; and that, by this help, it is in our power also either to omit our duty, or to do it, a sufficiency of this grace being still afforded us, according to that, 2 Cor. xii. 9, "My grace is sufficient for thee." Hence, 2 Tim. ii. 21, "If a man purge himself, he shall be a vessel unto honour." By virtue of this grace it is in our power to approach to God: James iv. 8, "Draw nigh to God, and he will draw nigh to you. Cleanse your hands, ye sinners, and purify your hearts." We may also, by the free will we have to resist this grace, harden our hearts.

2. Hence Pharaoh's obduration is ascribed often to his free will, Exod. viii. 15, "And Pharaoh, seeing this, hardened his heart." And, 1 Sam. vi. 6, "Why do you harden your hearts as Egypt and Pharaoh did harden their hearts?" And so David crieth to us all, "Harden not your hearts," Psalm xcv. 8, and Ezek. xviii. 31, "Cast away from you all your transgressions, and make you a new heart and new spirit; for why will you die, O house of Israel? for I have no pleasure in the death of him that dieth, saith the Lord God; wherefore, turn yourselves, and live ye."

3. Behold how God himself declares that, by the grace he offers us, we may make ourselves "a new heart, a new spirit; turn ourselves and live." God speaks clearly in Deut. xi. 26, "Behold, I set forth in your sight this day benediction and malediction: benediction if you obey the commandments of our Lord; malediction if you obey not, but revolt from the way which now I show you." Again, Deut. xxx. 15, "See, I have set before thee this day life and good," and contrariwise, "death and evil." And, ver. 19, "I call for record this day heaven and earth. I have set before you life and death, blessing and cursing: choose

therefore life." See here the choice left to our free will. So, Josh. xxiv. 15, "Choose this day whom you will serve." And, Philem. xiv., "Without thy mind I would do nothing, that thy benefit should not be as it were of necessity, but willingly." And, 1 Cor. vii. 37, "He that standeth steadfast in his heart, having no necessity, but hath power over his own will, . . . doth well."

4. Behold we have power over our own will to do that which is less perfect, or that which is more perfect. For as it is there said, "He who giveth in marriage doth well; he that giveth not doth better." And we have power over our own will to do either. Yea, God's grace so enables our power that, John i. 12, "As many as received him, to them gave he power to become the sons of God." By this his power, we cleanse our hands, purify our hearts, cleanse our whole selves; we, Matt. xii. 33, "make the tree and fruit good." And as it is said, 1 John iii. 3, "Every man that hath this hope in him purifieth himself." Hitherto of free will in doing good.

5. How free will comes to lead us to all our evil, St. James tells us, chap. i. 14, "Every one is tempted when he is drawn away of his own lust, and enticed." Hitherto no sin, but "then"—when? I pray note this,—"then when lust hath conceived, it bringeth forth sin." Then sin, and only *then*, is hatched, *when* free will yields herself in concupiscence, so as to consent to what is suggested. "Ye did not hear: ye did choose that wherein I delighted not," Isaiah lxv. 12. The texts also in the following Point confirm free will.

POINT XXXII.

HOW THIS FREE WILL IS STILL HELPED WITH SUFFICIENT GRACE.

1. IF God gave us not always that grace which is of sufficient force to excite us to the effectual performance of all the good which we are bound to do, or to the avoiding of all the evil which we are bound to avoid, our free will could neither do the one, nor avoid the other. All the former texts, then, which so clearly prove that we, by God's help, can, if we will, do what we are bound to do, and can avoid what we are bound to avoid, do consequently prove that God always gives such grace to both effects as wants nothing of perfect sufficiency to produce them, but our free consent. Hence St. Paul thus exhorts us, 2 Cor. vi. 1, "We, then, as workers together with him, beseech you also that you receive not the grace of God in vain." Excellently the Rhemists upon this text: "It lieth in man's power and free will to frustrate, or to follow, this motion of God," as this text plainly proveth; which really is the very self-same that the Council of Trent says, sess. vi. 5, "That by God's exciting and helping grace we are disposed to convert ourselves by freely assenting and coöperating to the same grace; so that, God touching the heart of man by the illumination of the Holy Ghost, man is neither void of all action, he receiving that inspiration; for he receives it so, as having in his power to cast it away; neither can he without the grace of God move himself." And therefore it followeth in the fourth canon: "If any one shall say that the free will of man, moved and excited by God, doth coöperate nothing at all by giving her consent to God exciting and calling, by which he may dispose himself to the grace of justification, and that he cannot dissent if he will, let him be anathema." Let those hearken to this who

hearken so much to the Jansenists. And let us go on to speak of this sufficient grace, which, in the next Point, we show more fully to be offered to all. Of this grace, Isa. v. 4, "What could have been done more to my vineyard, that I have not done in it?" For, Prov. i. 24, "I called you, and you refused." And that you may not say he only called, and did not stretch forth his hand to help you to come, the next words are, "I stretched forth my hand, and no man regarded: but ye have set at naught all my counsel." And, Isa. lxv. 12, "When I called, ye did not answer; when I spoke, ye did not hear; and did choose that wherein I delighted not." Though they did choose thus against God's call, yet this his call was so sufficient to have moved them, that God tells Ezekiel (chap. iii. 6) that if he had sent him with so strong and powerful preaching to barbarous and unknown people, "They surely would have heard thee. But the house of Israel will not hear thee; for all the house of Israel are impudent and hard-hearted." They will not be moved by those calls which would move others. And because they answered like Protestants, chap. xxxiii. 10, "If our transgressions and our sins be upon us, and we pine in them, how shall we then live?" God commands the Catholic doctrine to be thus delivered, "Say unto them, As I live, saith the Lord, I have no pleasure in the death of the wicked, but that the wicked turn from his way and live. Turn ye, turn ye, from your wicked ways; and why will you die, O house of Israel?" Note how still he saith he excites them sufficiently; otherwise vainly had he said, "Why will you die, O house of Israel?" For they might reply, "We cannot but die, because thou givest us not the grace to live."

2. And as God said of Ezekiel's preaching that it was sufficient to have converted barbarians, though the Jews would not be moved by it, so, Matt. xi. 20, of Christ it is said, "He began to upbraid the cities

wherein were done most of his miracles, for that they had not done penance. Woe to thee, Corazin; woe to thee, Bethsaida: for if in Tyre and Sidon had been wrought the miracles that were wrought in thee, they had long ago done penance in sack-cloth and ashes." Though the Jews would not repent, yet hence I am sure that Christ did sufficient for that end. Hence the most just exprobation both here and Matt. xxiii. 37, "Jerusalem, Jerusalem, how often would I have gathered together thy children, as the hen gathereth together her chickens, and thou wouldest not!" I would; "thou wouldest not:" therefore justly it follows, "Behold, your house shall be left desert." Again, Rom. x. 21, "All the day long I have stretched forth my hands unto a disobedient and gainsaying people." Again, Apoc. iii. 30, "Behold I stand at the door and knock: if any man hear my voice and open the door, I will come in to him." Whence again, 1 Tim. ii. 4, "Who willeth all men to be saved, and come to the knowledge of the truth." And therefore the same apostle, Rom. ii. 4, "Dost thou contemn the riches of his goodness, patience, longanimity? but according to the hardness of thy heart thou heapest up to thyself wrath." Behold a free will, able to contemn the very riches of God's goodness in still giving graces, and with so much patience and longanimity expecting the effect of them, still, by man's voluntary malice, made fruitless. Of such a soul it is said, Apoc. ii. 21, "I gave her space to repent of her fornication, and she repented not." You cannot blame a poor man for not dining, because you gave him space to dine, unless you also give him meat wherewith to dine: so God could not complain of our not repenting, because we had time, unless also he offered us grace to repent.

POINT XXXIII.

THIS SUFFICIENT GRACE IS DENIED TO NONE, CHRIST DYING EVEN FOR REPROBATES.

1. It is evident in Scripture that no grace is given to any, but by the merits of Christ consummated with his death. "He hath blessed us with all spiritual blessings in heavenly things in Christ," Eph. i. 3. So that if you see (Point XXX.) grace given to all, to make the keeping of the commandments possible to all; if you see (Point XXXI.) that our free will is still by God's grace able to do good; if you see (Point XXXII.) this free will still helped by sufficient grace to avoid evil and do good;—you must needs by all this see that this grace can come only from Christ's death; and therefore this grace, being so often proved to be offered to all, by the same texts it is also proved that Christ died for all. Call to mind how many (according to what was proved, Point XXIX.) do become reprobates, who by virtue of Christ's death once received the gift of heavenly grace in baptism. The like grace was by Christ's death given to that just man, of whom Ezekiel cited there (No. 5) saith, "that his justices shall be forgotten," because he persevered not, "and in his iniquities he shall die." He therefore became a reprobate. And thus it is true which God said to Abraham, Gen. xii. 3, "In thee shall all the families of the earth be blessed." And, Gen. xxii. 18, "In thy seed shall be blessed all the nations of the earth." Now, as St. Paul saith, Gal. iii. 44, "The blessing of Abraham comes on the Gentiles through Christ Jesus." There is none, therefore, to be excepted from being partaker of this blessing, seeing that all the families of the earth, and all the nations of the earth, do enjoy it. Yet it is evident that many among these families and nations be *reprobates*. Reprobates, therefore, enjoy many blessings

by Christ's death, which could not be if Christ did not die for them. By the merits of Christ's death many are called, yet of these many few are chosen, Matt. xxii. 14. Why? Hence, Ezek. xviii. 23, "Is the death of a sinner my will, saith our Lord God, and not that he convert from his ways, and live?" Which without grace from Christ he could not do. Again, chap. xxxiii. 11, " I will not the death of the impious, but that the impious convert from his way, and live. Why will you die, O house of Israel?" And so, Prov. i. 24, to those to whom he said, " I have called, and you have refused; I have stretched out my hand, and you have not regarded;" he shall say likewise, " I will laugh when your destruction cometh as a whirlwind," ver. 27. They therefore shall be destroyed and perish, who by Christ's death and merits had many graces, helps, and callings given them. Note that in Christ the will with which he called them was a serious will, of which, 1 Tim. ii. 4, " He will have all men to be saved, and to come to the knowledge of truth." See in the former Point the many evident texts cited to this effect. Hence it is said, Rom. ii. 4, " He showed the riches of his goodness to those who despised it, treasuring up wrath to themselves." Who are those but the reprobate? Again, 2 Pet. iii. 9, " Willing that none should perish." And, Rom. v. 6, " Christ died for the impious, or ungodly." And most clearly, 1 John ii. 2, " He is the propitiation for our sins; and not for ours only, but also for those of the whole world." The whole world comprehends more reprobate than elect. He, then, who died for the whole world, did also die for the reprobate. Wherefore St. Paul more than once warns us not to be the occasion of damnation to those for whom Christ died. So, Rom. xiv. 15, " Destroy not him with thy meat for whom Christ died." He, therefore, for whom Christ died, may be destroyed and perish eternally. Again, 1 Cor. viii. 11, " Through thy knowledge shall thy weak brother perish, for whom Christ died?" And again, 2 Pet. ii. 1, "False teachers bringing in damnable heresies, even denying the Lord who bought them, and bringing upon themselves swift destruction." Hence you see that even those who have brought upon themselves destruction, have done this by denying him who bought them at the price of his blood and death. He therefore even died for those children of perdition. Whence holy fathers often say, "that son of perdition Judas" did shed that blood with which he was redeemed. Let us then all be, as is said, 2 Cor. v. 14, "Judging this, that if one died for all, then all were dead." St. Paul has not proved, by Christ dying for all, that *all* were *dead*, if any man could be found for whom Christ did not die. And that no one should presume to say that any such man could be found, St. Paul's next words are, "Christ died for all." The Council of Trent, sess. vi. c. 3, citing these words, saith, "But though he died for all, yet all receive not the benefit of his death, but only those to whom the merit of his passion is communicated." Hence it is said, 1 Tim. iv. 10, "We trust in the living God, who is the Saviour of all men, especially of those who believe." A Saviour he is to all men, by giving what sufficeth to save all men; but this sufficiency is effectual to salvation only in the truly faithful, whose works answer to their belief, and therefore chiefly he is their Saviour. Yet it is true that, speaking generally of us all, 1 Cor. x. 13, "God is faithful, who will not permit you to be tempted above what you are able." But now it is most evident that God doth daily permit us to be tempted beyond our own power, because no power we have of ourselves, as of ourselves, is able or sufficient to resist those temptations which daily set upon us. Seeing therefore it is clear Scripture, "That God will not suffer us to be tempted above what we are able," it hence demonstratively followeth that God's grace sufficiently enables all men to resist any temptation, whatsoever falls upon them. This is that which we properly call giving sufficient grace to all men, though all will not resist the temptations which they were able to resist. Even as he sufficiently by nature enables most men to lift their hand up to their head, though some for laziness will not do it. Now the grace sufficiently enabling all to resist all kind of temptations is given them through the merits of Christ dying for them.

POINT XXXIV.

HOW OUR GOOD WORKS DONE IN GRACE, AND BY THE HELP OF CHRIST'S GRACE, ARE MERITORIOUS, AND MERIT LIFE EVERLASTING.

1. THIS is a point in which our adversaries are pleased to be much scandalised, because many of their teachers have notably belied us; insomuch that you shall find few who are not apt to think that we hide our doctrine, as ashamed of it. Whereas we do plainly and clearly tell them that none of our works deserves any heavenly reward, as it is the work, and even the very best work of man, done only by our natural free will. But we all, and every one of us, teach that those only good works are meritorious which are done first by a soul dignified with God's grace inherent in her (according to Point XXVIII.), and we say that the value of this action making it meritorious proceeds from this grace. Secondly, we say no man can do any such meritorious action, without the actual grace of God exciting him thereunto. Thirdly, we say the grace of God must be aiding and assisting him all the time he doth any such meritorious action. All this is taught by the Council of Trent, sess. vi. chap. 16. We add, that even to such actions done in this manner, God, if so he had pleased, might have given no reward. But he was pleased to promise

and to give this heavenly reward out of his free gracious goodness, he being moved by the merits and passion of Christ, from which all the foresaid graces flow, to accept, for his sake, all those works as rewardable; the said works, by his grace, being made worthy to be accepted of, so as to be recompensed by that heavenly reward, which God hath mercifully promised to them. This is our doctrine.

2. And in the very beginning of the world God taught this doctrine, saying to Cain, Gen. iv. 7, "If thou do well, shalt thou not be accepted?" When Abraham was ready to offer Isaac, God by an angel said to him, Gen. xxii. 16, "By my own self have I sworn, saith the Lord, because thou hast done this thing I will bless thee," &c. Behold a large blessing for this thing. David also, Psalm xviii. 20, "The Lord rewarded me according to my righteousness: according to the cleanness of my hands hath he recompensed me." And, Psalm xix. 11, "That in keeping God's precepts there is great reward." And his son Solomon saith, 1 Kings viii. 32, "God is justifying the righteous, to give him according to his righteousness." And that zealous prophet speaks thus, 2 Chron. xv. 17, "Be you strong, therefore, and let not your hands be weak; for your work shall be rewarded."

3. How often hath St. Matthew this doctrine! First, chap. v. 12, "Be glad, and rejoice; for your reward is great in heaven." Here the word which, both in Greek and Latin, is put for reward, doth properly signify the very wages or hire due to the work. Secondly, in several places of the sixth chapter, Christ exhorts us to the secret performance both of our fasts, of our alms-deeds, and of our prayers; and he tells us that otherwise we lose our reward; but if we do them in secret, "thy Father which seeth in secret will repay thee." Thirdly, chap. vi. 20, "Lay up for yourselves treasures in heaven." Fourthly, chap. xvi. 27, "He shall reward every man according to

his works." He saith not according to his mercy, but according to their works. Fifthly, chap. xix. 27, "We have left all, and followed thee; what therefore shall we have?" To them thus expecting a reward, Christ gives no check, but makes them a promise of having, on account of their works, "an hundred-fold in the present, and life everlasting in the future life." Sixthly, chap. xxv. 23, "Because thou hast been faithful over a few things, I will place thee over many things. Enter into the joy of thy lord." Note here many things given in heaven because such a man lived faithfully. So, seventhly, chap. xxv. 34, "Come, ye blessed of my Father, possess, &c. For I was hungry, thirsty, &c. And you gave me to eat, drink," &c. Note the word FOR, that is, *for this very cause come possess the kingdom*. So if a prince, taken by his enemies in war should be rescued by a common soldier, whom he presently preferring to be a colonel, should say, "I make you a colonel; for I was taken, and you freed me;" who can doubt but that these words clearly affirm the cause of this great reward to be the soldier's great merit? So contrariwise where, in that chapter, it followeth, "Depart, ye cursed, into everlasting fire; for I was hungry, and you did not feed me," &c., every one will confess that the particle FOR manifestly signifies the cause. My eighth and last text is that of St. Matt. x. 43, "Whosoever shall give to one of these little ones a cup of cold water only, in the name of a disciple, Amen, I say unto you, he shall not lose his reward." Other texts might be alleged out of other evangelists, as Mark x. 21, "Go, sell whatsoever thou hast, and thou shalt have treasure in heaven." And again, John v. 29, "They that have done good things shall go forth into the resurrection of life." Behold the reward of good works. And again, Luke xiv. 14, "For feasting the poor, recompense shall be made in the resurrection."

4. But to proceed: how often doth St. Paul in-

culcate this doctrine! As, first, 1 Cor. iii. 8, "Every one shall receive his own reward, according to his own labour." Secondly, 2 Cor. iv. 17, "For our light affliction, which is but for a moment, worketh for us an eternal weight of glory." Note the word worketh, which really signifieth the cause. Thirdly, 2 Cor. ix. 6, "He that soweth sparingly, shall reap also sparingly; and he that soweth bountifully, shall reap bountifully." Note here alms-deeds made the seed of glory. Fourthly, there again, ver. 10, "As it is written, He distributed, he gave to the poor (but with what effect?), his righteousness remaineth for ever." Fifthly, Gal. vi. 9, "Be not weary in well doing; (why so?) for in due season we shall reap, if we faint not." Sixthly, Eph. vi. 8, "Knowing that what good soever every man shall do, that shall he receive of our Lord." Seventhly, he seeks in his converts the doing of good works, by reason of the reward they shall receive for them. So, Philip. iv. 16, "Ye sent once and again to my necessity; not because I desire the gift: but I desire the fruit that may abound to your account." Behold St. Paul desired the increase of their merit. Eighthly, 1 Tim. vi. 7, "Charge them that are rich, that they do good, that they be rich in good works, ready to distribute. Laying up store for themselves, a good foundation against the time to come, that they may lay hold of eternal life." Ninthly, 2 Tim. iv. 8, "There is laid up for me a crown of righteousness, which our Lord, the just judge, will render to me in that day; and not only unto me, but," &c. It is his mercy to promise heaven to our good works; it is his mercy to give us that grace which confers all the meritorious value upon these works; it is his mercy to excite us by actual grace to perform such works, and to accompany and assist us whilst we work. But it is his justice and righteousness to give that reward, which his mercy made these works able to deserve. So that now, as a just judge, he rewards our merits, though they be his gifts. Tenthly, Heb. xi. 24, "Moses refused to be called the son of Pharaoh's daughter, choosing to be afflicted with the people of God, esteeming the reproach of Christ greater riches than the treasures in Egypt. For he had respect unto the recompense of reward." Behold how much Moses valued the recompense of the reward due to so meritorious an act as that was. And, eleventhly, Heb. x. 35, "Cast not away your confidence, which hath great recompense of reward." I might end all these texts with that of the Apocalypse, xxii. 12, "My reward is with me, to give every one according as his work shall be."

5. But I thought fit to add, that we Roman Catholics do so extol the dignity of good works, in regard of that value given them by the grace of Christ, merited for us by his passion, that we say these works, thus dignified, make us worthy of heavenly bliss. And this we prove by Scripture. St. Paul, Col. i. 12, "Who hath made us meet to be partakers of the inheritance of saints." And, Apoc. iii. 4, "But thou hast a few names in Sardis, which have not defiled their garments, and they shall walk with me in white, because they are worthy." Hence, Psalm xviii. 20, "The Lord shall reward me after my righteous doings. According to the cleanness of my hands shall he recompense me." See Point XXVIII. Nos. 2, 3.

6. Against so many and so clear texts, our adverraries chiefly object, first, that the Scripture says, Isa. lxiv. 6, "We are all as an unclean thing, and all our righteousness as filthy rags." I answer, this is said of us, and our good works done merely by us, as we are left to ourselves, born and grow up in sin, and not aided, nor cleansed and dignified by God's grace. And it is a strange inference of our adversaries, to draw from hence that our best works done in grace, and by the help of God's grace, are all deadly sins. For so in the texts cited, David could not be "rewarded after his righteousness, and according to the

cleanness of his hands." Neither should there be any of so undefiled garments as to " walk in white because they are worthy." Again, how saith St. James, chap. ii. 21, " Was not Abraham justified by works, offering Isaac? Seest thou not how faith wrought with his works, and by works was made perfect?" How so, if both his faith and his works were deadly sins? What? Doth God thus reward deadly sin? Or could such a sin be a work justifying Abraham? In the texts, No. 6, it is said that God will repay us *for fasting, praying, giving alms in secret.* How is this true, if all these works be deadly sins in us? Tell me how it is possible by heaping up deadly sins to do what Christ bids us, that is, to heap up treasures in heaven. The young man, of whom I spoke, was told that by selling all, he should purchase a treasure in heaven. How then? Was this selling all a deadly sin? If selling all be a deadly sin, then to say, If thou wilt be perfect, go and sell all, is to say, Go and do a deadly sin, if thou wilt be perfect. Is that the one thing that was wanting unto him? And thus I might argue out of most the above-cited texts. I am sure Christ saith, Matt. iii. 10, " Every tree that brings not forth good fruit is hewn down and cast into the fire;" if the fruit of no tree be good, then every tree must be burned. St. James i. 26. Of the doer of the work, St. James saith, "This man shall be blessed in his deed." And St. Paul, Phil. iv. 18, calls the alms sent to him "an odour of sweet smell, a sacrifice acceptable, well pleasing to God." These alms-deeds, then, were not filthy rags.

7. Secondly, they object out of Luke xvii. 10, "When you have done all that you are commanded, say, We are unprofitable servants." I answer, this is true, that by all we do, or can do, even by God's grace, we are servants unprofitable to God; for all we do, or can do, profits him nothing. But we are servants profitable to ourselves. For heaping up treasure in heaven, and making friends of mammon to

receive us into the eternal tabernacles, are things very profitable unto us, as also to be good and faithful servants, and therefore to be placed over much, and enter into the joy of our Lord. St. Paul said, 1 Cor. xiii. 3, "If I shall distribute all my goods to be meat to the poor, and have not charity, it doth profit me nothing." Ergo, with charity it profits me much. Yea, though faithful servants be thus unprofitable to God, yet in regard of the service they do him, he saith, John xv. 14, "Ye are my friends, if ye do the things which I command you;" a thing of no small profit and honour. Again, is it not, think you, any profit to have "an hundred-fold here in this world, and life everlasting in the next," for leaving what they had for his sake? Is it not profit to us to say truly with St. Paul, Col. i. 12, "He has made us meet to be partakers of the inheritance of the saints," and "to walk with him in white, because we are worthy"? Apoc. iii. 4. Had he no profit by overcoming, to whom it was said, "He that shall overcome, and keep my works until the end, I will give him (in heaven) power over the nations, and he shall rule them with a rod of iron"? Apoc. ii. 26. "He that shall overcome, I will give to sit with me in my throne," Apoc. iii. 21. Do we not, then, by overcoming, profit ourselves in a high degree?

POINT XXXV.

IT IS LAUDABLE TO DO GOOD WORKS FOR REWARD.

1. As charity towards our neighbour is a most commendable virtue, so charity towards ourselves cannot but be most commendable. Wherefore, seeing these good works do profit us so very much, as we have seen in the last Point and last Number, I cannot possibly understand that paradox of our adversaries, saying they do ill who do well out of a desire to gain

176   IT IS LAUDABLE TO DO GOOD WORKS.

heaven. True it is a man may do well out of a more commendable motive; that is, to honour and please God. But because something is better than doing good for hope of reward, the doing good out of that hope doth not cease to be good. You say that faith alone is so good that it doth justify a man; and yet Scripture tells you that "of these three, faith, hope, and charity, the greater (and better) of these is charity," 1 Cor. xiii. 13. Faith is very good and commendable. Whence appears that nothing ceases to be good, because another act is better.

2. The Scriptures cited in the last Point evidently exhort us in our sufferings "to be glad and rejoice, because our reward is great in heaven; and to do our good work in secret, not to lose our reward, but to heap up to ourselves treasure in heaven, and to sell all to purchase treasure there, and in doing good works not to fail; for in due time we shall reap, not failing." May we not sow in hope of harvest? Did not St. Paul seek the first abounding on this account to those who had sent to his use? Did he not bid us "not to lose our confidence, because it hath a great reward"? Heb. x. 35; "and not to sow sparingly, that we may reap plentifully"? 2 Cor. ix. 6. Did not Christ himself say, "Make friends of the mammon of iniquity"? Luke xvi. 9. To what end this? To the end *that they may receive you into the eternal tabernacles*. But what can be more clear than that which I there cited out of Heb. xi. 24? "Moses denied himself to be the son of Pharaoh's daughter, choosing to be afflicted with the people of God; esteeming the reproach of Christ greater riches than the treasure of the Egyptians. For he looked to the reward; or (according to your Bibles), for he had respect unto the recompense of the reward." No less clear is David, Ps. cxviii. 112, "I have inclined my heart to do thy justifications for ever for reward;" and "for this reward he inclined his heart to do them," saith St. Augustine on this place, reading it as we

do. And so (as we read it) it is faithfully translated by the Septuagint out of the Hebrew, and so your translators might have translated it, if they had pleased; but they wilfully chose another sense, though they so much professed to follow the Septuagint.

POINT XXXVI.

WE LAUDABLY WORSHIP ANGELS AND SAINTS.

1. For the ground of this question, I lay this foundation out of Scripture, that as the angels are in heaven, so the souls of the saints go directly from hence to heaven, unless they have some few offences to clear in purgatory. Our souls sleep not until doomsday. Christ said to the good thief, "This day thou shalt be with me in Paradise." And therefore St. Paul desired to "be dissolved, that he might be with Christ." And again, 2 Cor. v. 8, "We are willing rather to be absent from the body, and to be present with our Lord;" therefore we may come to be present with our Lord, even whilst our souls are absent from our body. Neither do our English Protestants deny this.

2. This supposed, our doctrine is, that great reverence and worship is due to the angels and saints with God. Secondly, that they can hear our prayers. Thirdly, that they can, and will help us; and therefore it is laudable to pray to them, and that this doth not derogate from Christ's honour. Fourthly, that among the saints it is most laudable to pray to our Lady; and here we shall speak of the beads said to her honour. Fifthly, we laudably worship images of Christ and his saints. Sixthly, that we laudably worship their relics, and enshrine them richly, and place them as honourably as we can. Seventhly, that some places are more holy than others, sanctified by the presence of those relics, or by special graces given there; and for this reason we laudably make proces-

sions and pilgrimages to these places with all devotion. Eighthly, that we laudably keep feasts or holy days, as also fasts in the honour of Christ and his saints. Lastly, in these our fasts we laudably abstain from certain meats. All and every one of these nine things shall have their particular proofs in so many several points next following in the order here designed.

3. And, first, for the worship of angels or saints, note that the very self-same outward worship, yea, and adoration itself, may outwardly be given either as a civil reverence to persons of respect and great eminence, or it may be given to them out of a religious respect, in regard of the great sanctity and heavenly dignity in such a person; or, lastly, given in regard of divine perfection and infinite worth. When this respect is given thus outwardly, there passeth inwardly an act in our understanding apprehending the excellence which we honour to be either human, as in civil honour, or to be an excellence of singular though limited heavenly eminence, as in the worship of saints, which we call *Dulia;* or lastly, we judge that there is a divine and infinite excellence in that person, as it happens in the worship of God only, which we call *Latria*. Another act passeth in our will, answerable to that which was in our understanding, by which we have a will to make this outward worship or adoration to be either a civil honour only, such as is due to men of highest human dignity, or to make it a religious worship, though far from divine, such as is given to persons of eminent sanctity, or endowed with great heavenly gifts; or, lastly, we intend to make it an act of divine worship, as when we do it to God. Whence it is evident that, by doing of the outward act, it cannot be known whether the honour we do be merely *civil*, or *religious*, or *divine*.

4. [It is much the same with the words whereby the act of honour is denoted; that is to say, the *same*

WE LAUDABLY WORSHIP SAINTS AND ANGELS. 179

word does often signify *very different* kind of honour. To understand which, note that in the Hebrew Bible and in the Septuagint Version, made by learned Jews in Egypt about three hundred years before Christ, and in the Latin Vulgate, translated from the Hebrew by St. Jerome about the close of the fourth century, one and the *same* word—Hebrew, or Greek, or Latin—is used, where your translators do use different. So of Abraham's servant it is written, Gen. xxiv. 26, "The man bowed down his head, and *worshiped* the Lord." In the chapter before, at the seventh verse, your translators say, "Abraham stood up, and *bowed himself* to the people of the land." But the Hebrew hath the same word in both these places, and so hath the Latin. Take now a few out of many examples of the civil honour (or adoration) spoken of in holy writ, where inferiors show reverence to superiors, equals salute equals, and superiors condescend to their inferiors. Abigail "fell before David on her face, and *bowed herself* to the ground," 1 Sam. xxv. 23. "Jacob *bowed himself* to the ground seven times, until he came near to his brother," Gen. xxxiii. 3. "Bathsheba bowed and *did obeisance* unto the king David," 1 Kings i. 16. And the king Solomon "rose up to meet Bathsheba, and *bowed himself* unto her, and sat down on his throne," 1 Kings ii. 19. Now your translators here render variously one and the same Hebrew word; which indeed is the same as that in the first text quoted in this paragraph; the same as in Psalm xxix. 2, where they translate, "*Worship* the Lord in the beauty of holiness." You see, then, that the same Scripture word which denotes honour may signify honour very different in kind. When Isaac blessed Jacob, he said, Gen. xxvii. 29, "Let people serve thee, and nations *bow down* to thee, be lord over thy brethren, and let thy mother's sons *bow down* to thee." When Jacob blessed his children, he said, Genesis xlix. 8, "Judah, thou art he whom thy brethren shall praise; . . . . thy father's children shall *bow down* before thee." Here again, in the Hebrew, and in the Greek Septuagint, and in St. Jerome's Latin respectively, is found the same word as in Psalm xcv. 6, "O come let us *worship*" (*Venite adoremus*). The summary at the head of Psalm lxxii., in your Bibles, says, that therein David showeth the glory of Solomon's reign, and of Christ's kingdom under that type. Which indeed is most true. Now verse the eleventh you translate as follows: "Yea, all kings shall *fall down* before him." And, in regard of Solomon, it is a prediction of civil honour, or worship, or adoration, paid to an earthly monarch; but, in regard of the type, Christ our Lord, it is a prediction of divine adoration and homage. See, now, how the same word may denote things very different, as the same prediction may concern persons very different. I have used the word "adoration" in speaking of the honour paid to men, because of the words being so used in St. Jerome's version of the Bible, and because that word, after all, signifies only a salutation of hand to mouth, or of the face to the ground; which outward acts, as I have before explained, are determined by the act inwardly passing in our understanding.]

I add one very fit passage of 1 Chron. xxix. 20: "All the congregation bowed down their heads, and worshiped the Lord and the king." Exteriorly the bowing was both alike to the ground; but the inward act made this bowing as done to the king to be civil honour only,* and the like bowing as done to God to be divine honour or worship, and true adoration in the most rigorous sense. You cannot, then, blame us if, when we reverence saints, or pray to them, we bow, kneel, or prostrate ourselves to the ground even seven times. For if *civil* "worship"—for this word the

* [The Protestant commentator BROWN, in his "Self-interpreting Bible" (Glasgow, 1836), gives this comment on the text,—*i.e.* "did reverence *at once* to Jehovah and the king; but rendered *a different kind* of reverence, as is manifest, to either."]

last text hath—may pass so far without robbing God of his honour, why may not an inferior *religious* worship do the like?

5. But of this adoring for religious worship we have clear Scripture. Joshua, vi. 14, being told by an angel that this angel was but a captain of the hosts of our Lord, "Joshua fell on his face to the earth, and did worship." Behold, before we had worship given by the people to the king, here we have worship done to an angel, known to be an angel. By and by, in the Apocalypse, we shall see this very word of worship to signify the reverence which is to be given to God. Now I go on, and I observe that the angel was not only willing to admit of this honour, but commanded him also to show reverence to the very place made holy by his presence. "Loose," saith he, "thy shoes from thy feet, for the place whereon thou dost stand is holy." If any reply that we may with religious worship adore angels, as Joshua did, but not saints, behold the Scripture showeth this religious worship or adoration, due to spiritual excellence, to be laudably given to those who excel in sanctity even in this world. So, 1 Kings xviii. 7, Abdias, governor of the house of Achab, king of Israel, meeting with poor Elias the prophet, when he knew him, fell on his face, and said, "My lord, art not thou Elias?" And 2 Kings ii. 15, "And when the sons of the prophets which were to view at Jericho saw Elisha (who had divided the Jordan by smiting its waters), they came to meet him, and *bowed themselves* to the ground before him."* See you not here that it was not for any worldly excellence, but merely in regard of his spiritual excellence, that they thus bowed themselves to the ground before

* [And yet your Book of Homilies, at the close of the first part of the Homily against peril of Idolatry, says that "all godly men did ever abhor that any kneeling and worshiping, or offering, should be used to themselves when they were alive." Was Elisha ungodly?]

him? This spiritual excellence is incomparably more eminent in those who are now made co-heirs to Christ himself in the participation of all heavenly gifts and glory. To them, therefore, religious bowing or worship is far more due; and we are commanded by St. Paul, Rom. xiii. 6, 7, "To render to all their due: to whom honour, honour. Owe to no man any thing" which you do not pay him. This I stayed upon, because our adversaries often ask for a precept commanding us to honour saints. Behold I have given you one, which is a precept grounded in the very law of nature and equity, commanding us to render to each one what is due to him.

6. Again, Apoc. iii. 9, "Behold, I will make them come, and worship before thy feet;" words spoken to the angel of Philadelphia. If by this angel you say the bishop of Philadelphia is understood, then we prove, first, that, *à fortiori*, we may worship before the feet of the chief bishop of the Church. Secondly, we much more (*à fortiori*) infer, that we may worship before the feet of those who have a far greater excellence in virtue, grace, glory, as saints have above all men on earth. For, St. Matt. xi. 11, "He that is the least in the kingdom of heaven is greater than he;" that is, is greater than the great St. John Baptist was upon earth, though of him Christ himself said, "There had not risen a greater among the sons of women." St. John the Evangelist, then, knowing it to be true which he himself had written, that Christ "would make men come, and worship before the feet of the angel of Philadelphia," thought it his duty to adore before the feet of any angel, and hence he saith of himself, Apoc. xix. 10, "And I fell at his feet to worship him" (the angel); and again, chap. xxii. 8, "I fell down to worship before the feet of the angel which showed me those things."

7. Our adversaries object, that at each of these adorations the angel checked St. John for them, saying at each time, "See thou do not; I am thy fellow-

servant: worship God." Our answer is, that if the first adoration used by St. John had been of its own nature idolatrous and sinful, which is incredible, it proceeding from so great a prophet and so sublime a Scripture writer, yet at least being told so, and instructed by the angel to the contrary, as you say he was, he would never the second time have done that idolatrous and damnable sinful act both wittingly and willingly, and this so very soon after he had been warned not to do it. It was not, then, by reason of any unlawfulness in this action that the angel willed him not to adore or worship; but the angel refused at both times this honour upon some other consideration, to wit, out of singular respect unto him whom he knew to have been at the last supper admitted to lie on Christ's breast; and so he would not permit him to lie now prostrate at his feet, whom he also knew to be so highly favoured by God with so many admirable heavenly visions; moreover, to be a virgin; to be a priest, an apostle; and to be that very disciple whom Jesus so singularly loved; to be also a prophet and an evangelist. Therefore he would not admit of such profound respect at his hands, but humbly saying unto him, "I pray do it not, for I am thy fellow-servant," and thou either now art greater in God's sight than I am, or soon mayest come to be far greater. Worship and adore God, who hath so magnified thee. Yet St. John's humility working still upon him more, by seeing an angel so humble, and producing in him a mean conceit of himself, by still reflecting on what he was as of himself, and knowing what his master said, "That even the lesser in the kingdom of heaven was greater than the great St. John Baptist,"—to wit, according to the present state,—he therefore did the second time show the angel the honour he knew due to him. See above how Joshua worshiped an angel, which honour notwithstanding was also refused by the angel in this place, both for the former reasons, and for that he knew full well how much this great humility of his had advanced him yet higher.

8. Their second objection is that of St. Paul, Col. ii. 18, "Let no man beguile you in worshiping of angels." To answer this objection, note that the former passage of St. John happened to him when he was in banishment in the island called Patmos, Apoc. i.; whence it is manifest that St. John in his Apocalypse, now cited, used both these two several adorations, twice worshiping the angel, long after St. Paul had written these words forbidding the worship of angels, which words St. John understood either much better, or at least full as well as our Protestants understand them. And therefore he knew very well that in adoring or worshiping the angel two several times, he in neither of these times was seduced in the worship of angels. We therefore may adore angels as St. John did, and yet not be beguiled in this worship of angels, as St. John was not. Those, then, are rather seduced by wilful mistake of what this worship of angels is, who, to make us guilty of it, define it to be such a worship as must make St. John as guilty as they would make us. Therefore this text is vainly alleged against us, for holding only and maintaining such worship of angels as St. John used twice, and that long after he knew what St. Paul had written. This, then, serves our turn, that in what sense soever St. Paul is to be understood, he cannot be understood in a sense forbidding any thing which St. John did, and which we, with him, do practise. The truth is, St. Paul speaks only of such religious worship of angels as had been taught among the Jews by Simon Magus, who would have sacrifice offered to all angels, as well evil as good. (Epiph. Hæres. 25, Chrysostom, Hom. 7, in hunc locum.) And this is that which is condemned in the Council of Laodicea, c. 35.

9. There is another very pertinent exposition of this text in Tertul. l. 5, contra Marcionem. That is, that the apostle laboureth in that place to prove that

the new Christians should not keep the old Judaical law; and for this end he saith, "Let no man beguile you in the worship of angels," by saying that we owe so much respect to the angels, that although Christ had abolished the whole law, yet because that old law was given them by the ministry of angels, Acts vii. 50, it ought still to be kept out of respect to the angels, by whose ministry it was given. Again, some then taught that this, as a heavenly verity, had been revealed by some of the angels. But the angels, revealers of such doctrine, being angels of darkness, St. Paul calleth the Judaical observation of meats, maintained by these Christians out of this principle, the doctrine of devils, 1 Tim. iv. 1. Such also is the worship of angels, given them by such observances. And it is to be noted, that immediately before these words, he expressly spoke against the Judaical observation of meats, saying, "Let no man judge you in meat," Col. ii. 16. Of which text see more, Point XLV. Nos. 5, 6.

POINT XXXVII.

THE ANGELS AND SAINTS CAN HEAR OUR PRAYERS.

1. PROTESTANTS undertaking to reform all our pretended errors out of Scripture, can with no ground pretend to reform our error in believing saints to hear us, unless they can show some clear text to prove that saints cannot hear us. It is enough for us to go on still believing that we ever believed, unless they can show us Scripture to the contrary. They produce but one poor text, falling short of any clear proof. It is, Isa. lxiii. 16, "Thou art our father, though Abraham be ignorant of us, and Israel acknowledge us not. Thou, O Lord, art our father, our redeemer." I answer, that the Jews considering how enormously they had continually swerved from the life, example, and instruction of

Abraham and Jacob, did with great reason fear that they would not look upon them as their children, as that word "acknowledge" doth express. Wherefore, knowing God's mercy to be infinitely greater than that of the greatest saints, they hoped that he still would look upon them. They did not say Abraham and Jacob knew not their state or condition; but they conceived that they for their sins, well known to them, had all reason not to own them as children, and to say, "We know you not," as Christ shall one day to the reprobate.

2. Again, though we should grant that Abraham and Jacob did not know the state of the Jews then, when Abraham and Jacob were still in Limbo Patrum, it doth not follow that the saints now present with God, enlightened with the light of beatific glory, cannot, by virtue of that light, know all that passeth on earth, as far, at least, as any thing maketh to their felicity. For it is part of happiness to know how things pass with our dearly beloved friends, especially when we are in a condition to help them easily, as the saints are. Yet it is also false that Abraham even in Limbo knew not what passed among the Jews after his death. For he could tell Dives "that his five brethren had Moses and the prophets," Luke xvi. 29, though Moses and the prophets lived long after his death. See No. 4.

3. As our adversaries have but this one poor proof out of Scripture against us, so we have many for us. Jacob calls upon an angel to bless his children. No man would call upon one who could not hear. The text is Gen. xlviii. 16. I shall speak largely of it in the next Point, No. 2. Again, 1 Sam. xxviii., the witch whom Saul consulted, calling by her charms upon the devil, instantly was heard by him; for presently she did that which, without help of some ill spirit, could not be done. Shall devils hear witches presently, and shall saints want power to hear their suppliants? See what I here say, No. 7: "Raphael,

one of the seven which assist before the Lord," Tob. xii. 15, although he be there assisting, yet he truly told Toby, ver. 12, "When thou didst pray with tears, and didst bury the dead by night, I offered thy prayer to our Lord." If this be not canonical Scripture, yet at least it is most ancient ecclesiastical history, and of such credit that SS. Cyprian, Ambrose, Austin, Jerome, Gregory, the third Council of Carthage, and many more, held it Scripture, and consequently they thought it as true as Scripture, that saints could hear our prayers. And you must bring something more than your own imagination to discredit it on this account. Eliphaz, in Job, chap. v. 1, thus spoke to him: "Call, now, if there be any that will answer thee, and to which of the saints wilt thou turn?" This showeth the common practice of invoking angels in that time; for, as then, no saints but angels were in heaven. Whence the Septuagint, whom you use to extol, do here interpret the saints to be the holy angels. David supposed the angels to hear him when he sung psalms; whence he saith, "Before the gods (we truly read the angels) I will sing praise unto thee," Psalm cxxxviii. 1. No man will say, "I'll sing my song in the hearing of deaf men." The angels, then, could hear his song. Of the letters of Elias I will speak by and by, No. 5; and there I shall show that Elias after his death knew what passed, and took care for the people of God.

4. In the New Testament, Luke xv. 10, "There shall be joy before the angels of God upon one sinner having done penance." No act is more interior, and passeth more properly in the bottom of the heart, than the conversion of a sinner. Weeping, sighing, groaning, knocking of the breasts, may be done by hypocrites. The angels, then, who joy at the conversion of a sinner, must know this conversion, which they cannot know unless they know the bottom of the heart by divine revelation. Again, Luke xvi. 26, though there was "a great gulf fixed between the

souls of Abraham and Dives," yet God gave them some means to hear what each of them said. Can he, then, find no means for saints to hear us? Do not you Protestants say, Abraham's soul was then in heaven? Could he hear Dives from hell, and can he not hear from earth those who pray to him? Again, ver. 29, "Abraham said to him (Dives), They have Moses and the prophets." Moses and the prophets lived many a year after Abraham was dead; and yet, you see, Abraham knew there were such men who left such books to the Jews. Secondly, He knew their books were yet extant. Thirdly, That these writings of theirs were of no less efficacy to convert Dives' five brothers, than the preaching of a man risen from the dead would be. If you say this is but a parable, I answer that in parables the interlocutors must be made to speak sense and not nonsense, as it would be in one of Lucian's dialogues, to make Julius Cæsar discoursing with Alexander about what they had seen in Charles V., who lived so long after their time.

5. But I have reserved one passage of the Old Testament to declare in this place how saints, even then, knew what passed. Elias departed out of this life, whither God knows, the eighteenth year of King Josaphat, 2 Kings ii. 11; "Now Josaphat reigned five-and-twenty years," 2 Chron. xx. 31, so that seven years of Josaphat's reign passed after the departure of Elias. "Then Joram his son reigned for him," 2 Chron. xxi. 1. After some time of this Joram's reign, ver. 12, "There came a writing to him from Elias the prophet, saying, Thus saith our Lord, Because thou hast not walked in the ways of Josaphat thy father," &c. And then he tells him many particular wicked acts of his, all done after Elias was dead. Elias, therefore, being departed, knew what passed, and showed his great care to help God's people, his brethren, in writing this letter after his departure.

6. When saints come to heaven, they see far more by the light of glory than we can easily conceive. For, 1 Cor. xiii. 9, "Now in part we know, and in part we prophesy; but when that which is perfect is come, then that shall be done away which is in part." Hence St. Aug., l. 22, de Civit. c. 21, proveth that the saints in heaven have more perfect knowledge of what passeth here than we have. The light of glory far exceedeth the light of prophecy; and yet by that prophets knew many secrets of the hearts and things far out of their sight. Samuel saith to Saul, 1 Sam. ix. 19, "All that is in thy heart I will tell thee." And, 2 Kings v. 26, Elizeus said to Giezi, "Went not my heart with thee when the man turned again from off his chariot to meet thee?" So, Acts v. 4, St. Peter did see the deceitful heart of Ananias, saying to him, "Why hast thou conceived this thing in thy heart?" Note, that as the light of prophecy is not a glorious glittering without, but a quality inwardly inherent in the understanding, elevating it, even so the light of glory is no such exterior brightness, as some may apprehend, but it is an interior noble quality, and the noblest of all qualities inherent to the understanding, elevating, corroborating, and enabling it to a wonderful perfection in knowledge, so that it is able perfectly to see God himself. We, blind worms, very rashly make those blessed souls ignorant of our low affairs.

7. Hear, further, to what authority over the affairs of this world God raiseth his saints, that hence you may see how much it belongs to this their authority to know how things pass here below, Apoc. ii. 26, "He that shall overcome, and keep my works unto the end, I will give him power over the nations, and he shall rule them with a rod of iron. And as a vessel of the potter they (who slight them) shall be broken." He is a blind ruler over nations, who knows not what passeth even in the spiritual affairs of nations, which are those affairs that belong to his

ruling power. Again, chap. iii. 21, "He that shall overcome, I will give unto him to sit with me in my throne, as I also have overcome, and have sitten with my Father in his throne." Do you think saints, raised by God so high, have no means to know what we do below? Is it not said of the devil, Apoc. xii. 10, "That he accuseth our brethren night and day," which he cannot do unless he first knows in what to accuse us? A shameful thing it is to deny this knowledge to angels which we grant to devils. See in the next Point, No. 7, two evident texts out of the Apocalypse, showing the angels and saints to offer, and consequently to know, our prayers; and note that all I have said from the fourth Number to this place proves the self-same. The former texts speak indeed only of angels; but you see saints raised to as high light of glory as those angels; besides, they living so mixed with them, and still enjoying their conversation, it cannot but seem strange, that all the angels should rejoice at the conversion of a sinner, and the saints should know nothing of it. Again, it being proved that angels can hear us, you cannot, upon that account, deny prayers to angels to be lawful, seeing that they hear us as well as the saints living upon earth, whose prayers we may lawfully crave. If you say that we are not commanded to pray to them, I answer, so we are not commanded to beg one another's prayers. 'Tis sufficient that, as our spiritual necessities command us to do this, so they command us much more to do that. But of this in the next Point, No. 1. See there, No. 7, two more texts out of the Apocalypse showing saints to hear our prayers. For the twenty-four elders were saints, and not angels; yet they knew and presented our prayers made here on earth.

POINT XXXVIII.

THAT SAINTS CAN AND WILL HELP US, AND THEREFORE IT IS LAUDABLE TO PRAY TO THEM.

1. FIRST, Protestants often ask us where we have a command to pray to angels or saints? I answer that if there be many advantages accruing to us by the devout invocation of saints, then it is apparent that prudence and charity to ourselves ought to excite us thereunto; as it doth to seek shelter when it rains, without being called to go under shelter by the crier's voice, as they say some simple people are. It is as simple to exact a command in a thing of greater benefit. I say, moreover, that if there be a command to beg the prayers of saints living on earth, that command, *à fortiori*, urgeth us to beg the prayers of saints living in heaven, they being more willing and more able to help us. If there be no such command, yet we may without any command practise that laudably: so also may we laudably practise this without a command, seeing that they hear us, as well as the saints living with us. Why, then, may we not say to saints in heaven that which St. Paul said to saints on earth, "Brethren, pray for us"? Job's friends were commanded to go to Job to pray for them, as we shall show more fully No. 9. You all keep the Sunday. Where is that commanded to you? You answer, it is sufficient to see examples of it among the first Christians. So say I, it is sufficient we show you examples in Scripture of such as prayed to angels. For of praying to saints the Old Testament could not write, no saints being as then in heaven. The four gospels writ no farther than the ascension of Christ to heaven, before which no saint also was in heaven. Wherefore you need not wonder that in the four gospels you see no mention of praying to saints in heaven. In St. Paul's epistles you find him beg-

ging prayers of saints on earth. So, Heb. xiii. 18, "Pray for us." Seeing, then, that prayer to saints in heaven is more beneficial to us, it is also, by manifest consequence, more to be used by us. And as often as the Scripture exhorts us to promote our salvation and spiritual good by all means we can, so often doth it exhort us to use this means as much or more than begging the prayers of others upon earth. In fine, when a thing hath many spiritual goods in it, we are sufficiently invited thereunto without a command: so nobody commanded Timothy still to drink water, St. John to drink no wine, and to come neither eating nor drinking, nor his disciples to fast often. See Point XXII. It is sufficient that we obtain much good thereby.

2. That by praying to saints we obtain much good, I prove by proving that saints can and will help us, which all they supposed who called upon them; as Gen. xlviii. 15, "And Jacob blessed the sons of Joseph, and said, God, before whom my fathers walked, the angel that delivered (or redeemed) me from all evil, bless the lads." He calls first upon God, and then upon his good angel, to help those children; and he tells you that this angel delivered him from several evils. How Jacob prayed this angel is expressed, Hos. xii. 4, "Jacob prevailed against the angel, and he wept, and made supplication unto him." So Job's friend, following the practices of those times, did bid him call upon some saint or angel, as I showed last Point, No. 3. How well the angels wish us, their joy for the conversion of sinners testifieth. And if the evil angels are so restless in circling about to see whom they can devour, and accuse our brethren night and day, as I showed in the former Point, No. 7, the good angels are no less careful to seek whom they can defend, help, and save.

3. Hence that earnest prayer of that angel, Zach. i. 12, "And the angel of our Lord said, O Lord of hosts, how long wilt thou not have mercy on Jerusa-

lem, and on the cities of Judah, against which thou hast had indignation these threescore and ten years?" What call you praying, if this be not? Now hear with what effect this angel prayed for them: "And our Lord answered the angel good words, comfortable words." Behold here this angel would and could help our necessities. And of St. Michael in particular Daniel saith, chap. x. 21, "There is none that holdeth with me in these things but Michael, your prince." Chap. xii. 1, "At that time shall stand up Michael the great prince, who standeth for the children of thy people." In what doth St. Michael stand for God's people, if he do not so much as pray for them?

4. That by the merits of saints we may beg and obtain favours, I prove also thus. 1 Kings xv. 4, when wicked Abdias reigned in Judah, "For David's sake, our Lord his God gave him a lamp in Jerusalem, to raise up his son after him, and establish Jerusalem, because David had done right in the eyes of our Lord." When a hundred and eighty-five thousand Assyrians came to besiege Jerusalem, God by his prophet said to Ezechias, "I will protect this city, that I may save it for my own sake, and for David's sake, my servant," Isa. xxxvii. 35. That is, say the Protestants, for my promise made to David. But we say, if they seek over all Scripture, they will find no such promise made to David, of defending or protecting Jerusalem. Yea, we prove there could be no such promise, because Jerusalem, in the captivity, was not protected, but ruined.

5. The power which the prayers of saints have, and that they use carefully to pray for us, is often expressed in Scripture. Jeremy xv. 1, "Though Moses and Samuel stood before me, yet my mind could not be toward the people." By which manner of speech it appears that Moses and Samuel, long since dead, after their death used to pray for the people, and that their prayers were most powerful. So a king may say, Though my mother shall come to me and pray, I

o

will not hear her. You shall see Daniel of like merit and power with God in just such another text: Ezech. xiv. 13, "I will kill out of the land man and beast. And if these three men shall be in the midst thereof, —Noah, Daniel, and Job,—they, by their justice, shall deliver their own souls. Yet, though these three men were in it, saith our Lord, they shall deliver neither sons nor daughters, but themselves alone shall be delivered." Which he repeats again, verse 20; this joining of Daniel, a saint then living, with Noah and Job, dead so many hundred years before, showeth that these men by their prayers no less powerfully interposed themselves than Daniel living. Of Elias's care to assist his people after his death, we gave you a memorable testimony in the former Point, No. 5, in the famous vision of Judas Maccabeus, 2 Macc. xv. 12. First, Onias, who had been the high-priest, but was now dead, "stretching forth his hands, prayed for all the people of the Jews. After this there appeared also another man, marvellous for age and glory, and for the port of great dignity about him. And Onias said, This is the lover of his brethren. This is he who prayeth much for the people, and the whole city; Jeremy, the prophet of God. And he gave to Judas a sword of gold, saying, Take the holy sword, a gift from God, wherewith thou shalt overthrow the adversaries of my people." The event confirmed the truth of this vision. Origen, tom. xviii., in Joan., reflecting on this place, saith it appeareth that saints departed from this life have care of the people; as it is written, saith he, in the acts of the Machabees, many years after the death of Jeremy: "This is Jeremy the prophet, who prayeth much for the people." So that though the books of Machabees be admitted not as Scripture, but only as a true ecclesiastical history, we have from thence that the most holy high-priest and chief of God's only people believed that saints prayed for us and helped us, and that all the people who were said to be encouraged by this vision were of the same belief.

How far, then, is this from all novelty which can be proved to have been practised before the days of the Apostles; and this by an authority far greater than that of Josephus, or any such historian, to whom you would scorn to give a place in your Bible, as you do to the history of the Machabees.

6. Let us now come to the New Testament. What motive soever moved Dives, Luke xvi. 27, to pray to Abraham, saying, "I would beseech thee that thou wouldest send to my father's house, for I have five brethren, to testify to them, lest they also come to this place of torments,"—the very same motive will work far more upon the heart of departed saints to help us, their poor brethren, "from that place of torments," and promote us to those eternal tabernacles, of which Christ said, Luke xvi. 9, "Make unto yourselves friends of the mammon of iniquity, that when you fail they may receive you into everlasting habitations." Again, Apoc. ii. 26, "He that shall overcome, and keep my words to the end, I will give him power over the nations, and he shall rule them with a rod of iron." The saints having authority to rule nations so powerfully, as is here expressed by a rod or sceptre of iron, they exercise this their power chiefly by making intercession so powerfully to God for us as to obtain for us such graces as we stand most in need of, this their power being given to a spiritual end.

7. And as God, who is goodness and mercy itself in an infinite degree, doth, notwithstanding, not so show this his mercy and bounty towards those who never pray to him, as he doth to those who are incessantly begging his help, so saints chiefly are moved to aid those who are still begging their assistance; yet true it is that they are of their own accord helping us. So Raphael offered the prayers made to God by Toby, as we have seen in the former Point, No. 3. So, Apoc. v. 8, "The four living creatures, and four-and-twenty elders, fell before the Lamb, having every one harps and golden vials full of

odours, which are the prayers of saints;" which prayers, made by saints on earth, these saints in heaven did know and hear, for they presented them in golden vials. And, chap. viii. 3, "Another angel came and stood at the altar, having a golden censer. And there was given to him much incense, that he should offer of the prayers of all the saints upon the altar of gold which is before the throne of God; and the smoke of the incense of the prayers of the saints ascended up before God out of the angel's hand." Note that the angel, being before the throne of God, did there hear the prayers of saints in earth. Secondly, He did not only hear their prayers, but also " offer them up before the throne of God in a golden censer;" which he could not do if he had not known them. Thirdly, These prayers of the saints on earth, by being thus jointly offered up by the more fervent prayers of the saints in heaven, or holy angels, did become more acceptable to God. "For hence the smoke of the incense with these prayers ascended" more sweetly and pleasantly to God "from the hand of the angel." God indeed knows our prayers before the saints or angels offer them; but he knows that they mount up less powerfully when they be not seconded of their intercession. So God knew beforehand that all the people answered Moses, saying to him, "All things that our Lord hath spoken we will do," Exod. xix. 8. And yet the very next words are, "And Moses returned the words of the people to the Lord." Which words were well known to God before that Moses did return them; yet by returning them, he did make, by his joint mediation, this cheerful offer of the people more pleasing to God.

8. And because he did this to their greater advantage, Moses himself saith, Deut. v. 5, "I stood between the Lord and you at that time." This I note to answer the objection of our adversaries, saying, It is injurious to Christ to make any other mediator; "for one is our mediator." To be a mediator

is nothing but to stand between God and us, mediating for us. In this proper sense, Moses was a mediator between God and his people. The same, in the same sense, may be said of other saints; yet in that sense, that Christ is said to be our only mediator, we make no other mediator; for he is called mediator because he is so by his own worth, and by his merits offered for us fully satisfying God's anger, and capable of no repulse. "I did know that thou didst always hear me," said Christ to his eternal Father, John xi. 42. "He is heard for the reverence due to him," as St. Paul speaks. In this sense we make no saint mediator for us. We only beg of them to pray for us, as we beg of living saints, whom by their prayers we desire to mediate for us. St. Paul in this sense desired the Thessalonians to mediate for him to God. "Brethren, pray for us," 1 Thess. v. 25. And to the Hebrews, chap. xiii. 18, "Pray for us." And God himself bids Job's friends use the mediation, or intercession, of Job, promising to hear the prayers of this their mediator made for them, but nowhere promising to hear their prayers made without his mediation,—yea, rather intimating that he would not hear their prayers unless Job mediated for them, as I shall now show.

9. If you say it derogates from Christ's honour that any other should help to save us, I answer, that saints yet living upon earth help to save us. And so, Job xlii. 7, God tells Job's three friends, "My wrath is kindled against thee. Take, therefore, unto you seven oxen and seven rams, and go to my servant Job, and offer up for yourselves a burnt offering. And my servant Job shall pray for you; him I accept:" that is, his mediation shall avail to your pardon. Neither do we dishonour, but we rather honour, our Saviour, when we desire saints to pray for us. For by this we show the dignity of his merits to be so great, that by his merits saints are advanced to so great favour with God, that their prayers hence

come to be as effectual as were those of a Moses, who, living yet on earth, could obtain so often pardon for the whole people of Israel. From whence also it proceeds that the saints in heaven, as well as the saints here living, are in Scripture said to save others. Hence St. Paul, 1 Tim. iv. 16, "For in doing this, thou shalt both save thyself and them that hear thee." And St. James, chap. v. 20, "He which converteth a sinner from the error of his way, shall save his soul from death."

10. Neither, lastly, do we act against that precept of Christ, saying, *Come ye all to me;* as Paul did not act against the said precept when, after our Saviour had said these words, he himself went begging the prayers of the Thessalonians and Hebrews, in his epistles to them. For there are two ways of going to Christ. The first, immediately by ourselves, approaching reverently in prayer to him. The second and more powerful way is when we, humbly acknowledging our unworthiness and the meanness of our poor prayers, do procure the intercession of Christ's greatest friends to accompany with their joint mediation our humble petitions. And thus, though the centurion did not personally come to Christ, yet he is said by St. Matthew truly to have come to Christ: "There came to him a centurion," Matt. viii. 5. And yet St. Luke said he did not come to him; for, Luke vii. 3, only, "He sent unto him the elders of the Jews to intercede, beseeching him that he would come." And again, "When he was now not far from the house, the centurion sent friends to him, saying, I am not worthy that thou shouldst enter under my roof. And Christ marvelling, said, Neither in Israel have I found such faith." Behold this more humble way of coming to Christ, by our mediators and intercessors supplying our unworthiness, far preferred before the former way, and that even for the faith of the person so approaching: "I have not found so great faith, no not in Israel." Ponder well this passage.

POINT XXXIX.

THAT AMONG THE SAINTS IT IS MOST LAUDABLE TO PRAY TO OUR LADY: AND OF THE BEADS SAID TO HER HONOUR.

1. As we are far from honouring our Lady more than her Son, because we know that all the grace she hath, and all her power in the court of heaven, is wholly and entirely by her Son; so are we also far from equalising any saint in grace or power to the most blessed Mother of God, who even before she was his mother was by the archangel pronounced "full of grace," Luke i. 28. The highest saints in heaven are only styled servants of God. But our Lady is truly styled God's mother. "Whence is this to me, that the mother of my Lord should come to me?" Luke i. 43. In all well-ordered families, the power of the Lord's mother incomparably exceeds the power of all his servants. God, who hath commanded us in a special commandment to honour our parents, cannot, without impiety, be thought not to yield a special honour to his mother. "All generations shall call her blessed: because he that is mighty hath done great things to her," Luke i. 48.

2. Two things chiefly concur to eminent sanctity: exterior advantages to improve ourselves in grace; and interior assistance of the Holy Ghost to make the best use of those advantages. Our Lady, in the exterior occasions of improving herself in grace, had the greatest advantages that ever any creature had, even after she was declared "full of grace." She had our Saviour lodging in her womb nine months. And she knew who he was, and what graces he could bestow upon her, if she neglected not to beg them. She did see the humility of his birth, and beheld all that then happened. "But Mary kept all these sayings, and pondered them in her heart," Luke ii. 19. All that

we read of our Lord until he was thirty years old is, that "he lived subject to his parents. And his mother kept all these sayings in her heart," Luke ii. 51. She then had for thirty years together the benefit of his example to inform her, the benefit of his conversation to move her, the benefit of his instruction to teach her all she could desire to learn, or he desire to impart to her. When her Son began to preach to the world, and the people all said, "Never man did speak as he did," who can doubt but a mother so dearly loving such a Son did hear him more frequently and devoutly than any other, "still keeping and pondering" all in her heart. But her special harvest was in the time of his passion, which her compassion made also to be hers. Mothers will understand somewhat of the martyrdom she then suffered; but nobody can understand how much after his death and ascension her soul daily was improved by continual meditation of what she had seen, and also by the devout feeding upon the body of our Lord, which she made her daily bread. Now as for the interior assistance of the Holy Ghost exciting her to make the best advantages of all these occasions, we know that all such excitations and graces are dispensed by the hands of her own Son. Is not she, then, the likeliest to have the largest share in all these graces? which graces her Son also had instructed her to use so well to her best advantage, and to their hourly increase and improvement.

3. Hence it is, that as she surpassed all in the practice of virtue, so she is raised above all in supereminence of heavenly glory. Whence it followeth, that both love to God and love to her neighbour being most perfect in her, she, by them both, is most powerfully moved to afford to all such as devoutly call upon her all the assistance she is able. Wherefore, seeing her power is far surpassing that of other saints, we have all reason to believe her intercession to be most available for us.

4. Among other devotions which we use to pro-

cure this her so advantageous intercession, one is to say the Rosary, or beads, to her honour. Not that our Church commands any one to say these beads, but that she holds this to be a very commendable thing, which she knoweth full well to be but a late practice of piety, as also many other prayers are most pious, which were made long since the apostles' time. For you cannot prove that in their time any one prayer which is in your Common Prayer Book was used, except the *Pater Noster* and Creed. Will you say, then, that the use of them is not laudable? Let us, then, go on.

5. As the Psalter consists of a hundred and fifty Psalms, so, in imitation of that, the whole Rosary consists of a hundred and fifty *Ave Maries*. And as the instrument to which David did sing his Psalms was an instrument of ten strings, Ps. xxxii. 2, so we distinguish these hundred and fifty *Ave Maries* into several tens, that is, into fifteen tens if we say the whole Rosary, or into five tens if we say but the third part of it, as we do when our leisure or devotion reacheth not at once to the whole Rosary. Every ten is distinguished by a *Pater Noster*, said in the beginning thereof. For before we call upon our Lady we think it fit to call upon our Lord, from whom all the graces of our Lady did proceed, and from whom all must be given which we beg of her to obtain. For we do not acknowledge our Lady to be the giver of any graces, though her intercession be most powerful to obtain them to be given by her Son. When we use this devotion, we do indeed say ten *Ave Maries* for one *Pater Noster*. But the reason of this is, not that we honour our Lady more than our Lord, for we are so far from equalising her to him, that we confess her infinitely inferior to him; but the reason is, that it is fit we should set some time apart to honour her, or else we should honour her at no time. Now, as when we are busied in honouring our mother, we are not at that time busied in honouring our

father; so when we bestow this parcel of time in honouring our Lady, we only at this time honour our Lord so far as all the honour we do to his mother is done out of the respect we bear to her because she is his mother. We reserve other devotions to our Lord, which contain an honour of an incomparably higher strain than any honour we give to our Lady. For because our Lord died on the Friday, we to his honour abstain from flesh on all Fridays; because he did rise again on the Sunday, we honour his resurrection by solemnising all Sundays; because he fasted forty days for us, we to his honour yearly fast the forty days of Lent. No such honour is done by us to our Lady. Our adversaries will ask us, first, What authority we have for the *Ave Mary*. Secondly, Why we use this prayer just so often reiterated, and how we busy our minds in the mean time. You will soon know what to answer by the ensuing discourse.

6. We say, then, the first part of the *Ave Mary* was made by an angel; and he, as ambassador from God, used such words as he knew to be to God's mind, saying to our Lady: "Hail, full of grace, our Lord is with thee; blessed art thou among women," Luke i. 28. The second part came also from God; for, ver. 41, "Elizabeth was filled with the Holy Ghost, and she spake out with a loud voice, and said, Blessed art thou among women, and blessed is the fruit of thy womb." The holy Church addeth, "Holy Mary, mother of God (for she is in the next verse called mother of our Lord), pray for us sinners, now, and at the hour of our death, Amen." Which words are most full of piety, supposing, what we have proved, prayer to saints to be pious; for if we may pray to our Lord's servants, we may pray to his mother. Behold the whole *Ave Mary*.

7. Secondly, we use just the number of a hundred and fifty *Ave Maries* in the whole Rosary, because we would say a whole Psalter to her honour. If these had been a hundred and fifty several prayers, as there

be a hundred and fifty Psalms, who would have remembered them? But now, they being all but the same prayer so often repeated, and this prayer also so well known, any simple person, though he cannot read, can say this whole Psalter to our Lady without book. And it was made chiefly for a devout entertainment for those ignorant people who cannot read, though it be also an excellent entertainment even for the most learned, when either they have not light to read, or when, being wearied out with contemplation, or less disposed thereunto, they desire to walk, or pass the time devoutly without any overmuch tiring exercise. If any one adds an *Ave Mary* more or less than this number, he doth no other hurt than he, who, intending to say the whole Psalter, should say one Psalm less, or repeat one twice. These hundred and fifty *Ave Maries* are most conveniently divided into fifteen tens, to help us at every several ten to call to our memory and devout consideration some mystery of the life of Christ and our Lady. For the prime mysteries of their lives be reduced, very fitly and orderly, into fifteen mysteries, of which five be joyful, five be sorrowful, and five be glorious. To the honour of all these fifteen mysteries, we say the fifteen tens, when we say the whole Rosary. If we have not will or leisure to say the whole Rosary at once, then we say only the beads of five tens, honouring or pondering either the five joyful, or the five sorrowful, or the five glorious mysteries. When I say the first five tens, at each ten I will honour and attentively ponder with devotion one of the five joyful mysteries. As, first, the Annunciation of our Lady, when the angel announced unto her that God would become man, and she should be exalted to be his mother. Secondly, her Visitation, when visiting her cousin Elizabeth. "As soon as Elizabeth heard the salutation of Mary, the infant did leap in her womb, and Elizabeth was filled with the Holy Ghost, and cried out, Blessed art thou," &c., Luke i. 41. Thirdly, the Nativity of our

Lord. "A joy that shall be to all people, because this day was born to them a Saviour," Luke ii. 10. Her joy was greatest who was the mother in this joyful birth. Fourthly, her Purification, when Simeon, in whom the Holy Ghost was, "came in spirit into the temple, and took the child into his arms," showing him to all publicly in the temple, and declaring him to be "a light to lighten the Gentiles, and the glory of the people of Israel," Luke ii. 32. Fifthly, her finding the lost child disputing with the doctors in the temple, where they "all were astonished that heard him, upon his wisdom and answers," Luke ii. 47. "And he went down with his mother, and lived subject unto her, even till he was thirty years old; and she kept all his words in her heart."

8. When I come to say the second five tens, I will honour and ponder the five sorrowful mysteries. First, Christ's prayer in the garden. Secondly, his whipping at the pillar. Thirdly, his crowning with thorns. Fourthly, his carrying of the cross. Fifthly his being crucified, and dying upon the cross. All which, as Christ felt them most sensibly in his body, so our Lady, next to Christ, had a most tender feeling of them in her own soul. "And her own soul the sword of grief did pierce;" as holy Simeon prophesied of her, Luke ii. 35. When I come to say the third five tens, I will spend the time in saying each of them by meditating upon, and so honouring each of the five glorious mysteries. First, the resurrection of our Saviour. Secondly, his ascension to heavenly glory. Thirdly, his sending the Holy Ghost. Fourthly, the assumption of our Lady: when, as many holy fathers have taught, that body of hers, in which Christ took flesh, was, soon after its burial, not made food of worms, but with far greater reason made partaker of her Son's resurrection than were those many saints of whom St. Matthew, chap. xxvii. 52, saith, "Their graves were opened, and they rose. And they going forth out of their graves after his resurrection,

came into the holy city, and appeared to many." Fifthly, and lastly, I will, to her honour, consider her coronation, importing her special state in that heavenly glory in which she is looked upon and reverenced by all saints and angels as their queen, she being the mother of the King of Glory. "The mother of my Lord," Luke i. 43.

9. The intent of the holy Church recommending this devotion is, to teach all that use it, especially the more ignorant who cannot use books, how to employ their minds fruitfully in a most commendable meditation of mysteries most glorious to Christ and his mother, and most beneficial to our souls, whilst their lips are most devoutly busied in reciting words so pleasing to the mother of God; to which end the teachers of our Church, both by words and by writing, still are inculcating this true use of the beads.

10. Now, this number of fifteen tens, or of five tens, serving so fitly for the orderly practice of so easy a devotion, cannot be more easily observed than by letting one bead fall at each *Ave Mary*. And the beginning of the next ten can no way be more easily notified than to begin the said ten with a bead of so different a bigness that it may be easily noted, even in the dark, without any distraction. And the same different bead serves also to remind us of passing to the consideration of a different mystery, unless perhaps our soul hath other predominant pious thoughts or affections, which, tending to a very beneficial meditation, are better continued than interrupted. Now though many simple people use not these considerations, but attend only to the words they say, yet those words be so excellent, that this entertainment proves most virtuous, by their using the recital of them to honour Christ and his blessed mother.

11. Neither is the often repeating of the same prayers or prayer a thing blameworthy. For if after the saying of one *Ave Mary* we should use a less excellent prayer, yea, or no prayer at all, you could

not blame us. How, then, grow we to be blameworthy for using this so excellent prayer? He who should every hour say our Lord's Prayer, although he should do it three times each hour, is not to blamed, but commended. How, then, is he to be blamed who saith the Lord's Prayer three or fourscore times in one hour? Next unto our Lord's Prayer, no prayer hath greater authority or excellence than the *Ave Mary*. Why, then, are we blamed for using it so often in so short a space, whilst, as you think, you remain without blame, who use it so seldom? Our Saviour had the rarest invention that ever man had, and, if we may make bold to account any of his prayers more excellent than another, his prayer in the garden may seem to have been most excellent. And yet even then, as rare an invention as he had, "He prayed the third time, using the same words," Matt. xxvi. 44, and not inventing any new form. So likewise those four blessed six-winged creatures, Apoc. iv. 8, "Had not rest day and night, saying, Holy, holy, holy, Lord God Omnipotent." The oftener they said this one prayer over and over, the more fervour appears, even in so rare inventive spirits. All the publican's prayer was, "God be merciful to me a sinner," Luke xviii. 13; and, ver. 38, all the prayer of the blind man was, to cry again and again, saying, "Jesus, Son of David, have mercy upon me." And when they rebuked him to hold his peace, he cried much more, "Son of David, have mercy upon me." And thus he, by perseverance in the same prayer, obtained his request. Who doth not see a special power to stir up a great feeling of God's mercies in the Psalm one hundred and thirty-six, which containeth twenty-seven verses, and yet it doth twenty-seven times repeat those words, "For his mercy endureth for ever"!

POINT XL.

IT IS LAUDABLE TO WORSHIP THE IMAGES OF SAINTS.

[Ask an English Catholic at the present day, whether he deem it laudable to *worship* images, and he will probably reply, By no means; it would be folly and a sin. A captious disputant immediately lays his finger on this proposition of Mumford's, or on some passage in a Catholic prayer-book, where *worship* is declared to be paid to an image, or to the Cross, and proceeds to infer, that either the Catholic's disclaimer is insincere, or that he has become ashamed of, and renounced, a tenet maintained by his forefathers. The insulting and customary imputation of insincerity may be dismissed with contempt; but it may be useful to show here that there is no real inconsistency between such a declaration as we suppose, and a full admission of that for which Mumford contends : It is laudable to worship images *in that sense in which we* Roman Catholics *worship images.* Words fluctuate in their acceptation : their signification is enlarged or contracted, according to the usage of different times. Even contemporary writers or speakers do not always attach the same meaning to the same term. The term is equivocal; that is to say, it stands for different notions, and thus becomes the subject of denial and of affirmation without any *real* contradiction. Of this, the word "worship" is an instance. Ask a Protestant, Who is the object of his *worship?* He will reply, *God only;* and perhaps quote Rev. xxii. 9. And yet you may, perhaps, be able to remind him, that at the marriage-service he declared to his *bride,* "With my body I thee worship ;" or that he belongs to a City company, which is jealous of its title of "worshipful ;" or that as a justice of the peace he receives the customary address of "your worship." It would, nevertheless, be foolish wrangling to allege this against his declaration, that God alone is to be worshiped.

At the time when Mumford wrote (in the seventeenth century) the word under consideration was not so appropriated to express the honour due to God only, as custom seems to have appropriated it at the present day. That it was acknowledged to have great latitude might be shown from writers of the time. As an instance, the following passage from the Protestant Bible, translated in the early part of that century, may suffice: " Friend, go up higher ; then shalt thou have *worship* in the presence of them that sit at meat with thee," Luke xiv. 10. Here *worship* is paid to an humble, unpretending man.

No candid Protestant will, after considering these remarks, affect to find a contradiction in propositions which differ in sound only, and not in sense. He will admit the denial we have supposed an English Catholic to make; he will not demur to the assertion of Mumford, "It is lawful to worship the images of saints in that sense in which we Roman Catholics worship them." To uncandid readers this note is not addressed; still less to wilful and systematic misleaders of the ignorant. Of this class of men (when *they* affect to be scandalised) we must say, "Let them alone; they be blind leaders of the blind," Matt. xv. 14.

Thorndyke, Prebendary of Westminster (in the seventeenth century), thus speaks of the decree of the second Council of Nice (anno 787), which decree is in substance the same as that of Trent: "*That the decree of the Council enjoins no idolatry, notwithstanding whatever prejudice to the contrary, I must maintain as unquestionable.* So far is it from leaving any room for the imagination of any false Godhead, that it expressly distinguisheth that honour done to the image of our Lord Christ to be *equivocally* called worship, *i.e.* to be only so called, but not to signify the esteem of God. He that believes the Holy Trinity can no way attribute the latter; and therefore, *if he puts off his hat, and bows the knee to the image of our Lord, it shall be no idolatry.*" Epilogue iii. p. 363.]

1. IT is laudable, I say, to worship the saints' images, in that sense in which we Roman Catholics worship images. The very saints themselves we worship not with divine honour, as I said and largely declared, Point XXXVI. Nos. 3, 4, 5. And therefore it is a most unconscionable slander which our adversaries lay upon us, saying that we give divine honour to images. No, we give no such honour to the saints themselves, much less do we give it to their images, unless you think we worship the images more than the persons represented by the images. All that we Roman Catholics hold, as a point of faith, may be read by all men in the Council of Trent, sess. 25, where this council teacheth, "due honour and veneration to be given to the images of Christ and his saints, not that there is believed to be in them any divinity or virtue, for which they are to be worshiped, or that any thing is to be asked of them, or that any

confidence is to be placed in the images, as anciently was done by the Gentiles, who did put their hope in their idols, Ps. cxv. 8. But because the honour which is given to the images is referred to the persons represented by the images; so that by or through the images which we kiss, and before which we uncover our head, or lie prostrate, we adore Christ, and reverence the saints, whom these images represent." Behold the belief of our Church, teaching that all the reverence done before images (I pray note well this manner of speech), all the honour, I say, that is shown before the picture, resteth not in the image, but passeth through it, and resteth in the person represented to me by this picture. He that abuseth King Charles's picture or statue neither intendeth to show, nor showeth, any anger or disrespect to paper, or to stock or stone. All the abuse, by all men's judgment, is given to King Charles, represented by his picture in paper, or engraven in wood or stone. A further and an evident proof of all this is, that yourselves on the one side believe the sacrament to be only a sign or figure of Christ's body, and yet, on the other side, you count it no idolatry to kneel before this sacrament at the receiving of it, because that worship is done to the person signified by this sign. But that which presseth you far more is what St. Paul saith, "He that eateth and drinketh unworthily, is guilty of the body and blood of Christ," 1 Cor. xi. 27. Now of this being guilty of Christ's body and blood, it is impossible for you to give any other reason but that the abusing of the sign or figure of Christ's body is a high abuse done to the body itself. The same is proved out of 2 Sam. vi. 16, where of David's dancing before the ark it is said, "Michol saw David dancing before the Lord." You see the honour thus done as much to the ark as our bowing, or kneeling, or prostrating is done to the images, is referred not to the ark, but to our Lord, and is said to be done before him.

2. First, then, I say, we neither are nor can be

accounted guilty of idolatry upon this account. No understanding man can deny but this hath been the practice of the only true visible Church for a thousand years at least; therefore no idolatry can be in this practice. For idolatry destroyeth the very essence of a true Church. Moreover, the Scripture manifestly tells us, that all idols, after the coming of our Saviour, shall be quite abolished in his known and visible Church. For how can otherwise be understood that of Isaiah ii. 18, "Idols shall be utterly abolished;" that of Ezek. xxxvi. 25, "I will pour upon you clean water; and from all your idols I will cleanse you;" and, chap. xxxvii. 23, "Neither shall they defile themselves any more in their idols"? And therefore, Micah v. 13, "Thy graven images also I will cut off, and thy standing images out of the midst of thee." Therefore in Christ's Church there cannot be found the use of such images as were unlawful, that is, of such as should be made to be adored as gods; whence the next words are: "And thou shalt no more worship the work of thine hands." Now all these words are evidently spoken of what should happen after the coming of the Messias; for in the beginning of this chapter is the famous text prophesying that Christ should be born in Bethlehem; and then he prophesieth the ensuing benefits of his birth. Zacharias also speaking, chap. xiii. 1, of this time, saith, "In that day shall be a fountain lying open to the house of David; and it shall be in that day, saith the Lord of hosts, I will cut off the names of idols out of the earth, and they shall be remembered no more." And yet what a remembrance of idols would it be, to see all churches in the whole visible Church filled full of statues, images, and pictures, exposed all to be worshiped, if the worship used in these churches be idolatrous? A most urging argument and clear demonstration. Yea, among the Jews, prone as they were to idolatry, there was, by God's appointment, a religious use of images.

IT IS LAUDABLE TO WORSHIP IMAGES. 211

3. Thus God to Moses, "Thou shalt make a mercy-seat of pure gold. Two cherubim also thou shalt make of beaten gold on the two ends of the mercy-seat. Let one cherub be on the one end, and the other on the other end. And the cherubim shall stretch forth their wings on high, covering the mercy-seat with their wings," Exod. xxv. 17. And thus Moses, by the command of God, made the propitiatory, that is, the oracle or mercy-seat, of the purest gold. "Two cherubim also of beaten gold on either side of the propitiatory, even to the mercy-seat-ward were the faces of the cherubim," Exod. xxxvii. 9. It is no small sign of honour that these cherubim's pictures were made of gold, as also that they were placed before the oracle itself,—"the holy of holies." Hence St. Paul saith, Heb. ix. 5, "Over it were the cherubim of glory, shadowing the mercy-seat." When this tabernacle came to be placed in God's temple, "The temple itself had graven cherubs in the walls. And in the most holy house he máde two cherubim of image-work, and their faces were towards the house." So that the people adored towards them. "He made the veil of blue and purple-crimson, and wrought cherubim thereon." Note here how all the people kneeled immediately before these pictures when they prayed; "yea, graven cherubim were in the walls," as I said, placed before them, which way soever they turned, 2 Chron. iii. 7, 10, 13, 14.

4. There is also a memorable passage of Hosea the prophet, chap. iii. 4, where, lamenting the great desolation of the temple, he particularly also laments the want of that religious use of images in God's temple. "For, saith he, the children of Israel shall abide many days without king, without prince, without sacrifice, and without an image (or statue), and without teraphim;" that is, without images, which word of images some of your Bibles have; some put the word teraphim, which properly signifies a statue, image, or similitude, either of indifferent use,—as the

statue which Michol put in David's bed, 1 Sam. xix. 16, is called teraphim; or of an idolatrous use, as, Gen. xxxi. 19, "Rachel stole the teraphim (idols) of her father;" or of religious use, as in this place of Hosea, where the want of teraphim is bewailed, with the want of sacrifice and altar. And hence the ancient rabbis proved that images of angels are not contrary to the decalogue. The same we may say of the images of saints, not then used, because as then the saints were not in heaven. But their images now may so much the more be allowed, because they can be pictured in their own true likeness and shape, which cherubim and angels could not, no more than God. Where, for simple people, you may note that it little imports whether the picture be just like the person pictured; it is sufficient it serves perfectly to represent him: as the cherubim and angels were represented perfectly enough to our imaginations by their images or statues, which were nothing like them.

5. A further proof for images is out of St. Paul, Phil. ii. 9, 10, "He hath given him a name above all names, that at the name of Jesus every knee should bow." We have from hence, that because this name is above all names, therefore every knee is to bow at it. Why so? because it is a name representing Christ by our ears, as his image represents him to our eyes, only the image being a more lively representation, especially to those who know not the person, is the far more noble remembrance of the two. And as to bow at the name of Jesus was and is commanded the English reformed Church by their canons, so to bow at the more perfect representation of Jesus cannot be but as lawful an act of reverence to his person. The Jews out of reverence to God dared not to pronounce his most sacred name of Jehovah; for so you are pleased to read this name. Now as the honour done to the *name* of any person, so the honour done to the *image* of such a person redounds to the honour of that person.

6. But because our adversaries much blame us for using this honour before insensible creatures, let us see whether such honour is not used in Scripture before things wholly insensible of any honour. Yet behold, before I look into the Bible, and whilst I only stay looking upon it, I see Protestants cover their Bibles with curious covers, and placing them in decent places, and taking it very ill if any one should trample them under foot, or scornfully tear them in pieces. And all this is done by reason of the relation which the word of God hath to God himself. You know, and we shall tell you in the next Point, what honour was given to the ark, by reason of the relation it had to God in regard that from thence he gave his oracles to the priests. And, 2 Sam. vi. 16, it is said, "Michol saw David dancing before the Lord." Because he danced before the ark, he is said to do this "before the Lord." So when he kneeled or adored before it, it may also be properly said, David kneeled and adored before our Lord. And in this sense, when we kneel before any image of our Lady or saint, we may be said to kneel before our Lady, or before such a saint. This manner of speaking, which you account ridiculous and superstitious, is, as you see, the very phrase of Scripture in like occasion. Yea, adoration itself was used before the ark. David, Ps. xcix. 5, saith, "Worship at his footstool, for he is holy." Mark that the reason why worship is to be made at his footstool is, the relation which this footstool hath to him whose footstool it is; for he is holy: that is, for it is the footstool of him who deserves that worship should be done even at his footstool.

7. Our adversaries will make us believe that they can call to mind Christ and his passion as well and as frequently without seeing a crucifix, as by seeing it, which is contrary to all common experience. And the Scriptures teach our weakness and dullness to be much helped towards stirring up pious acts by the

outward use of these material signs: Numb. xv. 38, "Speak to the children of Israel, to make themselves fringes in the borders of their garments. And it shall be to you a fringe, that ye may look upon it, that ye may remember all the commandments of our Lord." These fringes were those phylacteries spoken of, Matt. xxiii. 5. We see that to help their dullness in remembering God's commandments this command is given them: so Deut. vi. 9, "Thou shalt write them upon the posts of thy house, and on thy gates." And you Protestants usually, for this reason, write them in great letters in your churches. Give us, then, leave, by images of our Saviour, to excite the memory of him. Now to their objections.

8. You first object, Exod. xx. 4, "Thou shalt not make to thee a graven thing (you read *image*), nor any similitude." But I pray go on: "Thou shalt not bow down thyself to them, nor serve them." I answer, these last words do tell you the sense of this commandment; that is, we are not to make any graven thing *to adore it or serve it*. And this is the sense insinuated in these words, "Thou shalt not make *to thee;*" that is, to be adored as God by thee, or served by thee.*

We neither bow to them with intention to adore them as gods, nor do we hold them so much as capable of being served by us. Again, the Hebrew word PESEL doth only signify a *graven thing*, though you did translate this word as if it had determinately signified a *graven image*. This you did purposely to

* [The prophet Amos, chap. v. 26, reproaches the house of Israel in these words: "Ye have borne the tabernacle of Moloch, . . . the star of your god which you *made to yourselves.*" Now St. Stephen, Acts vii. 43, cites the passage as follows: "Ye took up the tabernacle of Moloch, and the star of your god, . . . figures which ye made *to worship them.*" An inspired speaker is the best expounder of an inspired writer; nor can any doubt remain on the import of the expression in the decalogue, Thou shalt not make *to thyself.* It must signify, Thou shalt not make to worship, or serve as gods.]

IT IS LAUDABLE TO WORSHIP IMAGES. 215

make us appear idolaters. Certainly, if God had declared it unlawful to make graven images, he would never have caused the images of cherubim to be made in the ark, before whose only presence idols could not stand, as we see, 1 Sam. v. 7, by Dagon, so often cast down before it. Neither would Solomon have presumed to place round about the walls of God's temple images of cherubim. Wherefore, in this command, *idols* only are forbidden, and not such images as are not used as idols. Whence the Septuagint, whom you pretend to follow, hath the very word *Eidolon*, that is, idol; why, then, translate you graven images? If our images be idols, God hath not fulfilled his promise, to take out of his Church the worship of idols, as I said in No. 2.

9. Your other and only objection to any purpose is Exod. xxxii. 1; to answer which, I must note some things before I put it. First, The people being assembled against Aaron, said, "Arise, make us gods, that they may go before us." Secondly, Aaron, knowing that they meant such gods as they had seen worshiped in Egypt, made them a molten calf; neither can you think of any other reason why he made rather a calf than any other thing, but only because the Egyptians worshiped their god Apis, or Serapis, in the shape of a black calf with white spots, as St. Augustine testifieth, *De Civit.* l. xviii. c. 5. Thirdly, This calf being molten, they said, "These be thy gods, O Israel, which have brought thee out of the land of Egypt: which when Aaron had seen, he built an altar before it, and by the crier's voice proclaimed, saying, To-morrow is the feast of our Lord." Here comes your objection. The word which Aaron useth here for the Lord is the name Adonai, or Jehovah as you Protestants will have it, a name proper to the God of Israel; so that it seems they only worshiped the God of Israel. Neither is it, say our adversaries, credible that Aaron would do otherwise, or that he could call the Egyp-

tian god by the most sacred name of all names,—a name so especially appropriated to the God of Israel. Whence, say they, you commit idolatry, if through the images you worship the person it represents. For the Israelites, when they committed idolatry, did only through that calf worship the God of Israel, represented by it. And this seems strongly confirmed. For Jeroboam renewed the self-same idolatry, by making molten calves to the house of Israel; yet through these calves he only worshiped the God of Israel, calling him Baali, as appears by these words of Hosea, chap. ii. 16, "And it shall be in that day, saith our Lord, that thou shalt call me no more Baali." Where, you see, the God of Israel saith they called him Baali. Him, therefore, the Israelites worshiped, calling him Baali; and so through Baali they worshiped him.

I answer, that they did not in this their idolatry worship the true God, but false gods. The people themselves desired gods to be made them by Aaron, as is thrice in that chapter of Exodus expressed. And Aaron, knowing that they meant such gods as they had seen worshiped by the Egyptians, did for that reason make a calf, as I said. To this calf, or, if you will, to the Egyptian god Apis through this calf, they did offer sacrifice. Hence God said to Moses, ver. 8, "They have made them a molten calf, and have worshiped it, and sacrificed thereunto, and said, These are thy gods, O Israel, which have brought thee out of the land of Egypt." You see God himself saith they have worshiped it, and sacrificed thereunto; that is, to the very calf, and not to the true God. And they did not acknowledge that the true God had delivered them from Egypt, but they did attribute their delivery to the gods, to wit, the Egyptian gods. Wherefore the true God said, in that place of Exodus just now cited, "They have quickly revolted, forgetting me," who so very lately did so many wonders to deliver them, all of which they now ascribe to the Egyptian gods. And that you may see I say this most groundedly, I show the same expressly said in other Scriptures. Moses, speaking of this very act of idolatry here committed, saith, Deut. xxxii. 16, "They provoked him with strange gods." The God of Israel cannot be called a strange god. And the next words are, "They sacrificed to devils, not to God." And yet you say they sacrificed to the true God, which also is expressly contrary to the next words: "They sacrificed to new gods, that came newly up; to gods whom they knew not; to gods whom their fathers feared not." What more clear? David also manifestly, Ps. cvi. 19, "They made a calf in Horeb, and they worshiped the molten image; they forgot their Saviour, who had done great things in Egypt." A strange thing indeed it was, that all those strange wonders should be so soon forgot. But it is that very thing for which God so often blameth them. So that Moses, with great reason, wondered how Aaron could be brought to be partaker in this sin, and as astonished he asked him, Exod. xxxii. 21, "What hath this people done to thee" (for I am sure they must have used great violence and force to bring thee to this), " that thou hast brought so great a sin upon them?" Aaron, for his excuse, allegeth the violence offered to him. Now whereas Aaron proclaimed this solemnity as the solemnity of the Lord of Israel, he did so because he denounced that the very self-same honour should to-morrow be solemnly given to this idol which was formerly given to the God of Israel. And seeing that they resolved to give to this new god all other honours, they would also give him the honour of the highest name—Jehovah; a name yet famous among them. So you might lately see a Quaker say to James Naylor,* "Thou art my

* [A disciple of George Fox. "He believed himself to be set as a sign of the coming of Christ; and he accepted the worship which was paid to him, not as offered to James Naylor, but to Christ, dwelling in James Naylor." *Lingard*, xi. 83.]

Christ;" as St. Paul said of the Gentiles, Rom. i. 21, "That whereas they knew God, yet they did not glorify him as God. And they changed the glory of the incorruptible God into a similitude of a corruptible four-footed beast." So might we say of these Jews.

Now I answer what was added of Jeroboam's renewing this idolatry. For he also did worship false and strange gods, as appears by what God spoke by his prophet Ahias, 1 Kings xiv. 9, "Thou hast gone and made thee other gods, and cast me behind thy back;" so that he did not honour (for of him these words are said) the God of Israel in those idols, but casting him off, he honoured other gods; yea, in chap. xii. 32, "He sacrificed unto the calves that he had made." But how, then, say you, did they call the God of Israel Baali? I answer that, as a Quaker calling James Naylor Jesus Christ doth make Christ to be no better man than James Naylor, and so doth as good as call Christ James Naylor,—even so these Jews, taking Baali for their true God, did say that, in effect, their true God was no better than Baali; and so they vilified him as much as if they had called him Baali, giving all honour to Baali that was due to God, yea, even the honour of being their chief God, as we said of Aaron.

10. Thus I have answered at large this their best argument, upon which chiefly they must build their uncharitable and heinous accusation of the whole visible Church to have been guilty of the highest of crimes, that is, of idolatry itself. Alas, how far short doth this objection come of making good so foul an accusation, which is most injuriously made if it cannot be better proved than by this weak argument!

POINT XLI.

IT IS LAUDABLE TO WORSHIP THE RELICS OF SAINTS.

1. ALL the worship we give to the relics of saints is only such respect as insensible creatures are capable of, as to be kissed, costly enshrined, touched, worn, and used with reverence, &c. And all this is merely for the respect we bear unto the person whose relics they be. By the worship done to the ark, we shall fitly both prove and declare the honour of which such insensible holy things are capable. The ark of God was only that portable little chapel in which God was pleased to speak and impart his mind to the high-priest, consulting him with due ceremonies. And yet see, I pray, what honour God would have done to this ark, though it was a creature insensible of honour, and only capable of being honoured for his sake to whom it had relation. And this relative honour was exceeding great, and extended to manifold strange expressions of reverence. Yet all these honours were far from being idolatrous; yea, God by this so much worshiped ark confounded idolatry. For, 1 Sam. v. 4, "Dagon fell upon his face unto the earth before it." Let us see what reverence God declared due to the ark. When, without respect, "they had looked on the ark of our Lord, he smote of the people fifty thousand," chap. vi. 19; and, 2 Sam. vi. 6, "Because Uzzah put forth his hand to the ark of God, and took hold of it,—for the oxen shook it,—God smote him for his error, and he died by the ark." Whence David, fearing want of due piety in himself, said, "How shall the ark of our Lord come to me? And so he caused it to turn into the house of Obededom, where it was three months. And our Lord blessed him and all his house." We may, then, hope for blessings by wearing relics, by having saints' bodies buried in our cities, &c. And when Solomon placed the ark in the

temple, 2 Chron. v. 2-6, "He gathered together all the ancients of Israel, and all the princes of the heads of families of the children of Israel into Jerusalem, to bring the ark from the city of David, which is Sion." See here this most stately and goodly procession to bring the ark. "And all that were gathered before the ark sacrificed sheep and oxen, which could not be told nor numbered for multitude," ver. 6. And God graced this procession and translation of the ark by a miraculous cloud, filling the house of our Lord, "so that the priests could not stand to minister by reason of the cloud," ver. 14. Laugh not, then, at our processions made in translations of relics; this being done for the ark. Now of other relics. "Eliseus took the mantle of Elias, he smote the waters the second time, and they were divided this way and that way, and Eliseus passed over," 2 Kings ii. 14. Do you not see how Eliseus, yea how rather God honoured by a stupendous miracle the cloak of Elias? No wonder, then, saints' bodies should be more graced with miracles than their garments. Read what followeth there, chap. xiii. 20, "Eliseus therefore died, and they buried him. And the bands of the Moabites invaded the land the same year. And it came to pass as they were burying a man, behold they spied a band of men, and they cast the man into the sepulchre of Eliseus" (anciently they buried in the open field, making caves and grottoes capable of holding more bodies); "and when the man was let down, and touched the bones of Eliseus, he revived, and stood upon his feet." And will you be still scoffing at us for devout touching of saints' bones, when so casual a touch caused so great and stupendous a good to that man, as was the restoring of his life? Note, also, how God honoured Eliseus's bones by so miraculous an accident.

2. Now, to join the New Testament with the Old, I find that, for keeping with all reverence and rich enshrining of relics, we read thus, Heb. ix. 4, "In

the which (ark) was a golden pot, having manna, and the rod of Aaron that had budded, and the tables of the covenant." All these relics, so honourably placed in gold, and in the ark, were by consequence all hid by Jeremy with it, and in it. And so after the captivity, thus being miraculously found, were, with all pomp, placed in the temple, which was restored by Zorobabel, and amplified by Herod; and there they remained till Jerusalem, under Titus and Vespasian, was destroyed, and had not left a stone upon a stone. This is most to be noted, because Protestants scoff so much at us for believing the wood of the holy cross, and many such relics, to be preserved for so many years uncorrupt. Indeed, though this be no part of our faith, the probability of it is hence invincibly confirmed. For the tabernacle, and all things pertaining to it, was finished about the year of the world 2485. Now Christ was born after the year of the world 4000. He lived thirty-three years, and forty years after his death Jerusalem was overthrown; so that the ark and tabernacle, with their veils and curtains and other appurtenances, lasted well near 2000 years uncorrupt; and so the rod of Aaron, so much inferior to the cross, and the table of the law, yea, and the manna itself, though so corruptible by nature that what was gathered one day would grow full of worms the next day, unless it were the Sabbath. No wonder, then, many relics should keep, and be reverently kept, since Christ's time, which is far shorter than the space which these relics were kept, as appears by St. Paul. Let us go on.

3. What relic meaner than the latchet of a shoe? and yet St. John Baptist, the greatest prophet which had risen, said truly, John i. 27, "Whose shoe's latchet I am not worthy to unloose," for the relation it had to Christ. With what reverence, think you, would a St. John Baptist have touched that poor leather thong? Hence that devout woman, Matt. ix. 21, "If I may but touch his garment, I shall be whole."

And Jesus turning him, and seeing her, saith, Thy faith hath made thee whole." The faith, therefore, in this devout touch, was not superstitious. Note here how the cure was wrought by this exterior touch, with interior faith; see Mark v. 30, Luke viii. 46, who, vi. 19, saith, "The whole multitude sought to touch him. For virtue came out of him, and cured all." We indeed touch the relics with faith and reverence; but the virtue by which any favour is granted comes from the saint whose relics we touch, God giving him power to assist us for our devout recourse to him. Hence, Apoc. ii. 26, "He that shall overcome, and keep my words to the end, I will give him power over the nations." He shall have power to help even whole nations, but he shall have this power given by me: "*I* will give him," &c.

4. Note, also, that the very manner of applying other things to touch saints' bodies, and, after they have touched them, to apply them with devotion (a thing most jeered at by our adversaries), is, notwithstanding, a thing recommended unto us in Scripture, proposing the example of the first and best Christians in this point, Acts xix. 12, "There were also brought from his (Paul's) body, napkins, or handkerchiefs, upon the sick, and the diseases departed from them, and the wicked spirits went out." Do not, then, blame us for hoping to obtain some blessings by wearing saints' blood or bones, or other relics, which commonly have a far greater relation to them than those napkins or handkerchiefs had to St. Paul, merely in respect of a simple touch of his body, unless you dare venture to say that it is more to touch a saint's body, when his soul liveth in it, than when his soul lives with God in heaven. I pray tell me what hath a thinner relation to man than his shadow? Or what apprentice-painter of one day's standing will not be able to make a better image of such a man than his shadow is? And yet the first and purest Christians did hold the very shadow of saints in great venera-

tion, either because it was a kind of picture of them, or had some small relation at least to them. And God confirmed their devotion by a world of miracles, Acts v. 15, "Insomuch that they did bring forth their sick into the streets, and laid them in beds and couches, that at least the shadow of Peter passing by might overshadow some of them." Our Bibles have, "that they might be delivered from their infirmities." St. Luke immediately after saith, "Then came also a multitude out of the cities round about, unto Jerusalem, bringing sick folks, and them which were vexed with unclean spirits; and they were healed every one." Note here that there being so great a resort of all, and all being cured, surely many came devoutly from remoter parts to enjoy this favour. Blame not, then, our pilgrimages to his body itself at Rome where he is interred, seeing the Scripture showeth many to have come to his very shadow to obtain help.

5. The Point following hath so great connexion with this present Point, that as we desire the reader to note all here said for proof of that Point, so we desire him, for further proof of this Point, to have recourse to what shall be said in the Point following. And particularly in both these Points we earnestly entreat our adversaries to observe how many and how strong texts we bring for our doctrine in these points, and how few and how weak proofs they can bring out of Scripture to the contrary. It is a shame to them to appeal to Scripture in these points, or to say they will reform our errors in them by clear Scripture, which is here so clear against them.

POINT XLII.

SOME PLACES ARE MORE HOLY THAN OTHERS: WE THEREFORE LAUDABLY MAKE PILGRIMAGES AND PROCESSIONS TO SUCH HOLY PLACES.

1. OUT of holy Scripture it is evident some places were more holy than others; and for that respect choice was made of such places to perform the best acts of devotion. The great patriarch Abraham had digged a well, and there called upon God by that solemn oath which he made to Abimelech, Gen. xxi. 31, "Wherefore he called that place Beersheba, that is, the well of the oath." This is the place of which it is said, Gen. xxvi. 23, "And he (Isaac) went up from thence to Beersheba. And the Lord appeared to him that night, saying, I am the God of Abraham; I will bless thee, and multiply thy seed for my (dead) servant Abraham's sake." Hence the well was accounted a sanctified place. And you shall find, in chap. xlvi. ver. 1, that Jacob (or Israel) many years after taking his journey "with all things that he had, towards Egypt, came to the well of the oath, and offering there sacrifice to the God of his father Isaac (who there, as I said, appeared to Isaac), he heard God, by a vision in the night, calling him," &c. You see Jacob, with all his children, beginning his journey with a pilgrimage to this holy place; you see that purposely he makes choice of this place to offer there sacrifice. You see God in this holy place favouring him with a heavenly vision, as he had done his holy father Isaac in the same place. Doth not, then, God make choice of some particular places rather than of others?

2. The place where God appeared is to be called and held holy. So, Exod. iii. 5, God out of the burning bush to Moses saith, "Draw not nigh hither: loose off thy shoes from thy feet; for the place

whereon thou standest is holy ground;" to wit, made holy, and sanctified by the presence of God, or rather of an angel sent as God's ambassador. For, Acts vii. 30, St. Stephen saith, "There appeared to Moses an angel in the fire of the flame of a bush, saying, Loose off thy shoes; for the place whereon thou standest is holy ground." Whence it was the transitory presence of an angel appearing for that so short a time which did sanctify this place, and make respect and reverence due to it upon that account. Therefore, by good consequence, the permanent abode of a saint's body, resting in such a monument, may do the like; that is, may sanctify this place. This is also made evident by the mouth of that angel who exacted reverence to be done in the place where he appeared, Josh. v. 15, saying to Joshua, "I am the captain of the hosts of our Lord. Loose thy shoe from thy foot; for the place whereon thou dost stand is holy." The ordinary common field of Jericho was, by the angel's presence, made so holy that it was indecent to tread upon it with a shoe. Wherefore, those who come barefoot to the bodies of saints commit no superstitious excess in devotion.

3. Moreover, some places are far more holy than others. There was a place in which the propitiatory (or mercy-seat) stood, called *Sancta Sanctorum*, the holy of holies, or the holiest of all; to which place, for reverence to it, none approached "but the high-priest alone once a year, not without blood," Heb. ix. 7; thus offering sacrifice always when he entered this so holy a place, which is the highest act of worship. And because sacrifice was the highest act of worship, God would not permit that to be performed in any ordinary holy place. But he thus commanded the people of Israel, Deut. xii. 5, "To the place which the Lord your God shall choose out of your tribes to put his name there, even unto his habitation shall you seek, and thither shall you come; thither shall you bring your burnt-offerings and sacrifices."

Where I note that this place is called his habitation, or dwelling-place. In which sense some Catholics may say our Lady dwells at Sichem, or Loretto; for the choice God hath made of those places in order to bestow favours and graces on such as there implored our Lady's aid. Note also that, verse 26, how far off soever they lived, God commands "the things sacrificed and vowed to our Lord to be all offered here." So that pilgrimage to this holy place did always accompany this holy offering. His command doth justify the holiness thereof.

4. Yea, because the temple of Solomon, which was the place chosen, was the place thus sanctified, and made so peculiarly holy, the very ordinary prayers which men made when they came in pilgrimage to this place, and made them there, were upon that account more pleasing to God, and sooner heard by him. For, 2 Chron. vi. 20, "May thy eyes be open upon this house night and day, upon the place whereof thou hast said that thou wouldst put thy name there; to hearken to the prayer which thy servant prayeth towards this place. Hearken to the supplication of the people made towards this place." And the next verses are all full of blessings begged for them, who shall pray, or make supplication, or spread forth their hands in this house. Wherefore, for easier obtaining of all these blessings, a pilgrimage to this place was usually undertaken. For a pilgrimage is nothing else but only a going to some holy places for devotion. Those who could not go to the temple or Jerusalem would at least turn themselves towards these places when they prayed, as we shall presently see Daniel did.

5. At the first bringing of the ark into the temple there was a most solemn procession made, 2 Chron. v. 2, by the king, "Solomon himself gathering all the ancients of Israel, and all the princes of the tribes, and the heads of the families of the children of Israel, to bring the ark of the covenant from the

city of David." From that place, then, the procession began, the priests and Levites carrying the vessels of the Sanctuary, and at the people in Mount Moria the procession ended, with sacrifices without number.

6. Pilgrimages to this place, and processions at the same time, were used by the most holy kings of the Jews. So, 2 Chron. xx. 3, the most pious king "Josaphat feared, and set himself to seek the Lord, and proclaimed a fast through all Judah. And Judah gathered themselves together to ask help of the Lord." Then, ver. 13, "All Judah stood before the Lord, with their little ones, their wives, and their children." For with them they all came up in pilgrimage to this place, here making this so solemn supplication. And God, upon the very place, prophesied victory to them. And Josaphat the next day caused a procession of singers to the Lord, to go before his army singing that psalm, "Praise the Lord." "And when they began to sing praises our Lord turned the ambushments upon the enemy." Lo here the pious procession favoured from heaven with a stupendous victory! For they not fighting one stroke, their enemies by their own swords lay dead in so great a number, that "for three days they could not take away the spoils, for the greatness of the prey," vers. 25, 28. The fourth day "they entered into Jerusalem with psalteries, and harps, and trumpets, into the house of our Lord;" thus, by a pilgrimage and procession, returning thanks for so great a victory got purely by a pilgrimage, and processions accompanied with fasting and prayer, as we usually accompany our pilgrimages and processions. How often do Protestants read these places, and, for want of practice in these devotions, never understand them, or note them!

7. Again, what shall or can they say to that pious act of Naaman, general captain of Syria, cleansed from his leprosy by washing "seven times in the river Jordan"? God prescribed the waters of the holy land for

his cure, though he had better in his country, as he said, 2 Kings v. 12. But it is for a far other reason why I speak of Naaman; it is because, being heartily converted by this miracle, and resolved to serve only the God of Israel, he said to Eliseus, ver. 17, "Shall not, then, I pray thee, to thy servant be given two mules' burden of earth? for thy servant henceforth will offer neither burnt-offering nor sacrifice but unto the Lord." Where I observe that he, apprehending how hard it was for one of his quality to come in pilgrimage to Jerusalem and sacrifice there, and knowing himself, because he was a stranger, to be licensed to sacrifice elsewhere, would, notwithstanding, carry the earth of that holy land,—a land chosen by God for his service,—that upon the holy earth he might raise an altar, and so do his devotions in a holy place, as well as circumstances permitted. Yet how do our adversaries scoff at us if we bring a little earth from about our Lord's sepulchre, or Mount Calvary, upon which he shed his blood, more sanctifying that earth than ever earth was sanctified! When Daniel was captive, and could not go to the temple to pray, yet "His windows being open in his chamber towards Jerusalem, he kneeled upon his knees thrice a day, and prayed and gave thanks to his God, as he did aforetime," Dan. vi. 10. Behold, this was his usual devotion, to turn towards a holy place and pray, when, in his body, he could not go thither.

8. In the New Testament you have, Matt. ii., the three sages or kings coming an exceeding long pilgrimage, to adore in personal presence our new-born Saviour, although they knew full well that he did as well see and hear all the respect and devout prayers performed to him by them in their own countries, as far off as they were; yet they personally would show their respect by waiting on him in person. So we Catholics personally will honour St. Peter in presence of his body at Rome by going to that end so long a pilgrimage: although we full well know he could

hear our prayers made at our own houses, yet we know those prayers to be more acceptable to him, as hath been formerly showed concerning prayers made in holy places, especially when those prayers receive so great force from so painful and devout a pilgrimage. Again, in the New Testament, you have also, John xii. 20, "That there were certain Greeks who came up to worship at the feast." These Greeks were not obliged to the Jewish law; but their devotion exhorted them to this long pilgrimage. And though they were by birth descending from the Gentiles, yet their coming to worship makes it evident that they were true believers. Now, that this their pilgrimage was grateful to our Saviour, it appears by his divine providence ordering things so that they should be introduced in to see him at such a time as a voice came from heaven, saying, "I have glorified it (thy name), and again I will glorify it," ver. 28. Likewise Philip, by God's special providence, was sent to instruct, convert, and baptize that noble eunuch of Candace, queen of Ethiopia, who was to come to Jerusalem to adore, though he lived as far off as Ethiopia. A grateful pilgrimage to God, though not commanded him by God: see Acts viii. 26. Evident, therefore, it is that some places are to be held more holy than others, and upon that account we do laudably go in pilgrimages to them; that is, we go to them for devotion's sake to do our best duty to God in those places. Again, because our Saviour was transfigured on Mount Tabor, St. Peter calls that mount a holy mount, 2 Peter i. 18, "When we were with him in the holy mount." So say I; because our Saviour was so disfigured at Mount Calvary, and all besprinkled that place with his sacred blood, that is also a holy mount. And far more grateful to God be all the devotions which are made in that holy place.

9. There is a memorable passage of John, chap. v. 2, to confirm all that hath been said, or that is believed or practised among us, in this point: "For

there is in Jerusalem, by the sheep-market, a pool having five porches; in these lay a great multitude of persons, blind, lame, withered, expecting the stirring of the water. And an angel of the Lord descended at a certain time into the pond, and the water was stirred; and he that had gone down first into the pond after the stirring of the water, was made whole of what infirmity soever." Interpreters affirm this great and constant miracle, which was true, though the former Scriptures never did set it down, to have therefore been given to the water of this pond, which made so great recourse of pilgrims to that place, because the carcasses of the sheep sacrificed in the temple were washed in this pond, or else because the blood of them did run into it. Shall not the blood of martyrs, sacrificed for Christ, more sanctify any place where it was shed than the blood of sheep sacrificed in his honour? Scarce any relic hath less relation to the person whose relic it is than this miraculous pond had to that great Lord to whose honour these beasts were sacrificed. Yet this pond had an angel of God deputed to look after it. The miracle was constant and infallible; and so no wonder a great multitude of persons came from remote places in pilgrimage to this place. So also many came or were brought even to St. Peter's shadow, as we noted in the former Point, No. 5. His bones and other relics have a far stricter relation to him than his shadow.

10. Let no man think that miracles now cease. All England knows that our kings, by touching with certain ceremonies, cured the king's evil; and all France knows their kings do so to this day: the first for St. Edward's sake, the other for St. Lewis. Our Saviour speaks home when he saith, and he saith it without limiting any time, "He that believeth in me, the works that I do he shall also do, and greater than these shall he do," John xiv. 12. Believe to find no true belief where there are no true miracles. Christ himself, of himself, saith, John xv. 24, "If I had not

done among them works which no other man did, they had not had sin;" to wit, the sin of incredulity. No sin, therefore, it is to reject Luther and Calvin, and all such new teachers as never did miracle.

POINT XLIII.

THAT WE LAUDABLY KEEP FEASTS IN THE HONOUR OF SAINTS.

1. THESE feasts to many seem to have no ground in Scripture, and therefore are not to be kept, but to be esteemed unwarrantable. Yet we say, first, The Apostles may have instituted several feasts of our Lord and our Lady, though they thought that they sufficiently recommended them to posterity upon the warrant of tradition only. For they knew that upon tradition only the Sabbath had been kept from the beginning of the world until Moses, that is, for two thousand four hundred years. After which time Moses did first set down in writing this command. Yet at the very beginning of the world, Gen. ii. 3, "God blessed the seventh day, and sanctified it." See the second Point, No. 2. And thus we know, by tradition only, that we are not any longer to keep the seventh day, though God had sanctified it; but that we are to keep the Sunday in honour of his resurrection, which is the eighth, and not the seventh day.

2. Now it is a strange thing that we should be appointed by the Apostles to keep weekly a feast in honour of that day of the week on which Christ did rise, and yet should not be appointed to keep the feast of the resurrection itself. The Jews kept their Pentecost, for having received God's law in written tables. And shall not Christians keep a Pentecost for having received the law of grace, first divulged and written in men's hearts at the coming of the

Holy Ghost? If the resurrection of Christ be a mystery so great that one day in every week should be kept through the whole year holiday in honour of it, shall Christ's ascension be so far inferior that no one day in a year (and consequently no one in an age) is to be kept in memory of it? Had the Jews reason to keep the Feast of Tabernacles, because God preserved them living in tabernacles forty years in the wilderness,—a benefit belonging only to their fathers; and hath not the Church reason to institute a feast in the honour of Christ coming to live in the tabernacle of our flesh at his nativity? And another feast in memory of his giving us, under the shape of bread, his body to remain in all the tabernacles of our churches, and to enter so often into the tabernacles of our breasts; both inestimable benefits to us personally, and also to all our posterity? Had the Jews all reason to keep a Feast of Assembly, or collection, in gratitude for the peaceable possession of the land of promise; and have not we more reason to keep the solemnity of All Saints (our most holy fathers), who now are in peaceable possession of the land of the living and the inheritance of Christ, and from thence afford us help and assistance to come thither? Had the Jews sufficient reason to keep the Feast of Trumpets, Numb. xxix. 1, in grateful memory that their father Isaac was freed from being sacrificed by Abraham, God sending a ram to be sacrificed in his place,* —and therefore they always offered a ram in that feast,—and hath not the Church sufficient reason to keep a less solemn feast in grateful memory that our chief patriarch and head of our Church, St. Peter, was freed when Herod intended bloodily to sacrifice him to the good pleasure of the Jews, and when "prayer was made to God without intermission by

* [That the object of the Feast of Trumpets was to commemorate the deliverance of Isaac is not asserted in Scripture, but is merely the opinion of some Hebrew commentators. A Lapide, *on Lev.* xxiii. 25.]

the Church for him"? Acts xii. 5. "An angel of our Lord was sent the night before Herod would have brought him forth to deliver him," as well as to deliver Isaac, now upon the point of being slain. This I bring, because many wonder that we keep a feast (though less solemn) of St. Peter's chains, and of his delivery from them. As for the feasts of martyrs, because to them it is a greater benefit to suffer all torments, and consummate them by death itself, than to be freed by miracle from them, the Church hath all reason to solemnise the days upon which God glorified these blessed martyrs, by enabling them, first to undergo such extensive torments so courageously, and then crowned them with immortal bliss after their victory. The Jews also, besides these solemnities here mentioned, and besides their weekly Sabbath, had divers other feasts; yea, every new moon brought them at least one solemnity. And will you think that God's Church can have no reason nor authority to appoint any other feast than the Sunday?

3. I will therefore further show you out of Scripture, that besides the feasts appointed by God in Scripture, other feasts have been superadded laudably by the authority of the Church. By which will appear her authority to do this when she judges it expedient. The law prescribed the solemnity of *Azymes*, or unleavened bread, to be kept but seven days; yet, upon a peculiar occasion, it seemed expedient to the Church, then assembled, to add seven more, so says the Scripture, 2 Chron. xxx. 23, "The whole assembly took counsel to keep other seven days, and they kept other seven days." And the Scripture adds, ver. 27, in commendation of this great piety, "And the priests and Levites blessing the people, their voice was heard, and their prayer came up to his holy habitation of heaven." For as in holy places, so in holy times, prayers are more effectual, as here they were in a time made holy, or set apart for God's service, by the authority of the Church only.

4. Again, Esther ix. 20, upon the like authority it pleased the Jews "to establish this amongst them, that they should keep the fourteenth day of the month Adar, and the fifteenth day of the same yearly, as the days wherein the Jews rested from their enemies, and the month which was turned to them from sorrow to joy." And the Jews undertook to do this. And, ver. 27, "the Jews ordained, and took upon them, and upon their seed, and upon all such as joined themselves to them, so as it should not fail, that they would keep these two days according to their appointed time every year." Why? Did any Scripture command this? No; but the Church laid this obligation upon itself. "The Jews," says the Scripture, "took upon themselves and their seed." Christ's Church has no less authority in this kind than the Jewish Church had to impose an obligation upon "herself, and her seed, and upon all that will be joined" to her religion. We read also that because the Church so judged it expedient, a perpetual feast, with an octave, that is, lasting for eight days, was instituted, Mach. iv. 56, without any peculiar warrant from Scripture beside the common warrant of holding that warrantable which the Church appointed. Now, if the books of Machabees be not true Scripture, as we hold them to be, yet, at least, according to our adversaries, they contain a faithful ecclesiastical history, in which it is recorded in the place cited, "that they kept the dedication of their altar eight days." Moreover, "Judas," then highpriest, "and his brethren, with the whole congregation of Israel, ordained that the days of the dedication of the altar should be kept in their season, from year to year, by the space of eight days, from the twenty-fifth of the month Casleu,"—that is, November, ver. 59. This feast was kept by the Jewish Church until our Saviour's time, and that without warrant of Scripture. Yea, our Saviour himself observed it. For so we read, John x. 22, "And the feast of

the dedication was in Jerusalem, and it was winter." I know the feast of the dedication of the temple restored, 2 Esd. vi., was in February, and therefore in winter. But this being the winter before his death, it could not be in that part of winter which was spent as far as February, because our Saviour is there, by St. John and by the other evangelists, said to have done more than could be done between February and the 25th of March, upon which he suffered death. So that Beza himself, in his annotations upon this place of St. John, confesses this feast, which our Saviour kept, to have been the feast we speak of. A great proof also of using prayer for the dead. For had the institutor of this feast, who in that book is recorded to have used prayer for the dead,—had he, I say, been superstitiously given, Christ would never have kept feasts of his institution. Note here, also, the warrant for feasts of dedications so usual in our Church, yet so unheard of among Protestants.

POINT XLIV.

WE LAUDABLY OBSERVE FASTS, SAINTS' EVES, AND OTHER DAYS.

1. Out of the former Point we make this strong argument: the Church has power to oblige her subjects to keep such and such feasts, as has been proved; therefore she has the power to oblige her subjects to keep such and such fasting days, for the Scriptures speak universally of this obedience, requiring of us carefully "to hear the Church," Matt. xviii. 17, and saying, "He that hears you, hears me; he that despises you, despises me," Luke x. 16. As also, "Obey them that have the rule over you; for they watch for your souls," Heb. xiii. 17. Yea, though Scribes and Pharisees should, *by lawful succession,* "sit upon the chair of Moses," Christ himself

will bid us, "Do all, therefore, whatsoever they command. All therefore whatsoever they bid you observe, that observe and do," Matt. xxiii. 2. And if you say that we must obey only when they bring clear Scripture, you are refuted by the former Point, where you see so many feasts commanded without clear Scripture, which did nowhere appoint those feasts. She then may command fasts not commanded by Scripture.

2. And now I will show you fasts to have been commanded by the Church upon a day not appointed in Scripture, but only by the appointment of the high-priest or Church. So, "Josaphat proclaimed a fast to all Juda," 2 Chron. xx. 3. So Joel, i. 14, exhorts the Church to command an extraordinary fast: "Sanctify ye a fast." Also, upon a day not commanded by Scripture, Esdras the high-priest commanded a fast: "And I proclaimed a fast, that we might be afflicted before the Lord our God," 1 Esd. viii. 21. "And we fasted and besought our God for this, and he was entreated of us." And, Esth. iv. 6, "Gather together all the Jews, and fast ye for me, and neither eat nor drink three days, night nor day." And it was done according as it was commanded. And, Esth. ix. 27, "the Jews ordained, and took upon them, and upon their seed, so as it should not fail that they would keep these two days" of fast "every year." And, ver. 31, "they decreed for themselves, and for their seed, the fastings, and their cry." For fasting and crying to the Lord were fitly then appointed to be observed in the vigil or eve of this feast, as we usually fast in the vigils of our feasts: for devout fasting best disposeth our mind to devotion the next day. Moreover, you Protestants teach there be no counsels given us of God, but only precepts; if this be so, God himself commands you to fast, when he says, Joel ii. 12, "Turn ye to me with all your hearts, and with fasting, and weeping, and mourning."

3. We fast on Ember days, because those days are deputed by the Church to ordain and consecrate new priests and other ministers of the Church. And it is Christ's command, Matt. ix. 38, "Pray the Lord of the harvest, that he send forth workmen into his harvest." To obey this command the more perfectly, and to make our prayer, poured forth for so important a blessing, the more effectual, the Church with this prayer joins three days' fast. So of the most primitive Church we read, Acts xiii. 3, "When they had fasted, and prayed, and laid their hands on them, they sent them away," to wit, Barnabas and Saul; "so they being sent by the Holy Ghost departed." And, xiv. 3, "When they had ordained them elders (priests) in every Church, and prayed with fastings, they commended them to the Lord."

4. Moreover, by our fastings in each of the four seasons of the year, we consecrate these seasons and our lives to God, and more effectually petition for his blessings in and at all seasons. Christ said expressly, Matt. ix. 14, "That after the bridegroom" should be taken from his disciples (as he was at his passion), "then they should also fast," as much as the disciples of St. John and the Pharisees did. And there the Scripture says, "they fasted often." And you know the proud Pharisee brags that he "fasted twice a week." The Church knows by Scripture that it was expedient "to keep under our body, and bring it into subjection," 1 Cor. ix. 27; "and to approve ourselves in watchings and fastings," 2 Cor. vi. 5; and to "give ourselves to fasting," 1 Cor. vii. 5. For this reason it was that St. John, the greatest of prophets, taught his disciples "to fast often," Matt. ix. 14. Now there being so great good in fasting, and all God's greatest saints having practised it so much upon this account, as I showed out of Scripture, Point XXIII., it is a wonder that, among our ungodly saints, even *Good Friday* itself, on which we received a greater benefit than ever mankind received, should

have no more notice commanded to be taken of it than if Christ's death belonged not to us.

5. We fast the eves of several great feasts, so to be the better disposed to prayer the next day. By fasting also we imitate and excite those saints to help us whose feast we solemnise; thus more honouring them, and more powerfully inploring their intercession, by fasting joined with our prayers. We fast forty days in *Lent*, for even the most ancient fathers called this fast an *apostolical tradition*. And surely, if the Apostles had not, together with the other practices of our religion, delivered also this practice of fasting for forty days, no man afterwards could have had sufficient authority, and this through the whole multitude of Christians, to make them all believe themselves obliged to fast so often. Men love their belly too well to be brought so easily to such an insufferable burden as this seems to many. Nothing but a strict command of an undoubted authority could have made all Christianity accept of this great fast with that rigour which Luther found in the whole Church at his time. Some Protestants venture to say that Pope Telesphorus, who lived A.D. 141, was the first that commanded this fast. They should have said, he was the first that by written law commanded the more exact observance of this apostolical tradition, which by some men's neglect was grown to be less observed. If they make him the first introducer of Lent, then they must be forced to confess that in that primitive age the pope's authority was known for undoubted, and reverently obeyed even over all Christendom at that time; and this in a matter which pincheth many so hardly, that we see here in England neither the known laws of the land, made by those of their own religion, nor the king's proclamations pressing those laws, nor the penalties enjoined by them, can prevail half so much in this one nation, as the authority commanding Lent did, in those pure and primitive ages, prevail through all Christian nations. I must not end

this Point without observing, that the whole Church may stand obliged to observe such and such fasts, notified to her without any Scripture, by the sole attestation of Church tradition, delivering this obligation as imposed first by the Apostles or such-like lawful authority. For, from the days of Noah until Moses, that is above a thousand years, all were obliged thus "not to eat the flesh with the blood," Gen. ix. 4. See Point II., No. 2. A command made known to them only by tradition.

POINT XLV., AND LAST.

THAT WE LAUDABLY IN OUR FASTS ABSTAIN FROM CERTAIN MEATS.

1. OUR adversaries finding fasting so often and so highly commended in Scripture, and not knowing well how to find fault with it, they turn to pick a quarrel against our manner of fasting. For upon fasting days we abstain from flesh, and in Lent from eggs, yea, from white meats also in some places; for we hold that the more afflictive or laborious the fast is, so that it be discreet, the more perfect it is of its own nature, as being more satisfactory for our sins past; and by more taming of our flesh, more preventive of new sins, and containing a greater exercise of virtue, to the greater increase of merit. Not that God delights in our sufferings, as they are afflictive of us, but because he highly delights in them as they are so many ways beneficial to us. Hence, Joel ii. 12, "Turn ye to me with all your heart, and with fasting." Now to fast all day without eating any thing, is a thing over hard to be prescribed by precept to such a vast community as the Church is. The Church therefore, according to her prudent charity, hath thus moderated the matter. First, That we

should fast till noon, or thereabout, without eating any thing that may break our fast. Secondly, That the meat we then eat be not of flesh, which, being more nourishing, doth also nourish temptations. Thirdly, That at night we eat no supper; but a slight collation is permitted, for fear our night's rest should otherwise be lost, with prejudice of health. Other fasts be less strict, and are rather to be called days of abstinence, on which we only abstain from flesh. But other fasts we have yet more rigorous, as from eggs, and all that is made of eggs; from white meats, which no one, who has the sense of feeling, can deny to be a very considerable addition to the austerity of fasting.

2. This abstaining from certain nourishing and delightful meats is peculiarly recommended by Scripture as especially pleasing to God. First, The Nazarites, Numb. vi., were obliged to abstain from wine, though wine was the usual drink of their country, there being no beer. Secondly, Jerem. xxxv., The Rechabites in like manner, abstaining upon command from wine, are highly commended by God, and rewarded for it, ver. 18. Thirdly, St. Luke i. 15, "He shall be great before our Lord, wine and strong drink he shall not drink." Fourthly, The same great John Baptist's ordinary food was "locusts and wild honey," Matt. iii. 4. And even of this coarse food he did feed so sparingly, that Christ himself said, "He came neither eating nor drinking," Matt. xi. 18. Fifthly, St. Timothy could not be induced "to drink a little wine in the weakness of his stomach, and his often infirmities," until St. Paul, for this reason, advised him "not still to drink water," 1 Tim. v. 23. Sixthly, I might add that this kind of fast is the most effectual "to keep under our bodies and bring them into subjection, lest we become reprobate," as St. Paul said of himself, 1 Cor. ix. 27. Daniel says also of himself, "Flesh and wine entered not into my mouth for three weeks," Dan. x. 3.

3. Hence we may easily answer our adversaries' objections. First, then, they object, Mark vii. 15, "Nothing that is without a man entering into a man can defile him." For the sense is this: no meat of its own nature is polluting or defiling; though to eat meats that are forbidden doth pollute and defile the soul, as the apple defiled Adam's soul, as also the taking drink to excess pollutes the drunkard. And even after our Saviour spoke these words, eating of hog's flesh would have defiled the souls of the Apostles. Yea, and the first primitive Christians should have been defiled by eating blood or meats strangled. Not because those meats were still unclean, but because the Church thought fit, yea and necessary, to forbid at that time the eating of those meats, Acts xv. 28, "It hath seemed good to the Holy Ghost and us to lay no further burden upon you than these necessary things, that you abstain from meat offered to idols, and blood, and that which is strangled." So, Gen. ix. 4, for above a thousand years before Scripture, all were obliged "not to eat the flesh with the blood." And this no Scripture then either commanded or testified; yet even then not the meat, but the breach of the Church's commandment would have defiled them, and still defileth us, if we eat what the same Church still forbids to be eaten at the times forbidden.

4. Secondly, You object, 1 Cor. x. 25, "All that is sold in shambles eat, asking no question for conscience." I answer, that the apostle there only tells them that, though to eat in the temple of idols what is there offered up to the idol be unlawful (ver. 28), yet we must not have a scruple of eating what we see sold in the shambles, by asking questions, out of an overtimorous conscience, whether that ox, calf, or sheep sold there were not, before it was brought to the market, immolated to some idol. Now what is this to our purpose?

5. Thirdly, It is objected, Col. ii. 16, "Let no man judge you in meat nor drink, or in respect of a holy

day, or of the new moon, or of the Sabbath." I answer, by what is here added "of a new moon," it is manifest this text only speaks of fasts according to Judaical distinction between meat clean and unclean; all meats being now clean to Christians, still, as above, excepting blood and strangled meat, though sold in the shambles, for this is not contrary to what St. Paul said, "All that is sold in the shambles eat."

6. Fourthly, And chiefly they object, 1 Tim. iv. 3, "The doctrine of devils, forbidding to marry, and commanding to abstain from meats, which God created to receive with thanksgiving. For every creature of God is good, and nothing is to be refused which is received with thanksgiving." For as much as concerns our doctrine of abstaining from marriage, we have already answered this text in Point XX. No. 8. We must see now in what sense it is "devils' doctrine to abstain from meats which God created." It cannot be in that sense in which the Nazarites and Rechabites abstained from wine, and St. John Baptist from wine and strong drink, and from all meats almost but "locusts and wild honey, coming neither eating nor drinking;" or in which St. Timothy also abstained from wine; or in which all Christians, as then, abstained from blood, and what was "strangled or offered to idols." The abstinence of the Manichees was devils' doctrine; for they taught to abstain from meats "which God created," because they said that the "devil, and not God, created some meats." Against such men St. Paul, of all meats without exception, saith, "God created them." To attribute such meats to the devil's creation, and therefore to abstain from them, is to teach the doctrine of the devils. This doctrine of the Manichees was held by divers more ancient heretics, as the Rhemish Testament showeth in this place. Again, the doctrine of some Jew was the doctrine of devils, who taught that still we must make a distinction between meats clean and unclean, and abstain from these because the law was given by angels; and

they said that the angels had revealed that therefore this law was still to be kept, even by Christians. But these angels were angels of darkness, and this was truly "the doctrine of devils," though disguised in the shape of angels of light. This is the interpretation of the most learned Tertullian, as I also showed, Point XXXVI. No. 9.

THE END.

LONDON:
ROBSON AND LEVEY, PRINTERS, GREAT NEW STREET,
FETTER LANE.

www.ingramcontent.com/pod-product-compliance
Lightning Source LLC
Chambersburg PA
CBHW020807230426
43666CB00007B/889